FOREWORD BY JOSEPH NYE AND BRENT SCOWCROFT

Blind Spot:
America's Response
to Radicalism in the
Middle East

EDITED BY NICHOLAS BURNS AND JONATHON PRICE

CONTRIBUTORS INCLUDE:

James E. Cartwright, Jared Cohen, Ryan Crocker, Peter Feaver,
Michèle Flournoy, Richard Fontaine, Shadi Hamid, Bernard Haykel,
David Ignatius, William McCants, Vali Nasr, Farah Pandith,
Tom Pritzker, Sarah Sewall, Frances Townsend, Graeme Wood,
Dov Zakheim, Philip Zelikow

The Aspen Institute
One Dupont Circle, N.W.
Suite 700
Washington, DC 20036

Published in the United States of America in 2015 by The Aspen Institute

Cover design by: Steve Johnson and Rosanna Pitarresi
Interior layout by: Sogand Sepassi

aspen strategy group

"This book is dedicated to the people of Syria, Iraq, Lebanon, France and elsewhere who have experienced first-hand the brutality and depravity of the Islamic State. May this book help contribute to a world free of terrorist violence."

Preface

Nicholas Burns
Goodman Family Professor of the Practice
of Diplomacy and International Relations,
Harvard University

Jonathon Price
Deputy Director,
Aspen Strategy Group

When terrorists operating under the banner of the Islamic State launched their savage attacks in Paris on November 13, 2015 the world was reminded anew of just how complex a challenge this will continue to be for the global community. Nearly five years following the start of the uprisings in the Arab world, the Middle East is less stable, less secure and more troubled and violent than at any time in its modern history.

How to understand the threat of radical Islamic terror groups and how to counter it was the subject of the annual meeting of the Aspen Strategy Group in Colorado in August 2015. Our strictly non-partisan group did not agree on a uniform strategy for the U.S. and its European and Arab allies. But, there was consensus that this problem must continue to be one of the top priorities for the U.S. and other states for the decade to come.

In the U.S., reaction to the Paris attacks has been anything but uniform. Should we aim to contain or defeat the Islamic State? Should the U.S. arm the Syrian Kurdish groups that have been the most effective fighting force against the Islamic State? Should we send additional American Special Forces to coordinate our air attacks in both Syria and Iraq? We delved into still other policy disputes that continue in Washington. Given the humanitarian catastrophe underway in Syria—more than 260,000 people dead and over 12 million homeless—is it now time for the U.S., Turkey and other countries to institute a No Fly Zone in the northern part of the country to take away the savage barrel bombs of the Syrian government?

And, as we went to press just before Thanksgiving, Republicans and Democrats argued over whether the U.S. should continue to accept Syrian refugees. This dispute goes to the core of our identity as a nation of immigrants. For seventy years since the end of the Second World War, we have always opened our doors to people fleeing persecution in their own countries. But, the Paris attacks and the continued brutality of the Islamic State convinced many American politicians that we should close our doors in order to stem the threat of terrorism. Others argued that such a step would contradict the American tradition of welcoming refugees. Without a substantial change in American policy in 2016, we should expect this already disastrous humanitarian situation to worsen.

Considering all of the above: the rise of the Islamic State in both Syria and Iraq, the intensification of the Syrian Civil War, the massive flows of refugees and mounting death toll, it is now abundantly clear that the U.S. needs to develop a more comprehensive and effective strategy in the Middle East. Our hope is this book provides some ideas for the way forward.

The topic of this year's publication, *Blind Spot: America's Response to Radicalism in the Middle East*, has become a recurring subject for the group since the terrorist attacks of September 11, 2001. In 2003, the Strategy Group examined the contours and complications of American grand strategy in the Middle East. Two years later, the group mapped the Jihadist threat facing the United States, and in 2012, we debated the implications of the Arab Spring for the region. This year's book on America's response to radical extremism in the Middle East draws lessons from these earlier meetings and underscores the need for continuing U.S. engagement in the Middle East.

As with all the work of the Aspen Strategy Group, the volume you hold today would not be possible without our supporters and partners. We are proud that many foundations, individuals, and corporations agree with our underlying thesis: nonpartisan and open dialogue among a diverse group of individuals can bring forward new ideas and meaningful solutions to some of the major challenges the United States faces. The Aspen Strategy Group provides a forum where experts can take time to comprehend the issues better providing background and context to the challenges of the day while looking to find concrete policy solutions. Unfortunately, venues for this type of deep dialogue are all too rare. The Aspen Strategy Group has been working to promote and host this style of convening for more than thirty years.

At our meeting in August of 2015, we invited some of the world's most authoritative and original thinkers for our Aspen Strategy Group sessions in Colorado to help us think through this extraordinarily complex problem. We are grateful to the experts and opinion leaders who drafted the chapters in this book for their scholarship and wisdom. We hope that their collective knowledge and insights will illuminate the major challenges that a revolutionary Middle East poses for the global community.

We are also grateful to the individuals and organizations who invest their time and resources to bring these ideas to the Strategy Group and the wider public. We would like to extend the deepest thanks to the John Anson Kittredge Fund, the Stanton Foundation, the Markle Foundation, the Resnick Family Foundation, the Rosenkranz Foundation, the Margot and Thomas J. Pritzker Family Foundation, the DEF Family Fund, Bank of America, Mr. Moses Feldman, Mr. Simon Pinniger and Ms. Carolyne Roehm, Mr. Howard Cox, the J. Ira and Nicki Harris Foundation, Mr. Robert J. Abernethy, Ms. Leah Joy Zell, and some donors who wish to remain anonymous.

Of course this volume would not be possible without the invaluable contribution of the distinguished Aspen Strategy Group members and invited participants who wrote the papers in this volume or offered their advice and comments to the authors. We would also like to thank our Brent Scowcroft Award Fellows, Mary Clare Rigali and Ole Moehr, for all their work to produce both the summer workshop and this book. They are both well on their way to promising careers. We are grateful for the service of Gayle Bennett in proofreading and editing this publication.

Finally, we must acknowledge that the Aspen Strategy Group was just an idea, until 1984, when the "founding three", Brent Scowcroft and William Perry as co-chairmen and Joseph Nye as Director, gave the idea life. Now, as then, they remain some of the most respected thought leaders for their extraordinary service and commitment to the Strategy Group's mission of nonpartisan dialogue. The ASG would not exist without them.

As the Strategy Group looks back on more than thirty years of workshops and publications, we are more convinced than ever that we fulfill an important and unique role as a nonpartisan forum, where strategic thinkers from the right, left, and center sit down together without partisan acrimony to solve America's most difficult challenges. As long as they're willing to do so, the Strategy Group will have the round table ready for the next conversation.

Contents

Part 3

A TOOLBOX TO COUNTER ISIS

Part 4

THE AMERICAN STRATEGY TO COMBAT ISIS AND VIOLENT EXTREMISM

Foreword
by ASG Co-Chairmen

Joseph S. Nye, Jr.
ASG Co-Chairman
University Distinguished Service Professor
John F. Kennedy School of Government
Harvard University

Brent Scowcroft
ASG Co-Chairman
President
The Scowcroft Group, Inc.

Over the years, many groups have sought to reestablish an Islamic caliphate, most recently al-Qaeda in Iraq when it emerged in 2004. Yet, when the Islamic State (ISIS) seized Mosul, Iraq, in June 2014, it took the international community by surprise. ISIS appeared to transform into a new threat with global implications overnight, but in a region beleaguered with religious, historical, and political tensions, its explosion onto the scene could have been anticipated.

The Islamic State presents a whole host of new challenges for policy makers as the group's caliph, Abu Bakr al-Baghdadi, poses a vision of a caliphate that demonstrates endurance and innovation. Yet, ISIS is not alone on the region's stage. Al-Qaeda and its Syrian affiliate, Jabhat al-Nusra, and other groups still plot, train, and maintain influence in the Middle East and North Africa region. These and other radical groups in the region present complex challenges. Each has its own motivations, history, and aspirations. And, despite varied strategies of engagement-boots on the ground in Afghanistan, training of local forces in Iraq and Syria, targeted special operations, efforts at diplomatic and political solutions-these groups remain influential and effective; indeed, some have even flourished.

In response to the evolving challenges extremist groups present in the Middle East, more than seventy leaders in academia, business, government, and journalism convened in August 2015 to analyze the roots and implications of radicalism in the Middle East under the auspices of the Aspen Strategy Group (ASG). The ASG, a policy program of the Aspen Institute, was originally founded to focus on the U.S.-Soviet relationship and arms control, but the Group has since evolved to examine the most critical foreign policy and national security issues confronting the United States. At our meeting in Aspen, Colorado, in August, the Group endeavored to make sense of the region's many dynamics and intertwined challenges that have contributed to the rise in radicalism—with a particular focus on the surprising success of the Islamic State.

This is not the first time the Group has addressed this topic. Following 9/11, this bipartisan collection of policy and thought leaders extensively debated the future of American policy in the Middle East. Most recently, in 2012, we examined the wave of revolutions sweeping across the Arab world. This meeting underscored the necessity for maximum flexibility in Middle East policy in order to facilitate transitions to a better form of governance. In 2002, 2003, and 2005, we discussed the homeland security threats generated by terrorism and militant jihadism. In 2005, former ASG Director Kurt Campbell presciently pinpointed four imminent challenges in his concluding observations of our workshop: weapons of mass destruction, war in Iraq, sectarian conflict, and the role of the Internet. Now ten years later, our 2015 Summer Workshop conversations sought to define the new challenge from the Islamic State, examine the current U.S. strategy to "degrade and defeat" it, and look at alternative policy options for the U.S. government and its allies to consider.

Over the course of our meeting, we discussed the costs and risks associated with intensifying engagement in Iraq and Syria. We looked at the American response in the region with varied lenses: we used case studies in Egypt and Tunisia to guide our discussions on the roots and appeal of extremism; we examined the military toolbox of capabilities against Islamic terrorism; we discussed how deeply rooted sectarian tensions enabled the spread of ISIS. We also looked at soft power dimensions of the problem. The group also took a careful look at the Syrian humanitarian crisis. Massive humanitarian assistance to the refugees (at which the American military is very effective) would enormously increase our soft power. In addition, we need to develop a capacity to take down botnets, counter hostile social media accounts, and contest the cyber territory ISIS occupies on the Internet. The transnational dimension of ISIS–the global campaign on social media–cannot be solved by hard power alone, but the funding and coordination of our soft power strategy is inadequate.

Even if we defeat ISIS over the coming decade, we should be prepared for a similar Sunni extremist group to rise like a Phoenix from its ashes. The Middle East is going through a series of revolutions, and revolutions take a long time to resolve. The sources of revolutionary instability include tenuous post-colonial boundaries, arrested modernization as described in the United Nations Arab Human Development

Report, the failed "Arab Spring," and religious sectarianism that is exacerbated by the interstate rivalry between Saudi Arabia (which has promoted fundamentalist Sunni beliefs) and Iran (which is the largest Shia country).

Looking back at European history, wars of religion between Catholics and Protestants lasted for a century and a half, and came to a close with the Peace of Westphalia in 1648 only after Germany lost a quarter of its population in the Thirty Years War. But it is also worth remembering that coalitions were complex, with Catholic France aiding Protestant Netherlands against Catholic Hapsburgs for dynastic rather than religious reasons. We should expect similar complexity in today's Middle East.

This volume contains the commissioned papers and overarching strategic insights derived from the Aspen Strategy Group's 2015 Summer Workshop titled, "Blindspot: America's Response to Radicalism in the Middle East." The following essays capture the range of opinions on the roots, drivers, and sustainability of radical groups in the region. Although we did not arrive at a unanimous prescription for tackling this multi-layered threat, the lack of consensus reinforces the need for continued attention. We believe that the turmoil in the region will not abate in the near future; rather, the United States will have to carefully weigh the costs and benefits of action and inaction over the long term, understanding that timeliness will be an integral component of the American response.

We hope this book will serve as an extension of our conversations in Aspen by sparking open dialogue and generating innovative solutions amongst experts and government leaders. We also entreat young leaders, who only have memories of a war-ridden Middle East, to evaluate closely the history of the region, as they will be tasked with constructing its future.

Part  I

THE ROOTS AND APPEAL OF EXTREMISM

The Seventh Annual Ernest May Memorial Lecture

The History and Ideology of the Islamic State

Bernard Haykel
Professor of Near Eastern Studies
Princeton University

CHAPTER 1

Extremism in the Middle East and Beyond

Fighting and Winning the Ideological War

Farah Pandith
Adjunct Senior Fellow
Council on Foreign Relations

CHAPTER 2

Radicalization After the Arab Spring

Lessons from Tunisia and Egypt

Shadi Hamid
Senior Fellow
The Brookings Institution

CHAPTER 3

Extremism, Sectarianism, and Regional Rivalry in the Middle East

Vali Nasr
Dean and Professor
Johns Hopkins School of Advanced International Studies

"*Thinking of the Islamic State in purely ideological terms offers only a partial explanation of the jihadist phenomenon in Iraq and Syria. To understand its emergence and appeal, one also has to look at the brutal political, economic, and social realities of the modern Middle East.*"

—BERNARD HAYKEL

The Seventh Annual Ernest May Memorial Lecture
The History and Ideology of the Islamic State

Bernard Haykel
Professor of Near Eastern Studies
Princeton University

Editor's Note: Bernard Haykel presented the annual Ernest R. May Memorial Lecture at the Aspen Strategy Group's August 2015 workshop in Aspen, Colorado. The following is a paper written based on his remarks at the meeting. The Ernest May Memorial Lecture is named for Ernest May, an international relations historian and Harvard John F. Kennedy School of Government professor, who passed away in 2009. ASG developed the lecture series to honor Professor May's celebrated lectures.

Earlier this year a debate raged in policy and academic circles about whether it is appropriate to use the adjective "Islamic" when referring to the Islamic State and other militant jihadist groups like al-Qaeda. This polemic is centered on President Obama's unwillingness to use the word Islam in any form when discussing these groups. He does not want to dignify them, or their claims, by an association with the religion of Islam and the great civilization it fostered. Instead, the term of art for jihadists in Washington is "violent extremists," and the policy against groups like the Islamic State is called "countering violent extremism" or "CVE." While this label is inelegant, the White House has made what appears to be a prudential policy decision on how to contend with the jihadist phenomenon. It does not wish to offend Muslims, and even hopes to galvanize them to join the policy of CVE. After all, the overwhelming majority of Muslims does not agree with the Islamic State's ideology and views its ideologues and fighters as misguided and perverting both the message and image of the faith.

As a scholar of Islamic studies, my role—unlike that of the policy-driven politician—is to study groups like the Islamic State, to trace their claims historically and to explain their ideology and rise. To do so, it is important to see in what ways the Islamic State is tied to the history of Islamic theology and law, how it cites texts of revelation, and how it selectively appropriates and refashions the tradition of Islam for its political purposes. In addition, it is equally important to study the political, economic, and social context in which this jihadist group emerged. In other words, to ignore the Islamic background and content of the Islamic State's ideology or the material factors that led to its rise is to fail in the scholarly enterprise and to fall short in providing the policy maker, the student, and the public with an adequate understanding of the global phenomenon of jihadism.

So who are the jihadists of the Islamic State, what do they believe in, how and why did they emerge, and what do they want to achieve?

The Islamic State is a Jihadi-Salafi movement, which means that its members adhere to a strict literalist interpretation of the texts of the Quran and the sayings of the Prophet Muhammad. They privilege armed struggle (jihad) as a means for implementing their austere, intolerant, and muscular vision of Islam. Salafis—not all of whom preach armed violence; only the Jihadi-Salafis do—have been an influential minority sect throughout the history of Islam. In pre-modern times, Salafis were associated with populist movements, as when some of their scholars were rabble-rousers in 10th-century Baghdad or when in 18th-century central Arabia they led a revivalist movement better known as Wahhabism (named after the founder of the movement, Muhammad ibn Abd al-Wahhab, who died in 1792).

Modern Salafis often claim that ordinary lay Muslims, whether in the past or the present, have beliefs and practices that are closer to a Salafi conception of the faith because of its "simplicity" and its attachment to a textual literalism that conforms with an "authentic" or "original" Islam. Much of Salafism's appeal lies in such assertions, and those searching for a locus of religious identity in our disenchanted modern world find a fully packaged version of the faith here. This claim, however, is not true on a number of counts, one of which is that in numerical terms most Muslims in pre-modern times were not Salafis; rather, they belonged to such traditional schools of law as Hanafism and were greatly influenced by Sufism—a mystical form of the faith at odds with Salafism—and the cult of dead saints associated with the Sufis. It is nonetheless true that in modern times, Sufism has declined considerably throughout the Islamic world and Salafism does indeed appear to enjoy widespread appeal. What explains this rupture with the past?

Salafism's ideology and worldview has come to the fore in modern times for a variety of reasons. Some of these have to do with the decline in stature of traditional institutions of religious authority as well as the spread of mass literacy and the personal desire of those not trained rigorously in the religious tradition to engage directly with the texts of revelation. Also, an urban middle class has arisen with particular expectations and desires, such as a personal sense of autonomy and a refusal to accept traditional hierarchies of learning and social status. (In this respect, what we see happening in the Islamic world is similar, though by no means identical, to the Protestant Reformation in Europe.) Finally, the funding of religious education by Salafi petro-states like Saudi Arabia has globally spread this literalist and textualist version of the faith.

Some have argued that petro-dollar financing alone explains the rise of Salafism, and if this funding tap was closed, the phenomenon would dissipate. While no doubt important, Saudi Arabia's funding is not a sufficient explanation for this religious revival, nor can it explain how so many Salafis, especially the jihadists among them, are virulent enemies of the kingdom. The blame attached to Saudi Arabia provides an overly simplistic narrative. The spread of Salafi teachings is rooted more in the needs and anxieties of modern Muslims—for greater religious certainty, for example—as well as with the emergence of new forms of authority, than in who is funding what. Moreover, people do not change their core beliefs and traditions purely for pecuniary reasons, and more is surely at stake when this takes place. Furthermore, those who posit the transactional model of Saudi funding for religious change never account for those who take the money but refuse to change or convert. Yemen provides many examples of this phenomenon.

Salafis principally target other Muslims for not following their version of Islam. They accuse their enemies of corrupting the faith with beliefs and practices that violate the doctrine of the oneness of God by associating other beings or things with Him. Many Muslims, Salafis argue, have become feeble because they have deviated into error and lost the "true" message of the faith. Their grievance is about theological issues and the need for reform, but this quickly acquires a political and militant dimension with the Jihadis who are frustrated with the inability to effect change through nonviolent means.

Jihadi-Salafis adhere to an activist doctrine in which they show loyalty toward fellow brethren in the faith and exhibit enmity and militant hatred toward the unbelievers—this is called in Arabic al-wala' wa-l-bara'. As a consequence of this, Shia and Sufi Muslims tend to be vilified by Jihadi-Salafis as unbelievers and often suffer violence. Of course, any self-proclaimed Muslim who supports democracy or a system of government Jihadi-Salafis deem un-Islamic is equally condemned as an unbeliever. To make their arguments, Jihadi-Salafis cite the most violent verses in the Quran and Hadiths of the Prophet Muhammad, and they also draw selectively on a pre-modern legacy of textual sources and methods of interpretation. By far the most important authority for them is the medieval Syrian scholar Ibn Taymiyyah (d. 1328), whose oeuvre represents an ideological bulwark against non-Salafi heresies. Yet, it must be stressed that Ibn Taymiyyah's teachings were more sophisticated and nuanced than the teachings of those who claim to be his modern heirs in the jihadi community.

In the realm of politics, the Jihadi-Salafis condemn in categorical terms the modern world order because its values and principles are not rooted in Islam but rather in the infidel West. More specifically, according to them, the modern world has stripped God of His sovereignty as the sole lawgiver and also weakened Muslims by dividing them into territorial states whereby citizenship, not faith, is the basis for identity and allegiance. To make matters worse, the rulers of these Muslim-majority countries have been co-opted into this system and ultimately serve the interests of the dominant West. These rulers have thus become "apostates" who must be toppled. How to go about this task is a matter of dispute among the Jihadi-Salafis. Some, like al-Qaeda, argue that attacks against the United States—the superpower that supports these regimes—must be undertaken because they will provoke a military response from the U.S. that will ultimately radicalize Muslims. In contrast, the Islamic State favors controlling territory, building a state, and fomenting a civil war between Sunnis and Shia as the path toward a general radicalization and adoption of its ideology. For the Islamic State, the attack on the West is to be indefinitely deferred until victory locally, in the Arab world, has been accomplished.

The ultimate goal of the Jihadi-Salafis is to make Muslims as powerful as they once were, before the relatively recent dominance of the West over the globe. To do this, it is not sufficient to educate Muslims about the tenets of the faith; one must engage in acts of violence, both individual and collective, against the enemies. Only by terrorizing the enemy, including through the use of suicide bombing and mass slaughter, enslavement, and beheadings, can victory be attained. In addition, re-creating the unitary imperial state of the early Islamic period, the caliphate, is deemed important because it can guide and channel the energies of the community and serve as an ideal around which Muslims can rally. This is one reason why the Islamic State declared itself the caliphate immediately after a series of remarkable military victories in Iraq in the summer of 2014.

The ideology described above is on display in countless online treatises and books written by the ideologues of Jihadi-Salafism. On the Internet, there are learned tomes and sermons by scholars such as Turki al-Binali, a 30-year-old prodigy from Bahrain who defends and elaborates the Islamic State's teachings with rhetorical eloquence and flair. Al-Binali's catechism-like treatises on theology and law are taught to all new recruits before military training is undertaken. But this ideology has become more effective and potent, especially at recruitment, because it is associated with what I label the culture of jihad. Unlike al-Qaeda, the Islamic State's supporters are masterful at producing technically sophisticated videos that are then skillfully distributed through social media applications such as Twitter, YouTube, and Facebook. And these are not just gory beheading clips, but include a cappella chants, poetic odes, scenes of battles interspersed with images of medieval knights on horses, clashing swords, and violent video game scenes. Particular favorites are clips from the movie *Kingdom of Heaven* as well as the video games "Assassin's Creed: Revelations" and "Call of Duty." Joining the jihad has become cool and means that one can live in a reality that mirrors a virtuous past, which is a contemporary projection of a time full of righteousness, heroism, and justice. This sentiment is evoked by the so-called female poet of the Islamic State, Ahlam al-Nasr:

Islam has become a fortress again; Lofty, firm and great
The banner of God's Oneness is raised anew; it does not bend nor deviate

But no one should be fooled into thinking that the society and state established by the Islamic State is a perfect reproduction of the past, as its ideologues and recruits would want everyone to believe. Many of its practices and beliefs are innovations (e.g., a female-only morality police force) or constitute a distortion in the form of an amalgam of the old and the new (e.g., wantonly destroying archeological sites that represent no threat for the spread of polytheism and idolatry). A question the Islamic State avoids answering is why it should destroy such sites when the virtuous first generation of Muslims, who after all conquered these territories in the 7th century, did not see fit to do so. Finally, much has been made of the apocalyptic or millenarian character of the Islamic State's ideology. The argument is that the Islamic State is a harbinger of the end times in which the Muslims would be ultimately victorious over the forces of evil and unbelief. This aspect of the ideology is used for purely propaganda and recruitment purposes and is not to be taken seriously. A couple of factors guide my thinking here. Why is the Islamic State's English language magazine called *Dabiq*, a place in Syria in which one of the battles of the apocalypse takes place, whereas no such allusions are made so explicitly in its Arabic publications? Also, and more important, why does the Islamic State expend effort and funds in building state institutions, as it has been doing in both Syria and Iraq, when the end is nigh?

Thinking of the Islamic State in purely ideological terms offers only a partial explanation of the jihadist phenomenon in Iraq and Syria. To understand its emergence and appeal, one also has to look at the brutal political, economic, and social realities of the modern Middle East. Perhaps the most important factor in this regard has been the U.S. invasion of Iraq in 2003. This assault on, and reconfiguration of, Iraq effectively disenfranchised the once dominant Sunnis and imposed a political system in which the majority Shia Arab population became the new masters of the country. Under the leadership of Nouri al-Maliki, the former Shia prime minister from 2006 until 2014, the Iraqi state pursued a sectarian agenda that marginalized and persecuted the Sunnis. In response, the Sunnis became radicalized and turned to the ideology of Jihadi-Salafism, with its virulent anti-Shia stance, as the path for resisting the new political order. The Sunni transformation toward militant Islamism was gradual and was aided by the Arab Spring uprisings of 2011, which quickly sowed violence and chaos in neighboring Syria. The Syrian Sunnis—some 70 percent of the country's population—had also been politically marginalized and since 2011 were being brutalized by the Damascus government, which is identified as Shia. The ruling Assad family, and most of its military and intelligence forces, belongs to a Shia sect called the Alawis or Nusayris. The Islamic State represents the merging of significant elements from the Iraqi and Syrian Sunni communities, with the aim of toppling the regimes in Damascus and Baghdad.

There are several other factors that also contribute to the Islamic State's appeal and help it draw recruits from across the Arab world, the source of most of its soldiers. Virtually every Arab country is ruled by a corrupt and unaccountable regime that practices coercion to obtain consent from the governed. These regimes have hollowed out their societies by deliberately destroying most forms of civic association, seeing in these potential sources of organized opposition to their rule. And the population in all Arab countries is very young, often with 60 percent under the age of 30—referred to as the youth bulge. Unemployment rates are high, and merit and competence are rarely rewarded. Obtaining work and advancement is often due to being connected to the right patronage network, a system that is referred to as clientelistm. The state is often the dominant employer and economic actor in society, and inability to obtain a job in the public sector dooms one to a precarious existence. Without employment, finding a marriage partner becomes very difficult, which delays the possibility of starting a family.

These economic impediments to development, both personal and societal, affect Arab populations that now have access to information through communication technologies such as the Internet and satellite television. Arabs know and see for themselves that other populations, in China or India for example, have it much better. This knowledge generates expectations, but for many individuals, it also causes considerable personal frustration and even hopelessness that they might ever improve their lot in life under the existing political systems. And to make matters even worse, the Arab world has four failed states (Libya, Syria, Iraq, and Yemen) in which all semblance of order has broken down. The Islamic State offers a utopian alternative, and its propaganda trumpets a social order that is just and moral and in which corruption is severely dealt with. A number of videos, for example, display Islamic State soldiers and officials being crucified for stealing.

The phenomenon of the Islamic State is multifaceted and its appeal is not straightforward. Its distinctive interpretation of Islam—the ideology of Jihadi-Salafism—cannot on its own explain its rise and relative success, nor can the political and economic realities of the Arab world explain it either. Only by adopting multiple perspectives, which combine the ideological and the material, can one begin to understand how and why the Islamic State has risen and what its trajectory might be. Its goals lie beyond Iraq and Syria, inasmuch as its ideologues boastfully claim that world conquest and the establishment of Islamic rule everywhere is their ultimate aim. Its immediate aim is to consolidate power over the territory it now controls and to expand further in Syria and Iraq. Saudi Arabia, however, remains the ultimate prize, and the Islamic State has made no secret of its intention to conquer the kingdom. Control over the two holy mosques in Mecca and Medina, not to mention the country's oil wealth, would go far in confirming the Islamic State's claims about its legitimacy and that it is carrying out God's plan.

The Islamic State will certainly not achieve any such dramatic conquest, and we are now beginning to see it suffer military defeat at the hands of a coalition that includes the U.S., Iraq, and Iran, among other nations. Thus far, it has only been able to take over Sunni-dominated territory and has not defeated either Shia or Kurds on their own ground. As it begins to lose battles and territory, the Islamic State's sheen will quickly fade. What will remain nonetheless are the factors that have allowed it to flourish in the first place, namely an ideology of religious power and domination as well as political, social, and economic realities that provide a wellspring of recruits and supporters who feel deeply disenfranchised and increasingly marginal to the flow of history. Only by addressing seriously these underlying causes and grievances will the phenomenon of jihadism be effectively dealt with. No amount of "countering violent extremism" through the U.S. government's messaging against Islamic State propaganda will turn this violent feature of global politics into a thing of the past.

Bernard Haykel is professor of Near Eastern Studies at Princeton University where he is also director of the Institute for the Transregional Study of the Contemporary Middle East, North Africa and Central Asia. Dr. Haykel is the author of *Revival and Reform in Islam*, and *Saudi Arabia in Transition*, both published by Cambridge University Press. He is also the author of numerous articles on Salafism, al-Qaeda, ISIS, and Wahhabism. He has received several awards, such as the Prize Fellowship at Magdalen College, Oxford, the Carnegie Corporation and Guggenheim fellowships, and the Old Dominion Professorship at Princeton. Dr. Haykel appears frequently in print and broadcast media, including PBS, NPR, the *New York Times*, al-Jazeera and the BBC among others. Dr. Haykel earned his D.Phil. in Oriental Studies from the University of Oxford.

"Since 9/11, Muslim youth have experienced a profound identity crisis unlike any in modern history. They have craved answers, seeking purpose and belonging."

—FARAH PANDITH

Extremism in the Middle East and Beyond
Fighting And Winning The Ideological War

Farah Pandith
Adjunct Senior Fellow
Council on Foreign Relations

Executive Summary

Extremism inspired by groups like the Islamic State, al-Qaeda, and others constitutes the single most comprehensive, sustained and global ideological threat to our country since communism. Fortunately, the solutions for fighting and winning the ideological war are both available and affordable. To build a safer, more stable world, we need to diminish the number of recruits to extremism, and that means helping Muslim youth solve a pervasive identity crisis that has gripped them since 9/11. We need to flood the marketplace with counter-narratives articulated by credible, organic, and local voices that Muslims themselves create all day, every day in ways that are millennial friendly. Our soft-power strategy, woefully neglected thus far in this area, must become more entrepreneurial, innovative, coordinated, and comprehensive, and it must receive appropriate funding. We must deploy it through a central point with accountability to the president or Congress, and we must integrate it well with our hard-power strategy. Indeed, we will only defeat extremism if we go "all in" behind a thoughtful, hybrid approach. In the absence of such a strategy, backed by words and actions, extremism will continue to spread, pushing the world further into an abyss of lone-wolf attacks, atrocities, armed conflict, and disorder.

In a *Washington Post* piece appearing on July 23, 2015, Under Secretary for Public Diplomacy and Public Affairs Richard Stengel wrote that "we are puncturing ISIL's myths through a targeted, locally tailored social media campaign" and that "when it comes to the information war, we are gaining ground and momentum."[1]

If only that were true. Just a day earlier, FBI Director James Comey stated that the organization known as the Islamic State (IS) was a bigger domestic threat than al-Qaeda, winning recruits in America and abroad and increasing the FBI's need to monitor hundreds of IS-sympathetic young Americans. "We have to, as a country, figure out how to solve this," Comey said, building off of his springtime comments that the FBI is tracking terrorism suspects in all fifty states.[2]

As our nation grapples with the now regular occurrence of so-called lone-wolf attacks like the incident in Chattanooga, as we encounter a Middle East we no longer recognize, as we embark on a new status quo in regards to the Iran nuclear deal, as Congress holds hearings on "The Rise of Radicalization: Is the U.S. Government Failing to Counter International and Domestic Terrorism?," and as the administration tries to reconfigure the "New Beginning" with Muslims in a post "Countering Violent Extremism Summit" era, the threat from extremists is growing in the Middle East and beyond. Extremist voices are saturating the virtual world *and* the real world with their message of "us" versus "them." They are outpacing and outmaneuvering every government on earth with their youth-friendly and "hyper-cool" call to action. When you consider that one billion Muslims are under the age of thirty, the pool from which the extremists recruit, you realize the full scope of the problem. *Extremism inspired by groups like IS, al-Qaeda, and others constitutes the single most comprehensive, sustained, and global ideological threat to our country since communism.*

Many inside and outside of government believe the current scourge of IS in Iraq and Syria is a recent development, one rooted fundamentally in the Middle East, and one that can be contained primarily by military force.[3] Further, many believe that the key to defeating the extremists is deploying specific tactics, specifically those related to social media.[4] Most critically, many believe that IS's strategic significance derives primarily from its particularities—its organizational architecture, strategy, and goals.[5]

I assess it differently. As I've seen firsthand, the rise of IS and other extremist groups is a threat years in the making and global in scope, one that requires an *intellectual* solution in addition to a military one. The threat isn't really just IS. Though each extremist group does have its particular purpose, genesis, history, financial instruments, tactics, and philosophy, the common ideology underlying these groups is our real enemy. We might defeat IS militarily, but what about the next IS that emerges somewhere around the world, and the next one, and the one after that?

Fighting and winning the ideological war requires that we go beyond short-term thinking and consider all angles and implications. We must develop a strategy for the real threat we're facing, not the one we wish we were facing. Trapped in a "what do we call this ideology" game, our conversations have usually led us so far to conventional solutions. Instead, we must address the crux of the issue: Why are Muslim youth so vulnerable? What in their ecosystems has allowed poisonous ideologies to take root? What is distinct about the Muslim millennial experience, and what will their experience mean for their kids and our future?

The Essence of the Extremist Threat

Between 2009 and 2014, I served as the Department of State's first ever special representative to Muslim communities, visiting communities in eighty countries around the globe and focusing on Muslim millennials and countering violent extremism (CVE). Previously, during the administration of George W. Bush, I worked on the War of Ideas at the National Security Council. Later, I served for three years as senior advisor to the assistant secretary of state for European and Eurasian affairs, focusing specifically on CVE and pioneering new efforts in the aftermath of the Danish Cartoon Crisis. In this capacity, I visited Muslim communities in 55 cities and 19 countries across Western Europe. Secretary Condoleezza Rice and Assistant Secretary Dan Fried created this role for me so that our nation could engage with Muslim youth in Europe, a region that most in our government did not see as particularly relevant to America's waging of the ideological war.

My roles as a political appointee under Democratic and Republican administrations afforded me trust, legitimacy, flexibility, and unprecedented grassroots access in places senior U.S. government officials rarely went. I was given an extraordinary ability to make connections and spot trends across a demographic rather than just a region, irrespective of who was in the Oval Office. Meeting personally with thousands of Muslims, hearing their stories and fielding their questions, I came away with a new perspective on trends relating to Muslim youth.

The realities I encountered flew in the face of many of the theories and seemingly logical explanations that circulate about extremism. Conventional explanations cite the so-called Arab Spring,[6] the lack of democratic values,[7] the lack of jobs and education,[8] our foreign policy,[9] our domestic policies,[10] our immigrant narrative,[11] our separation of church and state,[12] and, frequently "the reformation within Islam."[13] Yet what young Muslim men and women were confronting—and still are confronting— was different and more unwieldy. Since 9/11, *Muslim youth have experienced a profound identity crisis unlike any in modern history. They have craved answers, seeking purpose and belonging.*

Nearly every day since September 12, 2001, Muslim millennials have seen the word "Islam" or "Muslim" on the front pages of papers on- and offline. They have grown up scrutinized because of their religion, and much of this attention is confusing to them. As a result, they are asking questions like: What does it mean to be modern and Muslim? What is the difference between culture and religion? Who speaks for my generation? While members of earlier generations might have turned to close-knit families and communities for help, millennials are tuning into unsavory figures encountered online and in other venues. They look to "Sheikh Google" for answers and seek direction from like-minded peers. This demographic is experiencing something no generation of Muslims before it has experienced. Communities, not to speak of governments, were not and are not equipped to deal with the mammoth impact of this crisis of identity.

Understanding the vulnerability of young Muslims, extremists prey on them, offering ready-made answers. They market their ideas with savvy and alarming expertise—from magazines to apps, YouTube sermons to hip-hop and poetry. The extremists—whether al-Qaeda, IS, al-Shabaab, the Taliban, or Boko Haram—understand that to gain recruits, they must cater to their target audience. They are winning recruits because right now their narratives are louder and reach more youth than any other.

The responsiveness of extremists allows them to build virtual armies of activists around the globe; these activists in turn recruit youth to become part of a real army that perpetuates violence in communities around the world and on battlefields in the Middle East. The Middle East landscape, of course, is critical. Many youth find it validating to see the "powerful and victorious" IS armies march, train, and behead on Arab lands. They fervently believe that IS and others are launching a new chapter in human history.

Monolithic Islam

Regardless of the specific group disseminating it, extremist ideology has two critical components. The first is the notion that Islam is a *monolithic entity*. Extremists perpetuate a notion that has been spreading for years in Muslim communities worldwide—primarily thanks to foreign money and influence—that there is only one "true" or "right" version of Islam, and its norms should govern all of life. Extremists do not tolerate diversity of thought or practice within Islam, and in this respect, they're changing the very nature of Muslim communities the world over. Aside from its theological implications, the notion of a monolithic Islam has a real-world impact, including the sectarian violence arching from the Middle East toward Africa, Europe, Asia, and even South America.

Insecure in their own local identities and traditions, millennials have imbibed the notion of a singular Islam, and they suddenly feel that *the kind* of Muslim they are matters. Islam has become a *lifestyle brand* not so different in its cultural significance from conventional lifestyle brands like Harley Davidson, Apple, and so on. Youth are recasting every conceivable element in their daily existence to demonstrate a devotion to a monolithic notion of their religion. I call it the "halalization" of everyday life: every practice, behavior, or consumer purchase now has to be "halal," or conforming to an interpretation of how a "real Muslim" should act. That keychain you carry or that scarf you're wearing now can be branded as "Muslim" if it's deemed "proper." Not every Muslim has bought into this way of thinking, but enough have to make the theme of monolithic Islam relevant, indeed critical, to our policy-making.

Halalization is a cultural extension and expression of rampant Gulf religious norms; in effect, the Gulf Arabs have colonized not merely the mosques and ideology of their co-religionists, but daily life itself. As I traveled from Amman to Beirut to Cairo as well as to Nouakchott, Nairobi, and New Delhi, parents pulled me aside and said, "My daughter is dressing like she lives in the Gulf because she thinks this is proper" or "My son has suddenly started pushing back on our traditions saying they are not correct." This change is so evident that the marketplace is now accommodating it. In New Zealand, a local entrepreneur created "halal water" (there is no such thing); in Belgium and Saudi Arabia, adult intimacy shops carrying "halal" products have taken off; and in Paris and New York City, retailers have developed "modesty" apparel lines for millennials.

Why should policy makers care about this trend? Because enforcing the uniformity of practice and intolerance enhances the impact of extremist ideology. Youth are creating clear lines about identity and enforcing notions of who they are, speaking about their Muslim-ness in ways their parents did not. Self-identifying as Sunni or Shia, not just Muslim, they are rejecting the ancient groups that live side by side with them, showing fierce loyalty to their version of Islam.

It's also vital that policy makers understand a related strategy of extremists. In addition to advocating and identifying themselves with a narrow set of "halal" practices, extremists underlie their claims to represent the one, true brand of Islam by methodically erasing centuries of Islamic diversity around the world. As I write this, Islamic heritage is being washed away—evidence of its existence destroyed—so that in the future, new generations growing up will know only the extremists' version of truth. Boko Haram's destruction of 9th-century Qurans in Timbuktu replicated practices initiated by Saudi Arabia for decades all over the world. The recent IS destruction of ancient Assyrian heritage or the Taliban bombing of the Bamiyan Buddhas must be seen not just as a cultural tragedy but as a critical tactic used to enforce a specific ideology. We will see more actions like this going forward, precisely because the extremists are playing the long game, looking to rewrite history itself.

It's vital that we move to buttress local Muslim cultures and traditions and to support Islamic diversity in both our words and our deeds. Rejecting the idea of the "Muslim World," for example, is an important start, but clearly we must do more, including undertaking a larger effort to preserve Islamic heritage. Otherwise, a generation of Muslims risks falling under the sway of an especially intolerant, divisive, and violent brand of ideology that is marketed incorrectly as "Islam."

"Us" versus "Them"

A second primary component to extremist ideology concerns a bifurcation of the world into "us" and "them." At every turn, extremists assert that they are fighting an epic war as Muslims with the rest of the world (not just the West). Islamic imagery and mythology, the conspiracy theories of America or Jews fighting Islam—these and other motifs convey the notion that if not for The Rest, purity and peace would reign for "real" Muslims. Of course, extremists have to be able to "prove" the accuracy of such storytelling. To do so, they manipulate facts and connect them to emotion. It doesn't matter to America's bottom line if a blogger in Rabat believes America is at war with Islam, but it absolutely does matter if he or she brings youth along to *do something* about it. The us versus them narrative is growing exponentially because of the extremists' vast audience and the megaphone the extremists possess to sell it.

Mobilizing Women

To spread both key dimensions of their ideology, extremists are mobilizing a strategy in which women play a central role. Like Muslim millennial men, Muslim millennial women have experienced the crisis of identity and so are equally susceptible to extremist thinking. Although at first extremists pursued tactics that seemed largely gender-neutral, more recently they have aimed specific themes and tactics squarely at women. In February 2015, for instance, IS's all-female al-Khanssaa Brigade uploaded to the Internet a "Manifesto for Women" intended as a DIY book for millennial Muslim women wishing to become part of IS.[14] It contained information about how women can live properly as Muslims—handy tidbits like why marrying at nine years old is OK, why women shouldn't work outside the home or wear modern fashions, and how a woman's function is essentially to help create more potential martyrs for the "holy caliphate."

Again, this manifesto is hardly a one-off experiment or a short-term tactic. For IS, women recruits are a source of battlefield combatants; witness the wave of Western women heading to Syria or the high profiles attached to female extremists like the Jordanian prisoner Sajida al-Rishawi or Charlie Hebdo accomplice Hayat Boumedienne. But IS also understands the power of women to influence their children (for evidence of that power, just look at the Tsarnaev brothers). IS seeks more attacks on The Rest, but it also knows that to be viable long term, it must claim the loyalty of women—to provide sexual pleasure, to keep house, to procreate, to help actualize the model of domestic life that IS idealizes, and most recently, to serve as ideological messengers the world over. If we do not develop strategies that address women, we will likely face a next generation of extremist warriors that have been indoctrinated at birth to keep the threat to us alive and real.

Going "All In" Against the Extremist Threat

The War of Ideas today is far deadlier than it was in the years after 9/11, because the young recruits are so vulnerable to persuasion, purpose, and passion. Extremist ideologies are a virus that infects individuals and spreads to entire communities, shattering lives, destroying families, stoking fear, and disrupting the global economy and stability. The extremists are outpacing and outmaneuvering us in the ideological space, and to stop them we must take courageous and intelligent action, applying known methods and deploying all of our tools, both hard and soft power. Unless we act decisively, surpassing what we've done since 9/11 to inoculate communities, we will face an even more serious situation globally. We are currently "just" primarily seeing the Middle East in crisis, but one can imagine a terrifying situation in which this kind of war is being fought in multiple theatres at once, accompanied by expanded and more frequent lone-actor attacks from Chattanooga to Chennai.

Extremists must be stopped, and they *can* be stopped. The solutions for fighting and winning the ideological war are both available and affordable. To build a safer, more stable world, we need to diminish the number of recruits to extremism, and that means helping Muslim youth solve their own identity crisis. We must drown out the voices of extremists by supporting new concepts, causes, and charismatic leaders in which the youth can believe. We need to flood the marketplace with counternarratives articulated by credible, organic, and local voices that Muslims themselves create all day, every day in ways that are millennial-friendly. These voices are out there—if we know where to look.

The problem is we haven't spent much time or treasure looking. The U.S. government has struggled since 9/11 to wage a War of Ideas. After 9/11, we attempted to engage in such a war against al-Qaeda and the Taliban. Seeking to thwart their recruitment efforts, we focused on countering their narratives of us versus them. These efforts took place under the umbrella of CVE, a concept that has become fashionable of late but that actually dates from the Bush administration. Back then, it was an uphill struggle to get the interagency to buy into CVE. Most policy makers in our country and abroad couldn't envision how we could develop organic voices on the ground that could push back against al-Qaeda's ideology.

Still, several visionaries did understand that although the U.S. government did not have street cred with average Muslim youth, we did have the power to build platforms to raise up voices and build movements of credible voices. Thanks to the commitment and open-mindedness of these visionaries, we took risks and experimented, seeding initiatives that allowed us to launch new efforts on the ground and creating a road map of what was possible. Sisters Against Violent Extremism (SAVE) was designed in the image of Mothers Against Drunk Driving to be grassroots, local, and responsive. Recognizing that European Muslim youth needed positive role models, we created the first pan-European professional network that activated a new narrative and inspired others. By partnering with individuals and community groups across Europe, we managed to lift up voices of Muslims who had influence within local neighborhoods and communities, establishing the basis for a grassroots countermovement that would oppose extremist manifestations and messages. We joined former extremists, victims of terrorism, entrepreneurs, bloggers, and women into layered networks dedicated to combatting the allure of the extremist narrative and ideology.

When Secretary Clinton learned of our accomplishments in Europe as conveners, facilitators, and intellectual partners, she asked me to take our activities global. As special representative to Muslim communities (2009-2014), I used the same approach I did in the Bush administration to mobilize Muslim youth. I worked with our embassies to create first-of-their-kind global networks, like Generation Change, a network of Muslim change-makers who were committed to pushing back against extremist ideology. I listened to what youth were saying about the changing nature of extremists' appeal and tactics and focused on helping connect social entrepreneurs, activists, and other organic voices. We also launched efforts like Viral Peace, a program to train credible voices to push back against extremists online. Further, we identified "black holes" where we knew more work had to be done, including the increasing phenomenon of the radicalization of women.

We must now dramatically scale up innovative, entrepreneurial CVE programs if we are to prevail. I'm not talking about engaging in a messaging war on Twitter. I'm talking about getting credible, local voices to inoculate their communities against extremist techniques and appeal. I'm talking about helping parents understand extremist tactics so they can educate their children about this threat. I'm talking about supporting the hundreds of grassroots ideas and initiatives in our country and around the world that reject extremist ideology. I'm talking about working closely with mental health professionals to understand the adolescent mind and to develop programs that can help stop radicalization. Ultimately, we need to monopolize the marketplace of ideas on- and offline, spawning credible voices that give new agency and purpose to this generation.

CVE efforts are still very much in their infancy. Though our government has tried to counter extremist narratives through formal channels, scarce attention has been paid overall to CVE. We haven't approached the ideological war with the same resources or respect we did the physical war, devoting ourselves to an integrated strategy of hard and soft power. We did not ask the kinds of questions around the ideology that would have informed us of things to come and the global appeal, and we did not restructure ourselves to get ahead of the extremists. As a result, the extremist ideology has spread, leaving us where we are today: facing a virtual army of recruits not just from other countries, but from our own.

We have become all too familiar with gruesome images of beheadings and other atrocities, the destruction of human heritage, and the warnings of attacks on the homeland. Yet, still we remain locked into thinking that we can deal with the extremist threat primarily through hard power alone. While we have seen an increase in the interagency conversation around the ideological war, and CVE is the currency everyone is floating, our overall strategy to defeat the extremists does not contain a sufficient soft-power dimension. Ironically, extremists have done what we have not. They have mastered the use of soft power to persuade, influence, and recruit their armies. In fact, they depend on it for their success.

Our soft-power strategy to date has been ad hoc, disrespected, uncoordinated, and unimaginative. We have been tripped up by what the U.S. government can do and what we would like others to do for us. Though we have mastered soft power in other arenas, we have not been able to sell the potential results of soft power because we have not had a cohesive soft-power strategy, much less a comprehensive strategy joining hard and soft power.

The latter would allow for an expanded vision of the ideological threat, mobilizing all of our powers of persuasion to achieve our goals. Looking at both the ecosystem as well as the particular tactics, we would develop layers of tools that complement one another on- and offline, specifically focusing on millennials and the generation that follows them. We would distinguish between what is best done within government and what must be done outside of it. We would build new partnerships and rebuild old ones and create new pressure points and areas of influence. We would learn from the past and scale up what is already working. We would mobilize mental health professionals. We would leverage all our diplomatic tools, focusing on American audiences as well as foreign ones. We would reorganize our U.S. government effort to provide appropriate levels of funding and personnel. And, most important, we would put a senior person accountable to either the president or Congress in charge of this effort.

We can't create an ideological countermovement on the backs of a few isolated government-funded programs. It requires much broader commitment and focus. *Our strategy must be a cohesive, integrated, coherent, and comprehensive approach to the threat we face. We must wage a battle on all fronts with money, accountability, and experienced personnel.* We must look at this like we would any other contagion, rooting out its hosts globally and destroying its defenses. The extremists seem all-powerful, but they are not. We have yet to unleash the full power of our skills in the soft-power space. When we truly go all in, we'll see how vulnerable the extremists really are. We might not ever rid the world entirely of extremism, but by reducing extremism's appeal and dramatically depleting the supply of new recruits, we can remove it as a significant threat.

The Future Is Our Responsibility

For the first time since 9/11, we are reawakening emphatically to the growing threat posed by extremists. At the moment, we are rightfully concerned about the potential of radicalized youth returning from battlefields to conduct terrorist actions. But in addition to the short-term impacts on public safety, we should be concerned about the longer-term ability of battle-hardened extremists to build new terrorist networks at home and extend existing ones by preying on youth. Extremists remain radicalized once they return. They are technologically savvy and understand how to use emotions to attract recruits. They also might command heightened and growing legitimacy in Muslim communities. Hard-power actions are a start—it is critical that we stop IS's momentum. But we need to do much more to prevent recruitment of new terrorists.

If we do not go all in, the extremist threat will continue to evolve in ways we do not yet fully understand. We know that the extremists are already recruiting among the four million refugees (including a large number of youth) who have fled fighting in Syria and Iraq. We cannot yet know the numbers or the impact that such recruitment will have on that region or other parts of the globe, but clearly this represents a dangerous and compelling threat. In addition, while governments are still trying to understand the extremists' recruitment of women, we are learning of children already training to be IS warriors. Referred to as "cubs," these children, once grown, will comprise a massive untested demographic. What do we know of adults who have been brainwashed to be violent when only seven or eight years old? In addition, do we yet know the full impact of U.S.-born extremist fighters returning home?

Despite the uncertainties, we can easily imagine what the world might look like if we continue to wage a half-hearted ideological battle. We will face the prospect of many more so-called lone-wolf attacks on the homeland. We could well see the proliferation of multiple IS-like groups at the same time, all clamoring for recruits, all expertly mobilizing technology to win them over, and all gleaning insights from a careful study of IS, just as IS previously gleaned insight from a study of al-Qaeda. The identity crisis underlying extremism will worsen, and younger Muslims will grow up perceiving extremism as an ever more credible ideology on the rise. More ancient sites will be destroyed worldwide, further cementing the extremists' narrative. And, of course, we'll see ever more gruesome atrocities circulated on the web as extremists continuously try to up the ante.

Concern about extremism has reached unprecedented levels in America. You see it in the statements of Secretary of Homeland Security Jeh Johnson and FBI Director Comey, and you see it in the statements of concerned parents across the country. With the start of a presidential campaign cycle that includes a revised focus on homeland security and foreign policy, the nation is beginning to talk about whether we can make a difference in the larger ideological war. Vast numbers of Americans now understand that what is happening over there has an impact over here. The question remains: Do we now have the political will and attention to develop a strategy commensurate with the extremist threat?

We should remember that the extremists might win—a possibility acknowledged recently by former CIA Deputy Director John McLaughlin in the *New York Times*.[15] If that were to happen, it would be a tragedy of our own making. Fourteen years after 9/11, we should not feel content with the pace of our efforts. Yet a strong effort now can still turn the tide. We can destroy the extremists' ability to recruit young Muslims. We can beat extremists at their own game, ending their exploitation of the Muslim identity crisis. Doing so won't cost a fraction of traditional hard-power solutions, but we will need to take a more entrepreneurial and innovative approach to policy-making. We must stop playing catch-up and get ahead of trends. We must not look at specific conflicts or extremist groups as if they are one-offs and instead take a broader view. As a nation, we must move swiftly, like nimble start-ups. We defeated communist ideology during the Cold War by mustering creativity and full-on dedication. We can and must do this again. The time to act is now.

Farah Pandith is an Adjunct Senior Fellow at the Council on Foreign Relations and a Senior Fellow at Harvard University's Kennedy School of Government. She is writing a book and driving efforts to counter extremism through new organizations, programs and initiatives. Ms. Pandith has served as a political appointee in the George H.W. Bush, George W. Bush, and Barack H. Obama administrations. She has served in various senior capacities focused on issues of countering violent extremism, democracy, development, and Muslim youth. Most recently, she was appointed the first-ever Special Representative to Muslim Communities by Secretary of State Hillary Rodham Clinton (2009-2014). She served in this capacity for both Secretaries Clinton and Kerry. Ms. Pandith traveled to more than 80 countries in this capacity and launched youth-focused CVE initiatives. She is also a key architect of the Women in Public Service Project. She was awarded the Secretary's Distinguished Honor Award. Her one of-a-kind programs in countering violent extremism have been singled out by organizations as diverse as the Bi-Partisan Policy Center and *Wired* magazine. Prior to this appointment she served as Senior Advisor to the Assistant Secretary of State for European and Eurasian Affairs where she was responsible for pioneering CVE strategies across Europe (2007-2009) and traveled to 19 countries and 55 cities across Europe. She served on the National Security Council as Director of Middle East Regional Initiatives focusing on "Muslim Outreach", democracy and Islam (2004-2007). She was Chief of Staff of the Bureau for Asia and the Near East (2003-2004) for the US Agency for International Development (USAID). She served at USAID from 1990 -1993 on the Administrator's staff and as the Special Assistant to the Director of Policy. She has been a consultant in the public, private and non-profit sectors. From 1997 to 2003 Ms. Pandith was Vice President of International Business for ML Strategies in Boston, Massachusetts. She is a member of Secretary of Homeland Security Jeh Johnson's Homeland Security Advisory Council, a Strategic Advisor to the Risk and Network Exchange (RANE) and the Institute for Strategic Dialogue. At Harvard, she is part of the leadership team of The Berkman Center for Internet and Society's Viral Peace Program, an initiative to counter extremism online, and a former Institute of Politics Fellow. She serves on the Advisory Board of the Women in Public Service Project, The Tribeca Film Institute and American Abroad Media. She is a Member of the Leadership Council of Women and Girls Lead, and on the board of the We Are Family Foundation. Ms. Pandith is the recipient of various global honors for her work including the Ring of Tolerance Prize. She was named by *Boston Magazine* as "one of 75 Bold Thinkers Shaping Our City" and was named one of the 100 Most Powerful Women by *Washingtonian* Magazine. She is part of the Smithsonian's The Network by artist Lincoln Schatz, a permanent exhibit at The National Portrait Gallery, and has appeared in print, radio, television and film from *The New York Times* to a documentary for the 9/11 Museum. Ms. Pandith received a Master's degree from The Fletcher School of Law and Diplomacy at Tufts University, and received an A.B. in Government and Psychology from Smith College. She has served as a Trustee of

Smith College and Milton Academy, and is currently a member of the Board of Overseers of The Fletcher School of Law and Diplomacy and the Smith College President's Council. She was awarded the Smith College Medal and the Distinguished Achievement Award by Tufts University. She was born in Srinagar, Kashmir, India, and raised in the Commonwealth of Massachusetts.

[1] Stengel, Richard. July 23, 2015. "The United States is gaining ground against the Hashtag Jihadis." *The Washington Post.*

[2] Condon, Scott. July 22, 2015. "FBI director reveals hidden threat of ISIS at Aspen Security Forum." *The Aspen Times.*

[3] Dathan, Matt. September 9, 2015. "ISIS and Assad must both be defeated by 'hard military force'; David Cameron signals UK is close to bombing Syria." *The Independent.*

[4] Cooper, Abraham. June 7, 2015. "To Defeat ISIS We Must Convince Twitter, YouTube to 'Unfriend' Terrorists." *The Algemeiner.*

[5] Meek, James Gordon. April 25, 2015. "ISIS an 'Incredible' Fighting Force, US Special Ops Sources Say." ABC News.

[6] Attkisson, Sharyl. March 12, 2015. "How Arab Spring Opened the Door to Terrorism's Ugly March." *The Daily Signal.*

[7] DiPuccio, William. November 1, 2012. "Islam and Extremism: What Is Underneath." The Gatestone Institute.

[8] "State Department spokeswoman floats jobs as answer to ISIS." February 17, 2015. Fox News.

[9] Taylor, Adam. March 9, 2015. "3 times U.S. foreign policy helped to create the Islamic State." *The Washington Post.*

[10] Schmitt, Eric. October 4, 2014. "U.S. Is Trying to Counter ISIS' Efforts to Lure Alienated Young Muslims." *The New York Times.*

[11] Ricks, Thomas E. January 29, 2015. "Some thoughts on how to change the narrative on violent Islamic extremism." *Foreign Policy.*

[12] Benen, Steve. September 17, 2014. "Religious right leader ties U.S. 'secularism' to Islamic State." MSNBC.

[13] Ali, Ayaan Hirsi. March 20, 2015. "Why Islam Needs a Reformation." *The Wall Street Journal.*

[14] The Al-Khanssaa Brigade. January 23, 2015. "Women of the Islamic State." See translation: www.quilliamfoundation.org/wp/wp-content/uploads/publications/free/women-of-the-islamic-state3.pdf.

[15] Arango, Tim. July 21, 2015. "ISIS Transforming Into Functioning State That Uses Terror as Tool." *The New York Times.*

"Radicalization, as it happens in real life, is inelegant. It's banal to say so, but different people radicalize in different ways."

—SHADI HAMID

Radicalization After the Arab Spring
Lessons from Tunisia and Egypt

Shadi Hamid
Senior Fellow
The Brookings Institution

Any discussion of Islamist radicalization lends itself to analytical confusion, particularly if we're looking for an elegant model of why people turn to political violence and terrorism. Radicalization, as it happens in real life, is inelegant. It's banal to say so, but different people radicalize in different ways. As we will see, trying to understand why a particular individual in a Tunisian slum radicalizes and decides to join ISIS will always be something of a mystery. Why him (or her) and not someone else in that same slum who experiences many of the same political and economic pressures?

As terrorism scholar Jessica Stern writes: "It is difficult to make gross generalizations about what leads individuals to do what they do in any area of life; difficulty in answering this question is not unique to terrorism experts."[1] For some, radicalization is a gradual process that takes place over many years—the product of accumulated experience. Others might be predisposed to radical politics, but it is only a catalyzing moment that pushes them not just to theorize or think about violence, but to act on it. Each individual interacts with his or her own socio-political environment in distinctive, often unpredictable ways.

When looking at individual-level radicalization, the goal is to understand the different pathways and contributing causes. A more fruitful approach, however, comes with widening the aperture and asking which contexts make the resort to violence among (some) citizens more or less likely, all other things being equal. This *probabilistic* approach lacks the thick description of individual-level stories of would-be or actual jihadists, but it tends to be more useful from a policy perspective. For example, Egypt is a strategically important country as well as a close ally. Accordingly, we are concerned about the things Egypt does—adopting repressive measures and a heavy-handed security mindset, for example—that provide a more enabling environment for terrorist activity.

Lastly, while it isn't the focus of this paper, we can also consider *organizational*-level radicalization. For example, the Egyptian Muslim Brotherhood is a mainstream, rather than a radical or extremist, Islamist organization. Yet, after the Egyptian coup of July 2013, a process of radicalization began at the individual level, with a growing minority of younger Brotherhood members advocating "defensive violence" and, more recently, economic sabotage to the dismay of an older, more conservative leadership-in-exile. But the use of violence is only one element of radicalization and not necessarily the most important. Younger Brotherhood members have adopted a more revolutionary posture, seeing the Egyptian state not as something to be reformed (the group's pre-2013 position), but as an enemy to be overhauled, purged, or even destroyed. Those who advocate "defensive violence" primarily make tactical arguments. However, these changing attitudes toward state institutions suggest a potentially deeper, philosophical shift, with profound long-term implications. This new, revolutionary politics has, over time, seeped up to the Brotherhood's leadership and organizational structures. It reflects not just a critical mass of individual Brotherhood members adopting different attitudes toward political change, but an *organizational* shift as well.

This paper is divided into two sections, one focused on Tunisia's unusually high contribution of foreign fighters to Syria and the other a case study of terrorism and insurgency in Egypt after the military's overthrow of President Mohamed Morsi of the Muslim Brotherhood. These two cases offer different insights into how radicalization occurs in the age of ISIS. Again, my main question of interest is: What kinds of contexts are more or less likely to produce higher rates of political violence?

Tunisian Foreign Fighters and Islamist Extremism in Syria

Despite deep ideological polarization, the democratic transition in Tunisia survived, flawed but intact. That's not to say there weren't darker undercurrents. As the democratic transition sputtered along, a disproportionately large number of Tunisians were looking elsewhere for hope and inspiration. More than 3,000 Tunisians found that inspiration on the battlefields of Syria, accounting for a shockingly high percentage of an estimated 22,000 foreign fighters.[2] According to the Tunisian interior ministry, as of April 2015, another 12,490 Tunisians had tried to leave to fight in Iraq, Syria, and Libya but were blocked by the authorities.[3]

One could spend days in the capital city of Tunis and not see a single sign. Yet if you were a young Tunisian, you almost certainly knew friends, acquaintances, and even family members who had gone to fight. This was the new normal. Internationally,

Tunisia was being fêted as a democratic "model," but many in the ultraconservative Salafi community felt that there was no place for them in the political process.

As mentioned above, understanding the causes of individual-level radicalization is something of a mystery, even (or perhaps particularly) for those who knew the person in question intimately. During a recent research trip to Tunisia, I interviewed a man I will call Yassine. Yassine's son, a business student at Manouba University, went to Syria and died fighting for ISIS in August 2013.

"It happened all at once," Yassine recalled. The son, whom I will call Hichem, began spending a lot of time at the mosque and going to the *fajr*, or dawn, prayer. He grew a short beard and started wearing a thobe, the telltale dress of Salafis. "I told him this isn't how we Tunisians dress, and he took it off," said Yassine. "But he got a passport without telling us. He would tell his mother everything, except this one thing. One day, on a Sunday, he didn't come home. He called to say he was staying with a friend, although that's not something he ever did."

How did a father, or anyone else for that matter, make sense of such a tragedy? Yassine had a number of hypotheses for why his son went to Syria, ranging from the lure of Internet jihadist forums to a Salafi preacher at the local mosque who "brainwashed" his son, inserting foreign ideas of *takfir*, or the excommunication of fellow Muslims. Yassine said that his son and other young Tunisians were initially attracted to Syria (as opposed to Libya, the Sinai, or even acting inside of Tunisia) because of the unfolding humanitarian catastrophe. Watching the slaughter of their Muslim brethren at the hands of the Assad regime, they were moved to act in whatever way they could. The groups that were most hospitable to foreign fighters were the Islamist rebel factions, the most powerful of which at the time was Jabhat al-Nusra. Far from the usual al-Qaeda franchise, Nusra, directing its fire against Bashar al-Assad and fighting alongside "moderate" Free Syrian Army (FSA) factions, enjoyed considerable legitimacy among Islamist and non-Islamist Syrians alike. After the falling out between Nusra and the Islamic State of Iraq, many Tunisian fighters, including Hichem, defected to what would become the Islamic State of Iraq and Syria, or ISIS.

Young fighters, with no real military experience, went to Syria not knowing what to expect. Some became disillusioned. Others like Hichem appear to have radicalized over the course of the fighting, particularly after joining ISIS. "In the final months, he was asking his mother to pray for him to join the ranks of the martyrs," his father recalls. This isn't necessarily surprising. War and radicalization go hand in hand, which makes it all the more important to distinguish between the initial motivations for joining an Islamist rebel group and how those motivations and ideological commitments evolve over time. In other words, a young Tunisian might, at first, be moved to join Nusra for "secular" reasons—to fight Assad out of a desire for revenge because their friends joined, or because those groups take better care of fighters or have more advanced weapons. Individuals are complex, so we should assume that their motivations are complex as well. This suggests that the decision to ally with one faction over another is based on some combination of all of the above factors. Of course, religion plays a role as well, otherwise we would see liberal Tunisians going to fight for, say, the FSA. Salafi-oriented Tunisians are more likely to see the Assad regime as a secular, infidel regime at war with pious Sunni Muslims. They are more likely to see jihad as religious obligation. For them, it doesn't matter that they are Tunisian and the people they're ostensibly fighting on behalf of are Syrian; they are all Muslims, bound together as members of a transnational *umma*. But while religion may be necessary, it is not sufficient.

One of the few survey-based studies of Syrian rebel motivations supports the broad outlines of Yassine's account. Drawing on interviews with over 300 fighters in 2013-2014, Vera Mironova, Loubna Mrie, and Sam Whitt found that the "many reasons given by Islamists for taking up arms are not that different from FSA fighters."[4] While 71 percent of Islamists cited the desire to build an Islamic state, only 25 percent said this was their main motivation. Interestingly, when they interviewed FSA fighters who defected to an Islamist group, "almost all mentioned reasons which were not expressly religious."

However, after spending a significant period of time with a particular Islamist faction, fighters are likely to adopt and internalize more and more of the group's ideology. In other words, the "Islamism" of Islamist rebels is, to an extent, *acquired*. According to the study, 74 percent of the Islamist respondents said they had become more religious since the beginning of the war. Daily immersion and indoctrination in a group's propaganda is difficult to resist. More fundamentally, the natural desire to belong and be part of a cause that transcends the individual—something that grows increasingly appealing when facing death—contributes to a powerful and self-reinforcing dynamic. The most radical groups, such as Nusra and ISIS, obviously take ideological coherence seriously. Accordingly, individual fighters, even those with reservations, have strong incentives to demonstrate ideological fervor in order to gain the favor of local and regional commanders. Fear also plays a role, particularly in ISIS, where openly expressing doubts about the organization can bring about an untimely death. With individual fighters demonstrating, or even overstating, their devotion to the cause, a kind of religious outbidding takes place, leading to a vicious cycle of radicalization.

While it may be more pronounced in the region, this cycle isn't necessarily unique to civil conflict in the Arab world. Moderates tend to lose out in revolutions and civil wars. The longer a society experiences chaos and disorder, the stronger radicals become. As radicals grow stronger, violence intensifies further, and so on. As Samuel Huntington writes in his classic 1969 work *Political Order in Changing Societies:* "Moderates remain moderate and are swept from power. Their failure stems precisely from their inability to deal with the problem of political mobilization. On the one hand, they lack the drive and ruthlessness to stop the mobilization of new groups into politics; on the other, they lack the radicalism to lead it."[5]

Almost by definition, gradualism loses its appeal in the totalizing fog of battle. When the goal is to vanquish an opponent, or merely stay alive, everything else fades in comparison. For the "moderate," the taking up of arms is done grudgingly, if at all. The radicals, however, embrace violence because they have lost faith, if they ever had it, in the possibilities of politics. Revolution is the only way, and revolution is about maximalist aims. Why, exactly, would people who are willing to kill and die for a cause care about being moderate? In their book *ISIS: Inside the Army of Terror,* journalists Michael Weiss and Hassan Hassan identify an unlikely, even odd, category of ISIS supporter: secularists or agnostics who "express deep objections about [ISIS] atrocities" but come to embrace violence as necessary.[6]

The Problem of Theodicy

In understanding individual-level motivations for joining ISIS, theodicy looms large. The problem of theodicy involves answering, or at least trying to answer, the question of why God permits evil in the world. Far from merely an esoteric exercise, the problem of theodicy impacts how religious movements interpret evil and, perhaps more important, how they respond to it. And there is little doubt that the post-Arab Spring period has featured a considerable degree of "evil": a list of massacres too long to recount, bloody civil wars, the resurgence of brutal authoritarianism, and so on.

Atheists and skeptics tend to see the existence of evil, and God's seeming indifference to it, as invalidating the very notion of the divine. Islamists, and particularly those of the Salafi-Jihadi strain, see the existence of evil—in the form of the oppression of Muslims, the abolition of the caliphate(s), and the brutality of war—as part of a cosmic struggle. If there is evil, then it must be fought. Here it is worth quoting a fascinating essay by the author Ziya Meral.

> While we were amusing ourselves with the myopic question of how religion leads to violence we have missed out on the main question: How does violence alter religion and religious believers? Exposure to violence and injustice, seeing no "why," and looking for a "how" to survive, requires theological responses in their rawest form: What is wrong with this universe? What is right? How do I understand what I see?[7]

Meral considers what might motivate a religiously unlearned jihadist. For many would-be French, British, or Tunisian fighters, the first question is not necessarily one of theology. In a May 2015 audio recording, ISIS leader Abu Bakr al-Baghdadi unsurprisingly highlights the realities of repression and displacement when calling on Muslims to make *hijra* to the Islamic State. "We call upon you so that you leave the life of humiliation, disgrace, degradation, subordination, loss, emptiness, and poverty," he says, "to a life of honor, respect, leadership, richness, and another matter that you love—victory from Allah and an imminent conquest."[8] The aspiring jihadist's point of departure, Meral writes, is a "moral reading of the universe through personal experience, and the finding that it is corrupt, chaotic, and unfair. That is why it was only after deciding to travel to Syria did two confused British gap-year-adventure jihadists order *Qur'an for Dummies*. He concludes: "By the time theological discussion of when and how Muslims can engage in violent jihad occurs, the more important questions will have already been asked and answered. Jihad is the last theological question."

The brutality of the salafi-jihadists, then, is in part the product of an already brutal political environment. Even if these would-be jihadists don't live in failed states themselves, they see those states all around them, and because of the powerful notion of a worldwide Muslim *umma*, they come to feel that injustice as if it were their own. This can be considered a form of "altruistic killing," to use Stern's evocative phrasing.[9]

Egypt, ISIS, and the Failures of Mainstream Islamism

In the previous section, I used the example of a Tunisian ISIS fighter to discuss how individual-level and societal-level factors interact. Here, I will focus more on the latter: How does a major change in political environment—in this case the July 2013 coup and the subsequent crackdown on Islamists—alter incentives for radicalization? Post-

Arab Spring Egypt offers a unique case study, allowing us to use what is sometimes called a "before-after" research design. As the political scientists Alexander George and Andrew Bennett write, this can be done by "dividing a single longitudinal case into two—the 'before' case and an 'after' case that follows a discontinuous change in an important variable."[10] What this requires is a "turning point," where the independent variable of interest—in this case the level of repression—undergoes a qualitative shift.

President Abdel Fattah el-Sissi came to power on a classic strongman platform, promising stability and security at a time when most Egyptians had grown exhausted from the uncertainties of the Arab Spring. This raison d'etre, though, has been undermined with each passing month: by any measurable standard, Egypt is more vulnerable to violence and insurgency today than it had been before. On July 1, 2015, 64 soldiers,[11] perhaps more, were killed in coordinated attacks claimed by Egypt's ISIS affiliate, which calls itself the Province of Sinai. It was the worst death toll in decades and came just days after the country's chief prosecutor, Hisham Barakat, was assassinated.

Since Morsi's overthrow, Egypt has witnessed an unprecedented increase in regime repression. On August 14, 2013, Egypt experienced the worst mass killing in its modern history, with at least 800 killed in mere hours. By March 2015, security forces had arrested more than 40,000 people.[12] Meanwhile, since April 2015, at least 163 Egyptians have been "disappeared."[13] Some human rights activists put the number as high as 800.[14] These abductions at the hands of the state take place outside the law or, in Egyptian parlance, "behind the sun." It is little surprise then that repression under the regime of Abdel Fattah el-Sissi is "on a scale unprecedented in Egypt's modern history," according to Human Rights Watch.[15]

Intuitively, we would expect that this kind of repression might make the resort to violence and terrorism more likely among at least some Egyptians.[16] But to what extent is this the case? How much does the increase in terror attacks *really* have to do with the coup and subsequent crackdown? Putting aside what we think for a moment, ISIS clearly thinks it benefited from Morsi's overthrow. In ISIS's first statement after the coup, spokesman Abu Muhammad al-Adnani, addressing the Muslim Brotherhood and other mainstream Islamists, says, "you have been exposed in Egypt."[17] He refers to "democracy" and the Brotherhood as "the two idols [that] have fallen."

Of course, jihadists had long been making this argument, particularly after Iraq's Muslim Brotherhood took part in successive U.S.-backed governments during the 2000s. Al-Qaeda and its ilk gleefully described the Muslim Brotherhood as *al-Ikhwan al-*

Muflisun, or the Bankrupt Brotherhood—a play on its Arabic name. But while al-Qaeda may have achieved a measure of sympathy in the Middle East after the September 11 attacks, it was never, and never could be, a real threat to the Brotherhood's model of political change. It was proficient at staging terrorist attacks but proved unable to carry its successes into the realm of governance. More important, al-Qaeda's vision for state-building, to the extent it had one, failed to capture the attention of the world or the imagination of tens of thousands of would-be fighters and fellow travelers.

The same cannot be said about ISIS, whose seemingly irrational apocalyptic vision[18] coexists with an unusually pronounced interest in governance. As Yale University's Andrew March and Mara Revkin lay out in considerable detail, the group has, in fact, developed fairly elaborate institutional structures.[19] Intellectually and theologically, ISIS is not just Baathist brutality in Islamic garb. Rather, it has articulated a policy toward Christian minorities based on a 7th century pact,[20] an approach to Islamic economic jurisprudence,[21] and even a heterodox theory of international relations.[22]

ISIS's successes in the realm of governance undermine a key premise of mainstream Islamists—that because of their gradualism, pragmatism, and "competence," they, rather than extremists, are better suited to delivering on bread-and-butter issues. In fact, the opposite appeared to be true: Brotherhood-style gradualism and a willingness to work through the democratic process *hadn't* worked. One senior Brotherhood official told me in February 2015, as we sat in a café on the outskirts of Istanbul: "If I look at the list of mistakes the Brotherhood made, this is the biggest one: trying to fix the system from inside gradually."[23]

Even those who otherwise abhor ISIS's ideology might find themselves susceptible to the argument that violence "worked," while peaceful participation didn't. It's an argument that ISIS and its affiliates have repeatedly tried to drive home: in one recruitment video, a young Egyptian man—a judge in one of the Islamic State's Islamic courts—tells the camera that "[Islamist groups that participate in elections] do not possess the military power or the means to defend the gains they have achieved through elections. After they win, they are put in prison, they are killed in the squares, as if they'd never even won . . . as if they had never campaigned for their candidates."[24] Needless to say, this particular pitch wouldn't have been possible in 2013, when Morsi was still in power, or even in 2012, when the Supreme Council of the Armed Forces was in charge. In short, the Egyptian coup—coupled with the subsequent massacres and never-ending crackdown—have given the arguments made by al-Qaeda in the 2000s more power than ever before.

This is all well and good, but what do the numbers have to say? According to the Tahrir Institute for Middle East Policy, July 2013, the month of the coup, saw a massive uptick in violence, from thirteen to ninety-five attacks.[25] This is especially striking considering that the previous month of June had been quite tense in its own right, and it seemed an opportune time for militants to take advantage of the June 30th anti-Morsi protests and the accompanying sense of insecurity among Egyptians. The number of attacks dipped in subsequent months—to sixty-nine in August and fifty-six in September—but remained significantly higher than before Morsi's overthrow. The pre- and post-coup discrepancy becomes even more obvious when we zoom out further: from July 2013 to May 2015, there were a total of 1,223 attacks over twenty-three months, an average of 53.2 per month. In the twenty-three months prior to June 2013, there were a mere seventy-eight attacks, an average of 3.4 attacks per month.

If the coup had little or nothing to do with this, it would stand as one of the more remarkable coincidences in the recent history of Middle East politics. Of course, other variables of interest, such as the flow of arms from Libya or ISIS's growing stature, may have contributed to these outcomes, but neither variable changed in mid-to-late 2013 to an extent that could account for such a sharp increase in attacks over such a relatively short period of time. Civil conflict in Libya and the role of competing militias resulted in a more porous border and an increase in arms smuggling as early as 2012. As for ISIS's stature, it wasn't even called ISIS before 2013, when it was known as the Islamic State of Iraq. And while ISIS was making important gains in Iraq throughout 2014, ISIS didn't register in a serious way in the broader region until the summer of 2014, when the group took over Mosul, Iraq's second largest city.

That leaves us with the coup and what it wrought—namely the Sissi regime's increasingly repressive measures—as the key event that helped spark the wave of violence. How many people who otherwise wouldn't have taken up arms, took up arms because of the coup and the crackdown? Obviously, there is no way to know for sure. The strength of Ansar Bait al-Maqdis (ABM), the group that eventually pledged allegiance to ISIS and renamed itself Sinai Province, is estimated to be in the thousands, so even a tiny increase of, say, 500 militants—representing 0.00055 percent of Egypt's overall population—would have an outsized effect. Recruitment, however, takes time, so it is unlikely this would have mattered in the days immediately after the coup. The more likely short-term explanation is that militants viewed the coup as an opportune moment to intensify their activities for two main reasons. First, the Egyptian military—an organization, like any other, with finite resources—was preoccupied with securing major urban centers and clamping down on the

Brotherhood. Second, militants likely wagered that they could capitalize on the wave of Islamist anger and anti-military sentiment.

ABM exploited the "narrative" of the local Sinai population, which was already predisposed to distrust state institutions after years of economic neglect and heavy-handed security policies. Not surprisingly, then, residents were more likely to oppose the coup than other Egyptians. The founders of ABM, many of whom hail from North Sinai, knew this as well as anyone. The jihadist group, before pledging allegiance to ISIS in November 2014, was almost entirely focused on police and military targets and would generally couch attacks as "revenge for the security forces' suppression of Islamist dissidents."[26]

Electoral results from 2011-2014 offer additional insight into patterns of political support in the Sinai. South Sinai has generally been more pro-regime and less supportive of militant activity due, in part, to its economic dependence on the tourism industry. North Sinai is a different story, however. In each of the four major electoral contests during the transition period, North Sinai voters supported Islamist positions and candidates at a significantly higher percentage than the national average (which was already quite high).[27]

While the coup and its brutal aftermath contributed to a sustained increase in monthly attacks—as well as an increase in the lethality of attacks—we still see considerable variation in militant activity. From November 2013 to July 2014, for example, there is a dip, with the monthly average falling to around twenty-two attacks per month. Yet, even at this lower point, the average number of attacks is still more than 640 percent above the monthly pre-coup average. Starting in January 2015, militant activity jumps up sharply again to 107 attacks, from only nine in December. Again, there are any number of factors that could have played a role in this new surge in violence, but there is one main variable that changes dramatically during this period and helps account for such an unusual uptick in attacks: the military's hasty creation of a "security zone" along the border with Gaza.

The establishment of the "security zone" and its aftermath

On October 24, 2014, at least thirty-three Egyptian soldiers were killed in what was until then the deadliest attack on security personnel since the coup. ABM claimed responsibility. In response, Egyptian authorities moved to establish a buffer zone, forcing as many as 10,000 residents[28] to evacuate their homes, some with only forty-eight hours' notice.[29] The Egyptian military's narrow security lens and harsh tactics have, in effect, further alienated local residents and helped fuel the insurgency. Shortly after the army began "relocating" villages, the number of attacks increased once again, but this time to previously unheard of levels. The first five months of 2015 saw an average of 114.6 attacks, with an all-time high of 138 attacks in May.

This is not to say that the creation of a buffer zone transformed people into ideological hardliners in a matter of weeks, but, rather, that groups like ISIS seek to exploit local grievances and depend on local sympathy to stage successful attacks. Zack Gold, a researcher who specializes on the Sinai, wrote that, due to the army's scorched-earth tactics, "whole swaths of North Sinai civilization no longer exist."[30] One resident of the border town of Rafah, after learning his home would be destroyed, said: "I won't lie. I'm more afraid of the army than the jihadis. When you're oppressed, anyone who fights your oppression gets your sympathy."[31] Another Sinai resident, according to journalist Mohannad Sabry, said that after ninety percent of his village was destroyed in a security campaign, around forty people took up arms. Through 2013, he knew of only five ABM members in the village.[32]

Conclusion

On the individual level, radicalization occurs as a result of accumulated personal experience, making it hard to devise a generalized model. In Tunisia, there appears to have been a perfect storm of factors, one amplifying the other. The economy continued to deteriorate, and those on the fringes—secular revolutionaries and Salafi radicals alike—felt that the political system, consumed by polarization and gridlock, stifled the dramatic change they were hoping for and expecting. Early on in the transition, Rached Ghannouchi and other leaders of Tunisia's main Islamist party, Ennahda, were optimistic that they could bring Salafis into the fold. Yet, those outreach efforts failed.

Ennahda may have won forty-one percent of the seats in the 2011 parliamentary elections, but that didn't necessarily mean there would be much room for those further to its right. What could Tunisia's Salafis really hope to accomplish by joining the messy give-and-take of electoral politics? Despite winning by a landslide, Ennahda, due to overwhelming secular opposition, wasn't able to include even a mere mention of the word *sharia*, or Islamic law, anywhere in the constitution. The things that Salafis wanted and believed in simply weren't on the table. Yet, they benefited from the democratic opening all the same. With more room to operate and organize than ever before, Salafi groups directed their efforts toward preaching, education, and indoctrination.

In addition, Salafism–as a movement and an ideology–was young and immature and hadn't had a chance to develop, due to the totalizing repression of the pre-2011 era. Without established Salafi networks that could channel the outpouring of religious sentiment in a constructive direction, Tunisian Salafism increasingly became a language of alienation and opposition, drawing strength from the forgotten suburbs of Tunis and impoverished cities like Kairouan.

In Egypt, the configuration of factors that have contributed to radicalization are clearer and, as we have seen, appear to be tied to discrete political developments inside the country. In a sense, here too there was a "catalyzing moment," but on the societal level. This moment was the Egyptian coup, which put into motion a series of events, reactions, and counter-reactions. These developments have enabled a gradual spiraling of violence—a spiraling that is only likely to intensify the longer Egypt's political conflict persists.

Shadi Hamid is a senior fellow at the Project on U.S. Relations with the Islamic World in the Brookings Institution's Center for Middle East Policy and the author of *Temptations of Power: Islamists and Illiberal Democracy in a New Middle East* (Oxford University Press), which was named a *Foreign Affairs* Best Book for 2014. An expert on Islamist movements, Dr. Hamid served as director of research at the Brookings Doha Center until January 2014. He is also a contributing writer to *The Atlantic*. Dr. Hamid received his B.S. and M.A. from Georgetown University's School of Foreign Service and his Ph.D. in political science from Oxford University.

[1] Stern, Jessica. 2014. "Response to Marc Sageman's 'The Stagnation in Terrorism Research.'" *Terrorism and Political Violence* 26: 607.

[2] Blanchard, Christopher M., Carla E. Humud, Kenneth Katzman, and Matthew C. Weed. May 27, 2015. *The "Islamic State" Crisis and U.S. Policy*. Congressional Research Service, at fas.org/sgp/crs/mideast/R43612.pdf, p. 2.

[3] "Tunisia blocks more than 12,000 would-be jihadists: minister." April 17, 2015. AFP, at news.yahoo.com/tunisia-blocks-more-12-000-jihadists-minister-202230331.html.

[4] Mironova, Vera, Loubna Mrie, and Sam Whitt. August 13, 2014. "Islamists at a Glance: Why Do Syria's Rebel Fighters Join Islamist Groups? (The Reasons May Have Less to Do With Religiosity Than You Might Think)." *Political Violence @ a Glance*, at politicalviolenceataglance.org/2014/08/13/islamists-at-a-glance-why-do-syrias-rebel-fighters-join-islamist-groups-the-reasons-may-have-less-to-do-with-religiosity-than-you-might-think/. See also Mironova, Vera, Loubna Mrie, and Sam Whitt. August 11, 2014. Fight or Flight in Civil War? Evidence from Rebel-Controlled Syria. Social Science Research Network, at ssrn.com/abstract=2478682.

[5] Huntington, Samuel. 1968. *Political Order in Changing Societies*. New Haven, CT: Yale University Press, p. 269.

[6] Weiss, Michael, and Hassan Hassan. 2015. *ISIS: Inside the Army of Terror*. New York, NY: Regan Arts, p. 163.

[7] Meral, Ziya. February 26, 2015. "The Question of Theodicy and Jihad." *War On the Rocks*, at warontherocks. com/2015/02/the-question-of-theodicy-and-jihad/.

[8] Groll, Elias. May 14, 2015. "I'm Back! Baghdadi Appeals to Muslims to Sign Up With Islamic State." *Foreign Policy*, at foreignpolicy.com/2015/05/14/im-back-baghdadi-appeals-to-muslims-to-sign-up-with-islamic-state/.

[9] Stern, 2014, p. 608.

[10] George, Alexander L., and Andrew Bennett. 2004. *Case Studies and Theory Development in the Social Sciences*. Cambridge, MA: MIT Press, p. 81.

[11] Ashraf Sweilam and Brian Rohan "Scores Killed as Militants Attack Egyptian Troops in Sinai." July 1, 2015. *Associated Press*, at http://bigstory.ap.org/article/1b81eb41285047158770af1e3772aaf7/militants-attack-egyptian-army-checkpoints-sinai-kill-30.

[12] Human Rights Watch, "UN Human Rights Council: Adoption of the UPR Report on Egypt," March 20, 2015, http://www.hrw.org/news/2015/03/20/un-human-rights-council-adoption-upr-report-egypt.

[13] Eltahawy, Mona. June 15, 2015. "Egypt's Vanishing Youth." *New York Times*, at www.nytimes.com/2015/06/16/opinion/egypts-vanishing-youth.html.

[14] Abe, Nicola. September 10, 2015. "The Vanishing: Why Are Young Egyptian Activists Disappearing?" *Der Spiegel International*, at www.spiegel.de/international/world/young-activists-disappear-amid-egyptian-government-crackdown-a-1052006.html.

[15] "Egypt: New Leader Faces Rights Crisis." June 9, 2014. Human Rights Watch, at www.hrw.org/news/2014/06/09/egypt-new-leader-faces-rights-crisis.

[16] There is a growing academic literature pointing to a "tyranny-terror" link. In a widely cited 2003 study, for example, Alan Krueger and Jitka Maleckova conclude that "the only variable that was consistently associated with the number of terrorists was the Freedom House index of political rights and civil liberties." Steven Brooke and I survey this literature, as well as the relevant data sets, in greater detail in an article we wrote in 2010: Hamid, Shadi, and Steven Brooke. February/March 2010. "Promoting Democracy to Stop Terror, Revisited." *Policy Review*, at www.hoover.org/research/promoting-democracy-stop-terror-revisited.

[17] "They shall by no means harm you but with a slight evil." August 2013. *Al Furqan Media*, at azelin.files. wordpress.com/2013/07/shaykh-abc5ab-mue1b8a5ammad-al-e28098adnc481nc4ab-al-shc481mc4ab-22they-will-not-harm-you-except-for-some-annoyance22-en.pdf.

[18] McCants, William. 2015. *The ISIS Apocalypse*. London: St. Martin's Press.

[19] March, Andrew F., and Mara Revkin. April 15, 2015. "Caliphate of Law." *Foreign Affairs*, at www.foreignaffairs. com/articles/syria/2015-04-15/caliphate-law.

[20] March, Andrew. May 5, 2015. "Experts weigh in (part 3): How does ISIS approach Islamic Scripture?" Brookings Institution, at www.brookings.edu/blogs/markaz/posts/2015/05/04-isis-scripture-march-dhimma.

[21] Revkin, Mara. May 13, 2015. "Experts weigh in (part 5): How does ISIS approach Islamic scripture?" Brookings Institution, at www.brookings.edu/blogs/markaz/posts/2015/05/12-isis-approach-to-scripture-revkin.

[22] Fadel, Mohammad. May 7, 2015. "Experts weigh in (part 4): How does ISIS approach Islamic scripture?" Brookings Institution, at www.brookings.edu/blogs/markaz/posts/2015/05/07-fadel-isis-approach-to-scripture.

[23] Interview with author, senior Muslim Brotherhood official, Istanbul, February 19, 2015.

[24] "داعش يدعو المصريين "للجهاد". December 29, 2013, at www.youtube.com/watch?v=GFsrJADJkqY.

[25] Egypt Security Watch Infographic, Tahrir Institute for Middle East Policy, at timep.org/esw/.

[26] Kingsley, Patrick. January 31, 2014. "Egypt faces new threat in al-Qaida-linked group Ansar Beyt al-Maqdis." *Guardian*, at www.theguardian.com/world/2014/jan/31/egypt-alqaida-terrorist-threat-ansar-beyt-almaqdis.

[27] For example, in the 2012 constitutional referendum, North Sinai registered a 78.3 percent "yes" vote compared to 63.8 percent nationally. In the 2012 presidential election, 61.5 percent of North Sinai voters cast their ballots for Morsi, compared to 51.7 percent nationally. See www.atlanticcouncil.org/blogs/egyptsource/official-results-98-1-percent-vote-in-favor-of-egypt-s-new-constitution-with-38-6-percent-voter-turnout pres2012.elections.eg/round2-results and pres2012.elections.eg/round2-results.

[28] Fahim, Kareem, and Merna Thomas. October 29, 2014. "Egypt Flattens Neighborhoods to Create a Buffer With Gaza." *New York Times*, at www.nytimes.com/2014/10/30/world/middleeast/egypt-sinai-peninsula-gaza-buffer-zone.html.

[29] Daragahi, Borzou. January 30, 2015. "Egypt's army and militants clash in Sinai." *Financial Times*, at www.ft.com/intl/cms/s/a1ce385e-a87e-11e4-bd1700144feab7de,Authorised=false.html?_i_location=http%3A%2F%2Fwww.ft.com%2Fcms%2Fs%2F0%2Fa1ce385e-a87e-11e4-bd17-00144feab7de.html%3Fsiteedition%3Dintl&siteedition=intl&_i_referer=#axzz3hNpf6Nxf.

[30] Gold, Zack. May 18, 2015. "North Sinai Population Continues to Sacrifice for Egypt." Tahrir Institute for Middle East Policy, at timep.org/commentary/north-sinai-population-continues-to-sacrifice-for-egypt/.

[31] Daragahi, Borzou. January 30, 2015. "Violence spirals as Egypt's army and militants clash in Sinai." *Financial Times*, at www.ft.com/intl/cms/s/0/a1ce385e-a87e-11e4-bd17-00144feab7de.html.

[32] "Assault in Sheikh Zuweid: A turning point in Egypt's fight against terrorism." July 2, 2015. Tahrir Institute for Middle East Policy, at timep.org/commentary/assault-in-sheikh-zuwaid-a-turning-point-in-egypts-fight-against-terrorism/.

"Sectarianism is a problem now because political instability has both exposed the skewed distribution of power and provided opportunity to change it."

—VALI NASR

Extremism, Sectarianism, and Regional Rivalry in the Middle East

Vali Nasr
Dean and Professor
Johns Hopkins School of Advanced International Studies

Sectarian conflict between Shias and Sunnis is perhaps the most significant political dynamic shaping the Middle East today. It is dividing populations, challenging political boundaries, fueling civil wars in the Levant and Arabian Peninsula, and rousing Islamic extremism and terrorism. Even in Turkey, the once dormant sectarian divide between Sunnis and Alevis (a distant offshoot of Shi'ism) has come to life in national politics in reaction to developments in neighboring Syria.

Arab states and Iran both saw threats and opportunities in the Arab Spring. Their attempts to manage and manipulate that tumult intensified sectarianism and entwined domestic security concerns with the regional rivalry between the Sunni camp of Saudi Arabia and its Arab allies (and also Turkey) and Iran, Iraq, and their Shia allies.

The Islamic State in Iraq and Syria (ISIS) emerged in this context. Its particular brand of ideology and politics reflects the sectarian imperative, which also gives its fanatical rage both strategic relevance and staying power. Sunni sectarian angst and fury has been surging, and, through the crucible of the Syrian debacle, it has found its voice in the most dangerous ideologies and extremist forces. The same constellation of ideology and emotions that plunged Iraq into extremism and war a decade ago is at play again, hardening the Sunni identity, strategic relevance, and political following.

ISIS, the Victory Front (Jabhah al-Nusra), and al-Qaeda affiliates (in particular, al-Qaeda in the Arabian Peninsula, or AQAP) all appeal to and represent Sunni sectarianism—and in that they compete with Sunni Arab states in defending and furthering Sunni interests. The Assad regime's butchery in Syria was the proximate cause for the formation of ISIS, but its meteoric rise to power in Iraq reflected deep sectarian divisions in that country. ISIS took advantage of Sunni frustration, but also financial and logistical support from anti-Iranian forces, to take over northern and western Iraq, posing as a Sunni sectarian army at war with the Shia government in Baghdad.

The Demographic Reality

Roots of the sectarian conflict go back to early Islamic history, but it is competition over power, rather than differences over theology, that propel this conflict today.

In the Middle East, despite fealty to nationalism and ethnic identity, politics in states with mixed sectarian populations are still organized along communal lines. There is identification with national and ethnic identities, but then sect decides the pecking order within those identities—especially as greater importance of Islam in politics divides rather than unites the two sects—and each has its own interpretation of Islamic law and conception of ideal Islamic order.

Shias constitute a significant portion of the Middle East's population (especially if one counts sects affiliated with Shi'ism or seen by Sunnis as a variation of Shi'ism—Alevis in Turkey, Alawites in Syria, Zeydis in Yemen). Shias are a majority in Iran, Iraq, and Bahrain; a plurality of Lebanon; and constitute sizable minorities in Pakistan, Persian Gulf emirates, and Saudi Arabia. Alawites could be as many as a quarter of Syria's population, Alevis a fifth of Turkey's, and Zeydis close to half of Yemen's.

Sectarianism is a problem now because political instability has both exposed the skewed distribution of power and provided opportunity to change it. Sectarianism is not causing instability in the Middle East; it is instability that stokes the conflict.

Collapse of Arab Political Order

The Arab world as we know it was a product of World War I. The war settlement decided territorial boundaries and, more importantly, the balance of power in political systems that preached nationalism but promoted communal domination of politics. Majoritarian rule excluded sectarian and ethnic minorities (Kurds in Iraq and Syria), and, in some cases, minorities excluded majorities (Shia in Iraq and Bahrain or Sunnis in Syria).

That order has imploded. First, the U.S. invasion shattered the Iraqi state in 2003, freeing Kurdish nationalism and paving the way for Shia ascendancy that in turn provoked Sunni resistance and the onset of sectarian conflict. Then, starting in 2011, the Arab Spring has had a similar impact in Syria, Yemen, and Bahrain—challenging entrenched state institutions to open the door to competition for power between minorities and majorities.

The Arab Spring promised change in the Arab world: elections, good government, and economic opportunity. But ending authoritarianism also means altering the sectarian balance of power within states and in the region. This presented Arab rulers, rattled by popular uprisings, with an opportunity: to use sectarian angst to defeat democratic aspirations.

Persian Gulf monarchies proved particularly entrepreneurial in exploiting sectarianism to navigate the Arab Spring. In Bahrain, a popular reform movement inspired by Tunisia and Egypt that at first included both Shias and Sunnis was defeated once it was cast as a nefarious Iranian-backed Shia plot to disenfranchise Sunnis. This also elevated the domestic call to reform to a regional security challenge. Gulf Cooperation Council (GCC) troops crushed the Bahrain uprising, and backed with popular Sunni support, Persian Gulf monarchies closed the chapter on the Arab Spring.

In the Levant, too, sectarianism served the aims of the same Arab states: the means to strengthen popular resistance to pro-Iranian regimes in Syria and Iraq. Here the Arab Spring embodied a Sunni challenge to minority (in the form of Alawites) and majority Shia rule, which was a theme Bashar al-Assad and Nouri al-Maliki promoted as well. Assad used fear of Sunni reprisal to rally Alawite and Christians to his own defense, precipitating a brutal civil war. Maliki doubled down on sectarian policies of his own to guard against the Sunni surge he feared would follow that sect's triumph in Syria.

Sunni sectarianism in the Levant enjoyed the backing of Saudi Arabia and its GCC allies, along with Turkey. That support went to the moderate opposition, but eventually also to extremist expressions of Sunni sectarianism in the form of ISIS and the Victory Front.

The opportunities and threats the Arab Spring put before Sunni Arab states (and Turkey), more than any change in Iranian capabilities and goals in the region, account for the intensification of sectarianism. That sectarianism helped defeat the Arab Spring in the Gulf, and promoting it in the Levant turned it into the bedrock of Saudi and GCC regional policy.

Exit U.S., Enter Iran

The crumbling of Arab order has unfolded in the context of two other important regional developments: first, the changing U.S. attitude toward the Middle East; and second, the shift in U.S.-Iran relations.

Energy independence, war fatigue, and the lure of Asia have combined to diminish the strategic importance America had long placed on the Middle East. Although the scales of crises that grip the region continue to consume much U.S. attention, still, America's inclination is to extricate itself from the region.

The American change of heart has precipitated a crisis of confidence among America's Arab allies. The fear of losing status, vulnerability to internal political pressures (which the U.S. administration has been quick to point out), and losing preeminence in the region is playing out in a more aggressive regional policy directed at Iranian influence.

That the U.S. would first discount the region's importance and, worse yet, see engaging Iran as important to its Middle East interests is a blow to the Arab conception of its preeminence and to the standing of Arab leaders who have gained legitimacy from it. America's Arab allies think the U.S. is responding to palpable Iranian power (which has led them to seek to demonstrate their own—in Syria and Yemen—with dangerous consequences).

There is also a resentment of the West's attraction to Iran—an ancient civilization with a sophisticated and educated population whose coming in from the cold could generate excitement in the West, as reengagement with China did in 1971. Of course, the fear is exactly that: much as China has dwarfed its neighbors to dominate the West's relations with Asia, so might Iran. The threat of the Iran nuclear deal to Arabs is not just Iranian mischief in the region but more so the transformational potential of the transactional nuclear deal—real change in Iran and an opening to a broader relationship.

The Arab response has been to seek U.S. reassurance of its commitment but, more important, to create their own bulwark against Iran—building up their military capabilities and, more important, limiting Iranian influence in the Arab world—and sectarian posturing is a part of that plan.

This was a successful strategy in containing Iranian influence in South Asia in the 1980s. There, Saudi Arabia marginalized Iran but at the cost of entrenching sectarianism and the culture of extremism.

The Arab goal is to roll back Iranian influence where possible and, otherwise, to demonstrate Arab will and power. Saudi Arabia has set the agenda here—using its energy policy, military, and regional alliances. Saudis have seen utility in building a theological firewall to check Iranian influence—making strategic use of Sunni animus toward Shia, which is viewed as a synonym for Iran.

A successful show of force would strengthen the hand of Arab rulers at home too. This is particularly important, as the force that has most completely embodied Arab Sunni animus against Iran and the Shia is ISIS—outshining Arab regimes in responding to the perceived Iranian and Shia threat. A large number of Saudis are fighting against Iranian interests in Syria and Iraq as part of ISIS.

Regional Scenarios

The inherent weakness of the Arab order—and the inability of states to peacefully resolve internal distribution of power—is not going away any time soon. An end to the Iran-Saudi regional rivalry would help, but regional stability would require a fundamental change in the regional security architecture, which in turn would demand American leadership and a greater engagement than is currently Washington's intention. It would also require a conscious decision by both Riyadh and Tehran to change their respective strategic calculus in pursuing their regional interests.

Iran and Saudi Arabia see their interests in zero-sum terms. They have staked their prestige and the domestic legitimacy that goes with it on a display of regional dominance. Saudis see Iran ascendant and fear that the nuclear deal confirms Iranian gains. In fact, they would like to compel Iran to choose between opening to the West and having influence in the Arab world—i.e., the U.S. would follow up on the nuclear deal with support for an Arab push to extricate Iranian influence from the Arab world. Iran views any retreat from its line of control as a costly defeat.

U.S. and Iranian interests converge in fighting ISIS in Syria and Iraq (as well as in Afghanistan), but not so when it comes to Hamas and Hezbollah or the fate of the Assad regime in Syria. The U.S. has a vested interest in protecting its traditional alliances, and that means assuaging Sunni anxieties by checking Iranian ambitions. It is easy to see how that would play out in the Palestinian territories or Yemen, but in Syria and Iraq, where the future of the Middle East is being forged, the U.S. will have a difficult time balancing its own interests with Sunni Arab demands. For Arab states, the heart of the matter in Syria is toppling the Assad regime. For the U.S., that is a desired outcome, but the urgent task at hand, much as in Iraq, is to deny ISIS and other extremists a path to power.

A further challenge facing the U.S. is checking the Saudi inclination to rely on Sunni sectarianism to manage the Iranian challenge. Saudis are quick to fight extremism at home, but the relationship between the two outside the Kingdom is far more checkered.

Neither Iran nor Saudi Arabia can realize their strategic objectives in the region. Iran's Persian and Shia identity constitute natural limits to its influence in countries and territories that are distinctly Arab and now far more Sunni in their self-conception. Iranian setbacks in Syria and Iraq, and most recently also in Yemen, attest to those limits. And Saudi Arabia's brazen Sunni sectarian posturing excludes Arab Shias, who turn to Iran for support. The current Saudi position toward Shias—as questionable

Muslims, if not heretics, and as Iran's fifth column—has the same effect on Shias at the regional level that Prime Minister Maliki's sectarian policies had on Sunnis in Iraq.

Ironically, by emphasizing Sunni sectarian identity to isolate Iran's clients in the Arab world and deny Tehran influence, Saudi Arabia is further legitimating Iran's role. In a Middle East defined along sectarian lines, the Arab-Persian divide cannot override common Shia identity. If stalemate sets in between Iran and Saudi Arabia, then ongoing proxy conflicts will unfold in theaters of conflict across the Middle East.

Implications for U.S. Policy

For the U.S. and its European allies, defeating ISIS is a strategic imperative. ISIS's ideology draws on Sunni sectarianism, and its military campaign in Iraq and Syria serve the regional aims of Iran's Sunni Arab rivals. ISIS's conception of a caliphate is construed as a political formula that harkens less to the early years of Islam and more to the distinctly Sunni caliphates that ruled Damascus and Baghdad—a revival of Sunni prerogative to regional power.

Viewed from Iran, ISIS and Saudi Arabia constitute a single anti-Iran and anti-Shia continuum. The two are locked into the same sectarian regional strategy.

For this reason, the two most important U.S. policies in the Middle East, the nuclear deal with Iran and war on ISIS, cannot be separated. If the nuclear deal holds, then U.S. policy in the Middle East will become more clearly focused on eliminating the scourge of ISIS. Success there would require an end to conflicts in Syria and Iraq, which would need the cooperation of both Iran and Saudi Arabia. That would be a challenge for American diplomacy. But failing to create a diplomatic framework that would include both Iran and Saudi Arabia would put the U.S. in the difficult position of relying on Iranian help in combating ISIS in Iraq—and potentially also Syria— while further alienating Sunni public opinion and Sunni Arab states.

One scenario the U.S. can ill afford is if Iran withdrew from fighting ISIS for control of Sunni regions of Iraq and Syria—settling instead for defending Shia population centers and key strategic cities. That would leave the U.S. and Arab states to wrest control of Sunni regions of Iraq and Syria from ISIS. The U.S. would then have to commit greater resources to fighting ISIS.

It is tempting to think that the U.S. could rely on Turkey or Arab states to defeat ISIS. Turkey has shown that its priority is not ISIS but combating the perceived Kurdish threat. It is also unlikely that Arab states would be willing or able to shoulder a meaningful part of that burden. Some have had a hand in the rise of ISIS; others are uncomfortable signing up for an inter-Sunni war. The burden of breaking ISIS in Syria and Iraq and denying it entry into Libya or Afghanistan would fall on U.S. shoulders.

The U.S. could see the nuclear deal as an opportunity to pressure Iran into change. Shorn of its nuclear umbrella for a decade or more, Iran is more susceptible to pressure. The promise of successful containment makes the nuclear deal a strong lever in managing Iran. Success here would require a strategy for defeating ISIS that would not need or rely on Iran's cooperation. That is tantamount to "dual containment" of both Iran and ISIS.

U.S. policy in the Middle East has to be directed at promoting regional peace and security—to relieve pressure on U.S. resources and attention. That is a daunting task in the midst of a raging regional rivalry that extends from the apex of states to the ranks of their citizens. Containing one side or the other will neither end the conflict nor produce the peace and security America needs. The problem lies in the ambitions and strategies of both sides in this conflict.

In the short run, the U.S. will have to guard against the actions of both Iran and its Sunni rivals when they threaten American interests, but then collaborate with them when American interests demand it. In the long run, however, it is only by bridging the gap—a regional framework that would include both Iran and Saudi Arabia and its GCC allies—that the U.S. can imagine the kind of stability in the Middle East that would allow American foreign policy to shift its focus and resources elsewhere. That requires greater U.S. engagement—diplomatic as well as, if not more so than, military—and solving the Syrian crisis could be the all important first step.

Vali Nasr is Dean of The Johns Hopkins University School of Advanced International Studies. He is a Middle East scholar, author, foreign policy adviser and a commentator on international relations. Dr. Nasr is a Fellow at the Brookings Institution. Before joining Johns Hopkins University, SAIS, Dr. Nasr taught international politics at Tufts University's Fletcher School of Law and Diplomacy. From 2009 to 2011, Dr. Nasr was Special Adviser to the President's Special Representative for Afghanistan and Pakistan. He has been a Carnegie Scholar, a senior fellow at Harvard University's Kennedy School of Government, and an adjunct senior fellow for Middle Eastern studies at the Council on Foreign Relations. Dr. Nasr is a member of the U.S. Department of State's Foreign Affairs Policy Board, a director of the Rockefeller Brothers Fund, and a life member of the Council on Foreign Relations. He has authored several books on foreign policy, Iraq, and the Arab world.

Part 2

"Ultimately, ISIS can be defeated only by a political process in Syria and Iraq that fills in the sectarian canyons that have allowed ISIS to grow."

—RYAN CROCKER

Fighting ISIS, Then and Now

Ryan Crocker
Dean
The Bush School of Government & Public Service
Texas A&M University

As we confront the reality that ISIS just isn't going away, it may be useful to consider where it came from and how we fought each other in the past. We have a long battle history with ISIS and its forerunners—in Iraq from 2003 until the withdrawal of our troops in 2011, and in Iraq and Syria since 2014. In our entire history, we have been engaged with only one enemy for a longer period of time: the Taliban in Afghanistan. Surely we have learned something about ISIS over the years.

We know, of course, that ISIS emerged from Abu Musab al-Zarqawi's militia, first becoming al-Qaeda in Iraq (AQI) with allegiance to Osama bin Laden. But the differences with al-Qaeda were apparent early, with Ayman al-Zawahiri's 2005 letter to Zarqawi criticizing his anti-Shia campaign (ten years later, Zawahiri seems to have altered his views). Shortly before we killed him in 2006, Zarqawi proclaimed as a goal the establishment of the caliphate and announced the dissolution of AQI in favor of the Islamic State. Those we fought during the surge in 2007 and 2008 made no claim of a caliphate. It would have been short-lived in any case, as the combination of coalition power and the Sunni Awakening rolled back AQI, first in Anbar and Baghdad and then through Diyala and Salahuddin. Then as now, we were fighting an alliance of al-Qaeda and former Baathists, the Naqshabandiya.

Then as now, attacking their finances as well as their fighters was a priority. An interagency task force that General David Petraeus and I co-chaired followed the money, much of which flowed from corruption in the Baiji refinery. Treasury officers were as important as infantry officers. Interestingly, ISIS and Iraqi security forces continue to struggle for Baiji. It's all about the money.

Then, our relentless pressure badly hurt and almost eliminated AQI. Almost. Pockets remained in Mosul among a population that feared the Shia government in Baghdad and the Kurds more than AQI. Given the political crevices in which they could hide, even 150,000 U.S. troops could not completely finish the fight. In 2010, we trapped Zarqawi's successors, who committed suicide to evade capture, and the era of Abu Bakr al-Baghdadi (aka Ibrahim Awwad al-Badri) began.

Two events the following year gave a dramatic boost to the fortunes of the new amir and his cause. In the spring of 2011, the Syrian civil war began, and in December, the last U.S. forces left Iraq. The tiny political crevices of late 2008 became canyons just three years later, and Baghdadi had the space he needed to create his caliphate.

Where are we now, as we enter the second year of a campaign to degrade and defeat ISIS? Simply put, the means we are employing are not adequate to achieve the ends we have stated. After thousands of coalition air strikes, ISIS has not been degraded. It holds two provincial capitals in Iraq and has advanced in Syria. We should not be surprised—it took the surge in Iraq to beat back ISIS/AQI to the point where its sole mission was survival. There is no surge now, unless we count the Iranian-backed Shia militias in Iraq, known as the Popular Mobilization Forces, whose objectives seem to be deepening the Sunni-Shia divide and challenging the authority of Prime Minister Abadi.

We will not significantly degrade, much less defeat, ISIS by airstrikes alone. We could not have defeated AQI with just air power. So what are our choices? First, we could stop making the hole we have been digging for ourselves deeper. When we talk about 7,000 air strikes, what ISIS and its followers hear is that they are standing up to the full military strength of the infidels and their puppets in Arab capitals. When we say a 60-nation coalition is arrayed against a solitary ISIS, its leaders hear that they can defy the world. We seem to be incapable of effective messaging against ISIS, but at least we could stop doing their messaging for them.

More profoundly, we need to assess how grave the ISIS threat is to U.S. national security. How likely is a major ISIS-authored attack on the homeland? If we conclude it is unlikely, we should shift our stated end from degrading and defeating ISIS to containing it. Containment is effectively what we are doing now, and by shifting our stated goal, ends and means would be in alignment. If, however, our judgment is that ISIS is likely to mount such an attack, then it is imperative that we expand our means to match our currently stated ends. One way to approach this would be to develop a plan on how we would retaliate if ISIS does attack, and then carry it out preemptively: imagining another 9/11 and acting to ensure it doesn't happen.

I leave this crucial analysis to others far better equipped to carry it out than I am. Certainly an argument can be made that ISIS differs from al-Qaeda in at least two critical ways that may make it less of a threat to us: First, holding territory is critical to the ideology of ISIS—the caliphate must be physical. With something concrete to lose, the reasoning goes, ISIS is unlikely to take action that would precipitate it. Second, ISIS is focused on the near enemy—the Shia and unbelievers, such as Christians and Yazidis as well as apostate regimes in the region. The far enemy—us—is secondary. As Will McCants points out in this volume, public statements from ISIS place much more emphasis on exhorting the faithful to move from Dar al-Harb to the caliphate than to fight there. There is merit in these arguments, but I wonder if we want to bet the Empire State Building on them.

They do illustrate an important truth: ISIS cannot be defeated unless its territory is taken from it. An air war cannot do that—there must be boots on the ground. Whose boots? Certainly not ours. Our Muslim allies? The notion that Saudi Arabia, Jordan, Egypt, and/or Turkey will field a ground force in Syria is a hallucination. It would be a heavy lift to persuade them to go with us; they certainly will not go without us.

Some have argued that particularly in the wake of the nuclear agreement, the U.S. should make common cause with Iran against ISIS. This is a fundamental misreading of Iranian intentions, especially in Iraq. I have argued that to understand Iranian goals in Iraq, one must understand the recent history between the two countries, in particular the Iran-Iraq War from 1980 to 1988. It was the most vicious and costly trench warfare since World War I, leaving upwards of a million dead. For those like Quds Force commander Qasem Soleimani, who was commissioned in the Iranian army shortly before Saddam Hussein invaded in 1980, the war was a defining experience. Soleimani spent seven of the eight years of the war in combat, most of it on the Fao front, the bloodiest sector in a horrific conflict. Still in his 20s, Soleimani was made an acting division commander as officers around him perished.

Most Americans don't remember there was an Iran-Iraq War. No Iranian or Iraqi will ever forget it. And for Iranians like Soleimani, the war established Iraq, even more than the United States, as the dominant existential threat to the Islamic Republic. The one certain way to eliminate that threat is to eliminate Iraq as a unitary state. More than anyone else in the Iranian establishment, Soleimani is responsible for formulating and executing Iranian policy in Iraq, and he is well on his way to realizing the objective of permanent dismemberment of Iraq. In this, ISIS is his objective ally, not a dangerous enemy. The so-called Popular Mobilization Forces, for the most part Iranian-dominated Shia militias that killed thousands of Iraqi Sunnis—and hundreds of Americans—in 2006-2008, have now pushed into Anbar. It is every Sunni's nightmare. We are looking at an ISIS-controlled Jihadistan, an Iranian-dominated Shiastan, and an independent Kurdistan that will be under increasing Iranian pressure. An independent Iraq and America lose; Iran and ISIS win.

Is there another possibility—that the extreme brutality of ISIS and its horrific treatment of women and non-Sunnis who fall into their hands will lead to a popular resistance and the collapse of ISIS from within? We could hope, but hope is a poor policy. The question does highlight the importance of governance in a region that has seen very little of it. Corrupt, sectarian regimes in Damascus and Baghdad created an environment that allowed ISIS to establish itself, and there are indications it has understood that an ability to govern as well as swing the sword are essential to the future of the caliphate. Justice is harsh, but it is predictable. ISIS leaders have a reputation for not being personally corrupt in sharp contrast to those who came before. They seem to put a priority on services—getting the lights on, picking up the trash. Perhaps the single most important indicator of the staying power of ISIS is not its battlefield prowess but its ability to govern: Will Sunnis in areas under its control think their lives are better now? When ISIS took control of Palmyra, the West's concern was the fate of the antiquities. The focus of Syrian Sunnis was probably on something else—the liberation of political prisoners, almost all of them Sunnis, from Bashar al-Assad's notorious Tadmor prison.

Well, what about the Russians who have recently arrived in Syria with combat air support and armor? Could we combine forces against ISIS, even if it means tolerating Moscow's brutal client in Damascus? The Russian arrival could open a path to a political process in Syria, but it will not be through a U.S.-Russian alliance against ISIS. That would put us in the morally repugnant position of supporting a leader who has killed tens of thousands of his countrymen and bears more responsibility than any other individual for the massive refugee flows we are witnessing. It would also be the best recruiting tool ISIS could ever hope for: the infidels joining with the apostate butcher against the people of the true faith.

Russia is making a risky move. We should make it riskier: announce a no-fly zone. It would significantly reduce civilian casualties by stopping the awful barrel bombs and reduce refugee flows. It would signal to Sunnis that we are not tacitly supporting Assad and could create a climate more conducive to the development of Sunni alternatives to ISIS and al-Nusra Front. Most important, it could move Moscow to the negotiating table without insisting that Assad must stay. There would be the prospect of a moderate middle: the considerable majority of Alawis and the Sunni establishment that has stood with them out of fear of the jihadists, and Sunnis elsewhere who loathe Assad but have seen little alternative to ISIS. A long shot? Of course. Better than what we have now? Yes. Ultimately, ISIS can be defeated only by a political process in Syria and Iraq that fills in the sectarian canyons that have allowed ISIS to grow.

Finally, and woven through all of these issues is the question of U.S. engagement and leadership. They are largely absent in Syria and Iraq. In Iraq, we disengaged politically and militarily in 2011. The former may have had graver consequences than the latter. One does not end a war by withdrawing one's forces from the battle space. One simply leaves the field to enemies with more patience and greater determination—Iran and ISIS. In Syria over the same period, we have made a series of missteps, half-steps, and nonsteps: announcing that Assad must go in 2011 without the will or the means to make it happen, setting redlines that we didn't enforce, undertaking a campaign against ISIS that makes us look weak, initiating a belated and ill-conceived train-and-equip program for Syrian rebels, remaining passive as Assad's barrel bomb campaign approaches genocidal proportions, and failing to lead in the world's worst refugee crisis since WW II. A common theme in the calamities of the last four years in Syria and Iraq is the absence of U.S. leadership. Of course, we could not have prevented or ameliorated every bad thing. But we could make a difference. We still can.

Ryan Crocker is Dean and Executive Professor at the George Bush School of Government & Public Service at Texas A&M University, where he holds the Edward and Howard Kruse Endowed Chair. He retired from the Foreign Service in April 2009 after a career of over 37 years but was recalled to active duty by President Obama to serve as U.S. Ambassador to Afghanistan in 2011. He has served as U.S. Ambassador six times: Afghanistan (2011-2012), Iraq (2007-2009), Pakistan (2004-2007), Syria (1998-2001), Kuwait (1994-1997), and Lebanon (1990-1993). Born in Spokane, Washington, he grew up in an Air Force family, attending schools in Morocco, Canada, and Turkey, as well as the U.S. He received a B.A. in English in 1971 and an honorary Doctor of Laws degree in 2001 from Whitman College (Washington). He is a member of the Council on Foreign Relations, the American Academy of Diplomacy, and the Association of American Ambassadors. In August 2013, he was confirmed by the United States Senate to serve on the Broadcasting Board of Governors, which oversees all U.S. government-supported civilian international media. He is also on the Board of Directors of Mercy Corps International. Ambassador Crocker received the Presidential Medal of Freedom, the nation's highest civilian award, in 2009. In July 2012, he was named an Honorary Marine, the 75th civilian so honored since the founding of the Corps in 1775.

"For now, Syria is a lesson that a lack of clear U.S. policy can produce as disastrous an outcome as a military intervention."

—DAVID IGNATIUS

The Spread of the Islamic State in the Middle East

David Ignatius
Associate Editor and Columnist
The Washington Post

I. ISIS: Forwards and Backwards

"It is perfectly true, as the philosophers say, that life must be understood backwards. But they forget the other proposition, that it must be lived forwards." This observation was made in 1843 by the Danish philosopher Søren Kierkegaard in a journal entry, but it might have been written about the contemporary Middle East.

We have been living the Islamic State forwards, surprised at every turn, but we can perhaps begin to understand it backwards: although ISIS took most of the world by surprise when it swept into Mosul in June 2014, the group and its forebears had been proclaiming their goals for a decade. Like many consequential events, this one didn't sneak up on policy makers; they simply didn't see what was taking shape in front of them. ISIS told us exactly what it was going to do, and then did it. This was a secret conspiracy hiding in plain sight.

ISIS is mysterious in part because it is so many things at once. It combines Islamic piety and reverence for the Prophet and his companions with the most modern social media platforms and encryption schemes; its videos are "must see" for young Muslims because they combine the raw pornographic violence of a snuff film with the pious chanting of religious warriors; the group has the discipline of a prison gang (many of its recruits were indeed drawn from U.S.-organized prisons in Iraq), but it also has the tactical subtlety and capacity for deception of the most skilled members of Saddam Hussein's intelligence services, who were also pulled into the ISIS net. It appears less brittle than al-Qaeda because it cares less about religious doctrine and organizational hierarchy. As has been said of the Episcopal Church (forgive the comparison), ISIS is solid at the core but loose at the edges.

In this chapter, I offer a personal assessment of the Islamic State and its impact on the region. I draw upon my own reporting in Iraq, Syria, Jordan, and Lebanon over the past several decades, as well as commentary by others. Drawing any simple lessons from this story would be a mistake, I think. The errors of judgment that led to ISIS's rise have been too consequential for any easy prescriptive advice. Instead, I share a comment made to me in June 2003, as this terrible story was beginning, by Syrian businessman Raja Sidawi. Here's a passage from a July 1, 2003, column that quoted my friend's warning:

> "I am sorry for America," Sidawi said. "You are stuck. You have become a country of the Middle East. America will never change Iraq, but Iraq will change America…"

> This tragic sensibility—the sense that in most instances, things do not work out as you might have hoped—is generally lacking in the American character. Americans are an optimistic people: they have difficulty imagining the worst. That was why 9/11 was so shocking. Most Americans never considered that such devastation could be visited on them.

> Arabs grow up in a culture where it is always best to assume the worst. Sidawi rattled off the list of wars and disasters that have afflicted the Middle East almost continuously since he was born in 1939. That is the bloody history in which America has now enmeshed itself. "You will learn the culture of death," warned Sidawi.

And so we have.

What is ravaging the Middle East now is obviously deeper than ISIS. It has become commonplace over the last year to observe that we are witnessing the collapse of the post-Ottoman order—that the "lines in the sand" conjured in 1916 by Sir Mark Sykes and Francois Georges-Picot are being blown to dust. But we haven't reckoned with what that process feels like for the insurgents. ISIS has religious, psychological, and technological faces. But in some fundamental respects it is an anti-colonial movement that takes as its reference point the Muslim's great pre-colonial idea of power—an Islamic state, a Sunni caliphate. Even if ISIS is crushed, this idea of "our caliphate" is likely to persist, and return.

II. The Iraqi Roots of ISIS

A starting point in assessing the explosive growth of the Islamic State in the Middle East is the group's proclaimed goal of recreating the Muslim caliphate that spread in the region in the 7th century following the death of the Prophet Mohammed. This approach yields some interesting ideological and historical parallels.

The Quranic message of submission and jihad is as powerful now for believers as it was in 622, when Mohammed gathered his followers in Medina and began raiding neighboring areas. The historian Robert G. Hoyland describes this ideological spark in his book *In God's Path: The Arab Conquests and the Creation of an Islamic Empire*. It's the same idea that is evoked in the *nasheeds*, or Islamic chants, that provide the soundtrack for many ISIS videos today: "What is most striking is the very simple but powerful program outlined by Mohammed: form a righteous community (*umma*), go to a safe place (*hijra*), and from there embark on *jihad* against the unrighteous," notes Hoyland.

But religion alone cannot explain (except for the faithful) the spread of the first caliphate in the 7th century, any more than it can the rapid expansion of the current, self-proclaimed successor caliphate. The spark of jihad ignited and spread so quickly after Mohammed's death in 632 in part because it fell on the dry tinder of a region that was enfeebled by imperial wars and the exhaustion of the Byzantine and Persian combatants.

"The change was so sudden and unexpected that it needs explanation," wrote Albert Hourani in his landmark study, *A History of the Arab Peoples*. He noted archeological evidence that the prosperity of the eastern Mediterranean had been undermined by invasions and loss of agricultural techniques such as terraced farming. It was a region ripe for plunder. "The Arabs who invaded the two empires were not a tribal horde but an organized force, some of whose members had acquired military skill and experience in the service of the empires or in the fighting after the death of the Prophet," he wrote.

Reading Hourani's words, I couldn't help but think of the unlikely contemporary alliance between ISIS religious zealots and ex-Baathists who served in Saddam Hussein's most secret and brutal units.

The factors that allowed rapid conquest in the 7th century, as now, may also have included environmental causes. Hoyland's description of the days after the Prophet sounds hauntingly familiar: "Plausibly there were climatic and/or environmental stresses affecting large parts of Eurasia that were putting empires under strain and leaving them more exposed to the predations of steppe and desert peoples around them, but this needs further investigation."

How did the forbearers of ISIS get started in Iraq, and why were they successful in resisting direction from al-Qaeda's core leadership? This is largely the story of a rough-hewn, charismatic al-Qaeda recruit named Abu Musab al-Zarqawi. His story is well summarized by a former Western official who calls himself "Anonymous" in a recent piece in the New York Review of Books titled "The Mystery of ISIS." The author captures the paradoxical nature of Zarqawi's quest when he founded his group in 2003, called "Monotheism and Jihad" in its early days. As Anonymous observes: "Who then could have imagined that a movement founded by a man from a video store in provincial Jordan would tear off a third of the territory of Syria and Iraq, shatter all these historical institutions and—defeating the combined armies of a dozen of the wealthiest countries on earth—create a mini-empire?"

Zarqawi made his name challenging the grandees of al-Qaeda: the wealthy Saudi businessman Osama bin Laden and the Egyptian doctor Ayman al-Zawahiri. William McCants, in his excellent new book *The ISIS Apocalypse*, refers to Zarqawi as a "problem child." Where AQ Core planned meticulous top-down operations, Zarqawi fancied that he would instead emulate the romantic, crusader-conquering Nur al-Din Zengi, who drove the Westerners from Syria.

Zarqawi was convinced the Americans would invade Iraq, so he began building a base there in 2002; he was ready to ally with remnants of Saddam's intelligence network in 2003. Four months after the American invasion, his group brutally attacked three well-chosen targets—U.N. headquarters, the Jordanian embassy, and the Imam Ali mosque—that signaled the dirty war ahead. These bombs shattered the ground for reconciliation: Iraq would be a no-go zone for the international organizations that might have softened the burden of U.S. occupation; Iraq's links would be severed with its mainstream Sunni patron, Jordan; and Iraq would be cleaved apart by a vicious sectarian war between Sunnis and Shiites, whose coexistence had been a feature of modern Iraqi life. Zarqawi's game plan was set by late August 2003; at the time, the U.S. was still denying there was an insurgency.

My recollection of Iraq in late 2003 and early 2004 was of growing violence from Zarqawi's Sunni insurgency, yes. But even more, I was struck by the desperation of Iraq's Sunni sheikhs, who feared and in many cases despised the vicious Zarqawi, but couldn't get the tone-deaf U.S. officials in the Green Zone to take their problems seriously.

Take Fallujah, one of the early recruiting grounds for Zarqawi. This was a sprawling city just west of Baghdad along the Euphrates River. Its Sunni male residents all seemed to have served in the army or have been smugglers, or both. The tribal elders saw the intimidating power of Zarqawi and his mates; they wanted protection from the U.S. and a deal that would give the Sunnis a share of the post-invasion spoils. But their pleas were largely ignored. I visited Sheikh Khamis al-Hassnawi at his villa near the Euphrates in late September 2003. Beyond his banter about procuring an American wife (he seemed to have formed his impressions of the U.S. from *Baywatch*), he almost pleaded for American aid and persistence.

An American pullout from Iraq "would be a disaster," said Sheikh Khamis. "If coalition forces withdraw now, the strong will eat the weak, and people will start killing each other in the street."

That proved an accurate forecast of what occurred from 2004 on, before U.S. forces embraced a "clear and hold" counter-insurgency policy for Iraq. The Sunnis were a second thought for U.S. policy makers. For the social engineers in the Green Zone, the downtrodden Kurds and Shiites were the instruments for change in the New Iraq. If the Sunnis wouldn't go along, too bad for them. In this pre-surge period of growing insurgency and civil war, I remember one prominent National Security Council official telling me more than once that the answer for Iraq was the "80 percent solution"—in other words, Kurds and Shiites would build the new state regardless of the opposition of the 20 percent of the population that was Sunni. This view was recklessness dressed up as realpolitik.

As Zarqawi's toxic violence grew, especially toward Shiites, Bin Laden and his top deputies became concerned. Zawahiri warned Zarqawi to stop showing beheadings in his videos. McCants quotes his admonition that these ultra-violent images might excite "zealous young men" but would appall ordinary Muslims. "We are in a media battle in a race for the hearts and minds of our community," Zawahiri warned. The message, repeated by him and Bin Laden's chief of staff, Atiyah Abd al-Rahman, was, in effect: don't burn too hot; you'll burn yourself out.

The hotheads in Iraq didn't listen, especially on their pet project of declaring an Islamic state in Iraq. Zarqawi's first discussions of creating a caliphate date back to 2004, according to McCants. Al-Qaeda's supreme command disagreed; Bin Laden felt that moving too soon for power in Iraq and Yemen, the movement's two strongholds, would lead to premature defeat and would tarnish the brand. Bin Laden was so frustrated about the branding problem that he concocted nearly a dozen proposed alternative names for the group.

The U.S. killed Zarqawi in June 2006, leading many to imagine that the worst might be over. But his renegade followers went on to declare their state in October

2006, initially under the leadership of Abu Omar al-Baghdadi. The sectarian war that Zarqawi had launched against the Shiites was proving all too successful. Fifty or more bodies were found every morning in Baghdad; it was said that the Sunnis usually beheaded their victims; the Shiites drilled holes in their heads. Washington was still in denial: a *Washington Post* reporter who scouted the morgues to count dead bodies was accused by the U.S. commander and his public affairs officers of inflating the numbers.

"The decision to announce the State was taken without consulting the leadership of al-Qaeda," wrote Bin Laden's American media specialist Adam Gadahn in a message quoted by McCants. And over the next two years, it seemed that the prudence of al-Qaeda core leaders had been correct. President George W. Bush embraced Gen. David Petraeus's "troop surge" and the counter-insurgency philosophy that drove it. A counter-rebellion of tribal leaders that was already underway was christened the "Awakening" and received new money and attention. Sunni tribal fighters and U.S. special operations forces took the fight ruthlessly to al-Qaeda in Iraq (AQI)— ignoring its rhetoric about an Islamic State. And by 2009, the end of the surge years, the movement Zarqawi had created was *all but dead.*

But not quite. There were a few embers of Zarqawi's Islamic State, kept alive by the flicker of Sunni rage. The flame was nurtured at prisons such as Camp Bucca, where Sunni religious detainees were mixed with former Baathists, and the nucleus of a reborn movement began to take shape.

Did Americans know or care about the volcano that lay beneath Prime Minister Nouri al-Maliki's state? Apparently not. Maliki was proving corrupt and sectarian in his rule, displacing Sunnis from their few handholds of power in the new state. The Iraqi people sensed that Maliki was wrecking their country, and in March 2010 elections, they voted out his coalition in favor of a more inclusive group headed by the pro-American former Prime Minister Ayad Allawi.

In what can only be described as an act of folly, the U.S. contrived (with Iran as a silent partner) a horse-trading process that kept Maliki in power. Vice President Biden, who was in charge of the dickering, was fond of proclaiming that "politics has broken out in Iraq." Iraqi politicians concluded (probably correctly) that the Obama administration had decided to leave the country to its own machinations. Nobody imagined in Washington (and few seemed to understand in Iraq) that this future would empower as never before the Islamic State.

How did the Islamic State become so potent in Iraq and Syria in the years after Maliki's 2010 "reelection"? One way was through the group's deliberate, ruthless campaign of assassination against Sunni tribal leaders and the remnants of the Awakening movement in Anbar province. The best numbers I've seen were compiled by former U.S. Army officer Craig Whiteside in doctoral research while he was teaching at the Naval War College in Monterey, California. Between 2009 and 2013, by Whiteside's count, the Islamic State killed 1,345 Awakening members. In Jurf al-Sakhar, a strategic town south of Baghdad, 46 Awakening members were killed in 27 different incidents over this four-year period. This slaughter was hardly a secret: ISIS documented the drive-by shootings and point-blank assassinations in a video called "The Clanging of the Swords." Was anyone watching in Washington? Evidently not.

ISIS was able to seize Mosul so suddenly and dramatically in 2014 for two reasons. First, its assassination campaign had weakened Sunni resistance. Baghdad evidently didn't care; Maliki's government was probably as happy to see the slaughter of potentially powerful Sunnis as was ISIS. (Indeed, some Sunnis in Anbar told me they initially thought the assassination campaign there was the work of Iran-backed Shiite militias.)

The second reason for the rapid ISIS breakout was that it had used Iraqi prisons as its training camps, building trust, operations security, and a passionate hatred for the Shiite-led government in Baghdad. This was a guerrilla army in waiting, and ISIS staged a campaign called "Breaking the Walls" to free these captives and bring them into the fight. Whiteside estimates that between July 2012 and July 2013, there were seven successful prisons raids, culminating in a spectacular, well-organized breakout at Abu Ghraib. (It's notable that one of the first things ISIS did when it swept through Mosul the following June was to liberate the prison there, adding several thousand more fighters to its burgeoning ranks.)

Did anyone at senior levels of the Obama administration notice that, as W.H. Auden wrote in "Spain 1937," his great poem about the Spanish Civil War, "our fever's menacing shapes are precise and alive." Apparently not. In the run-up to the Mosul breakout, President Obama was still referring to ISIS and other post-Bin Laden terrorists as a "JV" team. Director of National Intelligence James Clapper admitted in an interview with me in September 2014: "We underestimated ISIL [the Islamic State] and overestimated the fighting capability of the Iraqi Army. . . . I didn't see the collapse of the Iraqi security force in the north coming. I didn't see that. It boils down to predicting the will to fight, which is an imponderable."

But ISIS's potency was certainly clear to Sunni tribal leaders. In April 2014, three months before the capture of Mosul, I interviewed Iraqi sheikhs from Anbar. One of them, Jalal al-Gaood, told me by phone what was happening in his home area of Albu Ali Jassim, west of Ramadi along the Euphrates River. "In the last week, violent extremists rampaged the police building and pushed people out," he explained. "The Iraqi military then began bombing and shelling the village, and the whole tribe moved out, 250 families."

Gaood offered a grim prediction: "Everyone tells me they've never seen what's happening on the ground now. Hell has come to these villages and towns. It's far worse than before." Sheikh Zaydan al-Jabari, a tribal leader from Ramadi, told me that day: "Iraq is not now a state. It is led by gangs."

Mosul was a wake-up call Obama couldn't ignore. But even after Obama successfully replaced Maliki with a less sectarian prime minister, the U.S. seemed unable to gain the trust of Sunni leaders and recruit the kind of force that could roll back ISIS's gains. In October 2014, on the morning after ISIS had gutted the pro-American fighters of his Albu Nimr tribe, Gaood told me that his pleas that night for help from Centcom went unanswered. "Every time the Iraqis meet with Americans, they just take notes," he complained.

Sheikh Zaydan from Ramadi said in October 2014 that the Sunni tribes wanted U.S. help again, claiming: "We want to create a strategic relationship with the Americans." Yet he scoffed at U.S. plans to create a national guard for the Sunnis, saying it was "wishful thinking," because Iraq's Shiites and Kurds would never agree. Until Sunni rights are respected, he said bitterly, "we will not allow the world to sleep."

I saw Zaydan again in June 2015, a few weeks after ISIS had overrun Ramadi (after bland reassurances from Centcom officials that the city would hold). Zaydan was seeking support for his tribal fighters. (Like several Anbar sheikhs, he had by now hired his own Washington lobbying firm.)

"Iraqis don't want to live under the Islamic State, but where are they supposed to go?" he asked me. Shiite militias had blocked the way to Baghdad for Sunnis fleeing Ramadi; ISIS, meanwhile, was offering amnesty to families who came back and turned over their sons to fight. These tribal leaders simply do not believe U.S. assurances that they're in this fight for real; they're selfish and self-interested, but can you blame them? They've been burned too often. The problem with the U.S. anti-ISIS strategy in Iraq is that it depends on a Sunni tribal movement that doesn't exist.

What lessons can we draw from the rise of ISIS in Iraq and the campaign against it?

First, anti-ISIS operations have been successful when they are launched from platforms that have strong operational and planning resources and well-trained and motivated fighters. Kurdistan is the obvious example, as I saw on a recent visit: Kurdistan Democratic Party peshmerga fighters under the Barzani clan have pushed ISIS west and south, and squeezed Mosul tightly. A visitor can drive unmolested today into Nineveh province and over the Mosul dam, which in the fall of 2014 was in ISIS hands. Patriotic Union of Kurdistan militias have held their own in the Kirkuk area, though there's growing concern that they are taking orders from Iran and its Quds Force. Similarly, Shiite militias have fought well in defending Baghdad, under Iranian supervision.

The problem remains creating a Sunni force that can help the Iraqi military push ISIS from Mosul, Fallujah, and Ramadi and then hold the ground. Such a force would have to operate from a secure base—not just a logistical base, but a base of trust, in which the Sunnis feel they are fighting for a part of Iraq that will truly be theirs post-ISIS. Iraq's Ambassador to Washington, Lukman Faily, has told me that he favors constitutional changes that would create the kind of Iraqi federalism that would truly give Sunnis some "skin in the game" and make a decentralized Iraq work.

Absent this essential political component, it's hard to imagine how the U.S. strategy can work. U.S. military power could drive the heirs of Zarqawi underground, but without Sunni empowerment, the insurgents will be back as ISIS 2.0 or 3.0. The "80 percent solution," we can now see, is shorthand for the dismemberment of Iraq. If some new balance can't be created in Iraq that allows Sunnis to govern their land, we must reckon with the stark warning of the CIA's former deputy director, John McLaughlin, to the *New York Times*: "If you add everything up, that these guys [ISIS] could win. Evil isn't always defeated."

III. How ISIS Grew in Syria, and How It Can Be "Degraded" There

As we disentangle the story of ISIS's growth in Iraq, we can at least see a coherent narrative. That's less true in Syria. The growth of the Islamic State there seems, in the famous French dictum, "worse than a crime, a blunder." We'll never know whether a more aggressive U.S. policy—arming the moderate opposition sooner or bombing Syrian command and control after President Bashar al-Assad used chemical weapons—could have produced a better outcome. But it's hard to imagine a policy that would have done worse.

Where ISIS had an organic growth in Iraq (in the sense that a metastasizing cancer can be called organic), in Syria it seems more a case of implantation. For all the mistakes in U.S. policy, the regional powers—Turkey, Iran, Saudi Arabia, Qatar—have taken truly reckless actions, making Syria a cockpit for their proxy wars. It was Turkey that allowed a northern border so porous that it offered ISIS and Jabhat al-Nusra what amounted to a logistical safe zone and an economic free ride. It was Iran that marched Hezbollah, a Lebanese militia whose rationale was fighting Israel, into Syria to save its client Assad. It was Saudi Arabia and Qatar, jockeying for regional influence, that funded a scattershot array of Sunni militias that were easy recruiting grounds for the extremists (and in this sense supported the extremists). And it was Russia that cynically stood by while its client bombed civilians and ravaged his nation.

Russia's recent move to send its own military into Syria to fight the extremists (and prop up a regime that protects Russian interests) is an act of pure cynicism. Yet U.S. strategy in Syria is so feeble (and its implementation so inept, as in the worst days of the Green Zone) that the U.S. seems willing to tag along behind Russia and the other regional players.

Perhaps Syria is like one of those Agatha Christie books where everyone had a hand in the crime.

Because I've had a chance to watch this Syrian tragedy unfold, I'll share some conclusions drawn from my reporting. My basic judgment hasn't changed in the last three years:

> --The best hope for the country's survival is a political solution that provides a new, post-Assad government.

> --But, such a political solution will be impossible without strong, U.S.-backed opposition that can merge with "acceptable" elements of the army to manage a transition from Assad.

> --This transition process will be fostered by safe zones, in the north and south, where Syrian refugees can be repopulated and the possibility of political compromise can be rediscovered.

> --And, finally, if these steps cannot be taken, the inevitable result will be the continuing growth of ISIS and other extremist groups and the full collapse of Syria into a failed state and terrorist haven.

I first visited Syria in the early 1980s. On a Syrian bus that passed through Hama just after the fighting ended, I was able to see the systematic destruction of Muslim

Brotherhood strongholds in February 1982. (I will never forget the gasps of the Syrian passengers on the bus as they saw the level of point-blank tank bombardment of residential areas.) Later, I was one of many Westerners who had regular conversations with Assad during the decade of 2000 to 2010 about what he claimed was his recognition of the need for political reform in Syria.

For all these reasons, I travelled to Damascus from Cairo in February 2011 with great curiosity. The Mubarak government had just fallen in the Tahrir Square revolution that marked the apex of the Arab Spring. The "barrier of fear," as was said in those days, had been broken across the Arab world. Young Arabs with their cell phones were waging what came to be called "hashtag revolutions"—drawing sudden crowds to demonstrations that had the simple, core demand of "power to the people." What would Damascus, scene of so many coups and counter-coups during its modern history, bring to this revolutionary moment?

Assad's advisers were buzzing about the president's plans for reforms. He knew that change was the only way to escape the deluge, one insisted. He knew the Baath Party was corrupt, said another. He knew the power of the Makhlouf family (i.e., his relatives) had to be curbed. This sense of a looming showdown increased on February 19: a policeman insulted a driver in downtown Damascus; when the man complained, he was attacked by the cops. It was a normal day in authoritarian Damascus—but not in the age of the cell phone and the hashtag. A crowd of hundreds quickly gathered in the Damascus streets and began chanting: "We are the people. The people won't be humiliated." Cell phone videos took the drama to the Internet, and into Syrian homes.

Assad (and his advisers) were wise that time. The minister of the interior arrived about 30 minutes after the protest started, apologized to the man who had been attacked, and escorted him away in his car. The police officers were disciplined. The crowd gradually ebbed, and some (doubtless with official encouragement) began chanting Assad's name. It was a bullet dodged.

The regime wasn't so lucky a few weeks later when protests spread in Daraa, the provincial capital south of Damascus. The Houranis (as the people of this region are known) are famously feisty, and they pushed the local police and military hard. The authorities, led by a bullheaded provincial governor, began firing back. Civilians were slaughtered, and the Syrian revolution had begun.

The Syrian revolution had several characteristics that made it especially disorganized (and prey to manipulation by ISIS and other extremists). First, it was a genuinely bottom-up movement, with each mosque gathering its own young men into brigades that would defend the local area and then (in theory) fight a larger war to overthrow the regime. The destruction of the Muslim Brotherhood in 1982 had been so brutal that the group lacked the discipline and organization inside the country that could have helped weld a strong opposition. The moderates were hapless. Even by the standards of militias in the Middle East, they lacked any coherent command and control.

A second Syrian factor was that, like in Iraq, the revolution began with strong sectarian hatreds. Sunnis appreciated the stability and "Arabism" that the Assad regimes had brought, but they felt humiliated by their subservience to a leadership that many derided as Alawite bumpkins from the mountains. (One popular Syrian anti-regime joke had a phrase that translated "from a donkey to a tank.") Amid this sectarian tension, Syrian minorities banded together behind the regime. Syrian Christians, an ancient and cultivated community, faced a special dilemma. Unlike in Lebanon, the Christians had no militia to protect them, only the Syrian Army. Unlike in Egypt, where Copts feel they are the true Egyptians, Syrian Christians felt marginalized.

(A small aside here on religion: I suspect that one reason Vladimir Putin has been so resolute in his defense of the Assad regime is that he feels a duty to protect his Orthodox brethren—including Syria's large and Russophilic Armenian community—from the depredations of Sunni jihadists. He sees this as a principled mission, not just an opportunistic one.)

Because of the disorganization of the opposition, and the sectarian character of Syrian society, the civil war got nastier after 2011. Inevitably, the opposition became more Sunni and proto-jihadist. Without a U.S.-led effort to bolster a secular opposition, it seemed likely that the extremists would get stronger.

To test these ideas about Syria, I decided to travel inside the country in October 2012 with the help of the Free Syrian Army (FSA). It was a short trip of two days, but I reached Aleppo (even then under savage bombardment) and came to three basic judgments. I'll repeat what I wrote on October 5, 2012, when I was smuggled back into Turkey.

> First, there aren't enough weapons for the rebels to defeat Assad's forces, and almost every Syrian I talked to thinks this is America's fault; second, the commanders of the Free Syrian Army are trying to exercise better command and control over what has been a disorganized, ragtag operation; and third, in this chaotic and under-resourced fight, the power of the Salafist jihadists—who ask only to be martyrs—appears to be growing.

It seemed clear that absent U.S. training and assistance, these problems would only get worse.

A CIA covert training program began, sort of, in 2013. Working with the Jordanian General Intelligence Directorate (GID), the agency has had some success in building a "southern front" that poses an increasing threat to the regime's control of Damascus. But the CIA's program has never worked adequately in the north. I've interviewed most of the pro-American moderate commanders who operated from Turkey: a former military science professor named Gen. Selim Idriss; a loud former Syrian Army Col. named Abdul-Jabar Akaidi; a roustabout guerrilla leader in Idlib named Jamaal Maarouf; and Hamza al-Shamali, the leader of the largest CIA-trained force in the north, known as Harakat al-Hazm.

None of them had the military leadership skills or command presence to create an effective opposition. Shamali's group, Harakat al-Hazm, got chased from its bases in Idlib by the jihadists from Nusra. "At some point, the Syrian street lost trust in the Free Syrian Army," Shamali explained to me in a 2014 interview at a safe house along the Turkish border. He bluntly admitted that many FSA commanders weren't disciplined, their fighters were poorly trained, and the loose FSA structure hadn't provided adequate command and control. Sadly, he said, "the question every Syrian has for the opposition is: Are you going to bring chaos or order?"

The U.S. tried to bolster these nominally covert Syrian missions with an overt "train and equip" program backed by $500 million in congressional support. At this writing, the program has been a dismal failure. A first "class" of 54 trainees was inserted into northern Syria and in mid-2015 was promptly attacked by extremist Muslims. Some in the White House seemed almost to gloat over the failure of the train-and-equip program—as if this showed that their reluctance to back Syrian rebels had been right all along. How nice it would be if American inaction—and its waffling, wobbling approach to Syria—could be described as success. Alas, not so.

I have believed since visiting Syria in 2012 that these are fixable problems, if the U.S. and its allies make a serious commitment to building a new Syrian army that can help stabilize a new Syria, post-Assad. But the halfway measures taken by the U.S. have only helped the jihadists.

Into the vacuum of the moderate opposition fell the extremists of ISIS and al-Qaeda. At first, all the momentum seemed to be with Jabhat al-Nusra, the al-Qaeda affiliate. When I asked an FSA commander in Aleppo in 2012 whether his men fought with Nusra, he answered: "Of course, they're the best fighters." If the FSA needed tough men for an assault, they would turn to the suicide bombers of Nusra, who were often foreign fighters looking for a ticket to paradise. I asked a Syrian doctor what he had learned from treating rebel casualties at the front. A large majority of those with serious wounds were from Nusra, he said. Inevitably, people, arms, and money began flowing to the fighters who were the toughest and best.

ISIS played a spoiler's game in Syria. It moved to Raqqa, an area adjacent to its supply lines into Iraq, and used it as a kind of logistics base camp for its bigger Iraq operations. Raqqa soon became the "capital" of the "state" and the destination point for thousands of foreign fighters. It prospered in part because it wasn't bombed by Assad's air force, which was leveling every other civilian area under rebel control.

You don't have to be a conspiracy theorist to understand why Assad allowed ISIS to put down roots: he needed a threat to show the West why his regime's survival mattered; he needed to demonstrate that there was a worse Syrian face than his own—that of Abu Bakr al-Baghdadi, who had become ISIS's leader. (If you are a conspiracy theorist, you would also note the strong intelligence connections that developed between the Syrian mukhabarat and AQI during the Zarqawi days.)

Friction between Nusra and ISIS remains as strong as the old infighting between Zarqawi and Bin Laden. That's one reason to think that the jihadists' power can be degraded over time in Syria. Propagandists for Nusra and ISIS take almost daily potshots at each other on social media. The U.S. and its allies are doubtless working to exacerbate these cleavages. Raqqa is now nearly encircled; as the squeeze really starts on ISIS forces there, Nusra will have to decide whether it wants to come to the apostates' aid or let them be pounded. Either way, they suffer in the eyes of followers.

Should Nusra be an equal target with ISIS? Prudence argues for a strategy that treats ISIS as the main enemy and Nusra as the next priority. For one thing, if ISIS is toppled, there will be a tipping effect away from extremist forces, generally. A second factor is that Nusra has seemed willing to make pragmatic deals where necessary. Israel is said to maintain intelligence liaison with Nusra along the Golan border; Jordan has similar intelligence links with Nusra in the Daraa area and southwestern Syria. The Qataris, who have given Nusra backdoor funding, see a chance of splitting Nusra soon into a moderate and radical wing. This may be wishful thinking, but it's worth exploring.

The only thing that can preserve ISIS power over the long run in Syria, where it's a transplant, is Assad's continued hold on power. That's why a campaign against ISIS that doesn't have a leadership-change component is short-sighted. Perhaps because Baghdadi knows that he is governing a "foreign-implant" caliphate, ISIS in recent weeks has been emphasizing its hearts-and-minds, community-friendly side. There were unconfirmed reports that Baghdadi himself had questioned the ultra-violence of ISIS videos. British newspapers reported that the best-known foreign fighter, Mohammed Emwazi (the notorious "Jihadi John"), was on the run.

In the last month, the factors that would make possible a Syrian settlement and defeat of ISIS have come into better focus. There are now, effectively, safe zones along the Turkish and Jordanian borders. This will squeeze the extremists and Assad, alike. Both goals are advantageous, but U.S. officials are right to fear a freewheeling regime collapse that opens the way for warlordism and terror across Syria.

A potentially positive new development is apparent interest from Russia and Saudi Arabia in exploring a political settlement. President Obama has talked about his conversations with Vladimir Putin on a Syrian transition process, and as I write, Secretary of State Kerry has met his Russian counterpart several times to discuss details. Meanwhile, Saudi Arabia is coordinating its policies for both war and peace more closely with Turkey and Qatar, two Muslim Brotherhood-linked regimes that once were anathema for the Saudis. For example, Ali Mamlouk, perhaps the leading intelligence figure in the Assad regime, went to Riyadh in July 2015 for talks about the shape of a possible settlement.

Will these positive trends ripen? Can Russia, the U.S., Saudi Arabia, and Iran somehow combine to bring an end to the charnel house of the Syrian war? For now, Syria is a lesson that a lack of clear U.S. policy can produce as disastrous an outcome as a military intervention.

IV. Final Thoughts

This paper has focused on the two places in the Arab world where the Islamic State has been most successful—Iraq and Syria. In both countries, the group benefited from existing sectarian tensions and years of war that left the regimes weakened and unable to contain the flash of motivated, violent extremism. The same characteristics are present in post-Qaddafi Libya, and it's no surprise that the Islamic State has put down roots there, as well.

Libya deserves more study than I have been able to offer here. It's a failed state on the Mediterranean, close to Europe's troubled southern periphery. It's said that ISIS foreign fighters in Syria (or on their way there) are being instructed to rebase in Libya. A serious campaign plan for Libya, ideally run through NATO, seems to me an urgent priority. The overall ISIS strategy won't be complete until this Libya component is in place.

It's useful to look at the countries where the Islamic State, so far, has had relatively little success, such as Jordan and Lebanon. What's their secret? One answer is simply the demonstration effect of the implosions in Iraq and Syria, across the Lebanese and Jordanian borders. There are ISIS cells in both Lebanon and Jordan, but the authorities have been successful in keeping control—for the simple reason that Lebanese and Jordanians cooperate with the security services. Each nation was nearly destroyed in the 1970s by the militant Sunni terror group that was the PLO. People know what they have to lose.

Lebanon and Jordan also benefit from special factors that help the anti-ISIS fight. Lebanon's dominant military and political presence is the Shiite Hezbollah, which is fighting a bitter war against Sunni extremists across the border and wants to keep them locked down at home. But in this effort, Hezbollah has had help from two noteworthy allies. The Christians of Lebanon see their protection as minorities in the defeat of Sunni jihadists, making them natural allies of Hezbollah. What's more interesting is that Lebanon's Sunnis, under the leadership of the Hariri family, have also been working effectively to check Sunni radicalism in Lebanon.

Jordan's special advantage is the experience of its intelligence service, over many decades, in combating extremists. The GID is a presence in every neighborhood, nightclub, bar, and mosque. Its tactics are often unattractive, but Jordanians know there is a thin line between order and chaos in their country, and Palestinians and East Bankers alike seem willing to support the GID.

A final advantage for Jordan was ISIS's stupidity in killing Lt. Muath Kasasbeh so brutally, immolating him in a cage. Jordanian officials weren't sure on the day of his killing which way the country would turn—against ISIS, for murdering the son of a tribal family from Karak, or against the king, for putting Kasasbeh in his warplane to drop bombs on fellow Muslims. Jordanians wisely turned against ISIS. That's the most useful evidence that, over time, the terror group's extremism is a net minus, rather than (as sometimes seems the case) a net plus.

And finally, what of ISIS's appeal to Muslim communities in Europe, Africa, North America, and Asia? Here, the psychological and technological factors that shape ISIS seem to me the dominant story. McCants describes the crass strategy that led Zar-qawi to post on the Internet bloody films celebrating his exploits—an approach taken to a new level of horror by his successors. "They opted for snuff films rather than al-Qaeda's usual pedantry and uploaded multiple links to videos in numerous sizes and formats. Extreme violence attracted eyeballs, and redundant links and decentralized distribution kept it online."

ISIS's theater of death has disturbing appeal for young Muslims around the world. Certainly, it speaks to the dispossessed, to the unemployed, to the marginalized, to those resisting secularization and seeking to live their faith. But perhaps a deeper truth is that this kind of hyper-violence appeals to adolescent, anti-social young men with too much testosterone and too little regard for other human beings.

Youth-gang violence is part of the social pathology of nearly every city on the planet. These crazy, super-violent forms of rebellion are not going to burn themselves out. They seem to be remarkably constant in all times and places. But seen as a social pathology, closer to gang violence than a global war, this problem should have a natu-ral demographic cap—given vigilant use of force by a U.S.-led coalition against those using deadly violence.

David Ignatius was born in May 1950 in Cambridge, Massachusetts. He received a BA magna cum laude in social studies from Harvard College and an economics diploma from King's College at Cambridge University. Since 2003, he has been the author of a twice-weekly, globally distributed column on global politics, economics, and international affairs. From 2000-2003, he was executive editor of the *International Herald Tribune*, and prior to that he worked at the *Washington Post* as assistant managing editor for business news from 1993-1999, foreign editor from 1990-1992, and editor of the Outlook section from 1986-1990. From 1976-1985, he was a reporter for the *Wall Street Journal*, serving as the Middle East correspondent from 1980-1983 and chief diplomatic correspondent from 1984-1985. He has written for numerous publications, including *Foreign Affairs*, the *New York Times Magazine*, and the *Atlantic Monthly*. He is the author of nine novels, including *Body of Lies*, which was made into a movie starring Leonardo DiCaprio and directed by Ridley Scott. His latest novel, *The Director*, is about hacking and espionage. He is a fellow of the Harvard Kennedy School's (HKS) Belfer Center and has taught as an adjunct lecturer at HKS.

"The increasing number of weak states in the Middle East and North Africa means that the Islamic State will continue to have room to expand."

—WILLIAM MCCANTS

Enduring and Expanding
How the Islamic State Offsets Its Territorial Losses

William McCants
Director, Project on U.S. Relations with the Islamic World
The Brookings Institution

The ideological fight against the Islamic State is unlike the ideological fight against al-Qaeda during the past fourteen years. Al-Qaeda appealed to anti-imperialist sentiment in the Muslim world to win support for its cause. Get the United States out of our lands, and its puppets will collapse. Countering al-Qaeda's message required changing perceptions of the roles it assigned to itself and to the United States. Thus, one of the West's most damning counter-messages was to show how many more Muslims al-Qaeda killed than Westerners. How could al-Qaeda be anti-imperialist when it was killing so many of the people it claimed to protect?

Conversely, the Islamic State's message is imperialist. It claims to be the kernel of a reborn Islamic empire that will retake Muslim lands. As long as it succeeds, its program is ratified in the eyes of many jihadists. No surprise, then, that control of territory is at the core of the Islamic State's ideology and claim to legitimacy, as evinced by its succinct slogan: "Enduring and Expanding."

One might reasonably conclude that taking territory away from the Islamic State would sap its credibility and allure. That is probably right in the long term, but it will be difficult to achieve because the Islamic State will exploit security vacuums in the Arab world to offset its territorial losses elsewhere and thus retain jihadist support for its project.

When the Islamic State proclaimed itself in 2006, it fell short of every single benchmark for state-building that it set for itself: monopolizing violence, administering justice, and tending to the economic well-being of its subjects.[1] Nevertheless, it demanded to be treated as a state because it aspired to do all three.

The incongruity between aspiration and reality invited criticism from other jihadists. A well-regarded Kuwaiti jihadist dismissed the Islamic State as a farce in April 2007. He argued that a proper Islamic state required *tamkin*, absolute control over territory. Only then could an "emirate" be declared—literally, land controlled by an emir. That's why Mullah Omar could declare an Islamic emirate in Afghanistan in the 1990s, but the Islamic State of Iraq should not.[2]

In response to the criticism,[3] the first emir of the Islamic State, Abu Omar al-Baghdadi, proclaimed that the Islamic State would endure despite the rhetorical and real firepower arrayed against it. He said that unlike previous failed attempts to create emirates:

> The State of Islam endures.
>
> It endures because it was built from the remains of martyrs and watered with their blood, by which the marketplace of paradise was assembled.
>
> It endures because God's confirmation for this jihad is clearer than the sun in the sky.
>
> It endures because it has not been contaminated by unlawful gain or a defective approach.
>
> It endures by the honesty of its leaders who have sacrificed their blood and by the honesty of the soldiers who have arisen to aid them. We reckon them as honest, and God is their Reckoner.
>
> It endures because it unites the mujahids and shelters the downtrodden.
>
> It endures because Islam has begun to ascend and rise. The clouds are lifting and unbelief is being defeated and disgraced.
>
> It endures because it is the call of the oppressed and the tear of the bereaved and the cry of the captives and the hope of the orphans.
>
> It endures because the unbelief of every religion and sect is arrayed against us and every cowardly, traitorous, misguided heretic has begun to cavil and speak evil of it. We are certain of the goal and the rightness of the road.
>
> It endures because we are certain that God will not shatter the hearts of the downtrodden monotheists, and oppressors will never gloat.
>
> It endures because God the Exalted promised in His unassailable revelation, "God has promised those of you who believe and do righteous deeds that

He will surely make you successors in the land, even as He made those who were before them successors, and that He will surely establish their religion for them that He has approved for them, and will give them in exchange, after their fear, security" (Q 24:55).[4]

In other words, as long as the Islamic State continued to fight as an effective insurgent organization, it could mollify its critics. And in 2007, the group was at the height of its power. But as the Awakening took hold and the State's attack rate plummeted as a consequence, the jihadist rank and file began to doubt the Islamic State's claims to be a state. "The Islamic State of Iraq is still in the right," a jihadist forum member wrote. "So why are things becoming so difficult for it (and) its enemies joining against it from all sides?"

The Islamic State's project might have been utterly discredited when it collapsed in 2009. However, other jihadists took up its banner and its project, helping the group mitigate the damage to its credibility until it roared back to life in 2013. Al-Qaeda in Yemen began using the Islamic State's black flag, not the flag of al-Qaeda Central, in its propaganda. And it adopted its program of state-building, which was at odds with Bin Laden's directive to focus on the United States. Al-Qaeda's secret affiliate in Somalia and al-Qaeda's North African branch followed suit. Jihadists online set up a clock, counting the days since the Islamic State's establishment. The organization was defeated in Iraq, but jihadists outside the country kept its dream of a caliphate alive.

The Islamic State itself got another chance to try its hand at state-building with the onset of civil war in Syria. The State created a secret branch in Syria, the Nusra Front, to accelerate the war and take advantage of the resulting security vacuums to control territory. When the Islamic State proclaimed that Nusra was actually a part of the Islamic State in April 2013, Nusra broke with the organization. The Islamic State responded by raising its flag over the cities it controlled in Syria, and its followers added a new word to its slogan. The Islamic State was no longer simply "enduring." It was also "expanding."

In the following months, the Islamic State began to receive oaths of allegiance from other jihadist groups outside of Syria and Iraq. No one had heard of many of them, but some, like Ansar Bayt al-Maqdis in Egypt and Boko Haram in Nigeria, were already terrorist powerhouses. These new "provinces" or affiliates of the Islamic State benefited from its popularity among jihadists and its propaganda expertise, while the State was able to make good on its claim that it was a caliphate on the march. Some of the smaller affiliates also started to grow, as in Libya, capitalizing on state collapse.

The increasing number of weak states in the Middle East and North Africa means that the Islamic State will continue to have room to expand. So even if the organization is defeated or, implausibly, utterly destroyed in Syria and Iraq, jihadists will have opportunities to implement its state-building project elsewhere, keeping the dream alive.

This does not mean the United States and its allies should cede these territories to Islamic State groups; we should defeat them where we can and contain them where we can't if they pose a threat to our interests. But we should also be realistic that the organization's ideological defeat, which is tied to its loss of territory, is unlikely given the security vacuums in the region and the proliferation of groups willing to follow the Islamic State's program. As long as there is instability, the Islamic State will continue to endure and expand, and its ideology will continue to find adherents as a consequence. Counter messages to the contrary will have little effect.

William McCants directs the Project on U.S. Relations with the Islamic World at the Brookings Institution. He is adjunct faculty at Johns Hopkins University and a former State Department senior adviser for countering violent extremism. His second book, *The ISIS Apocalypse: The History, Strategy, and Doomsday Vision of the Islamic State,* was published by St. Martin's Press in September 2015. Dr. McCants has a PhD in Near Eastern Studies from Princeton University.

[1] al-Tamimi, Uthman bin Abd al-Rahman, ed. January 7, 2007. "I'lam al-anam bi-milad Dawlat al-Islam," *Minbar al-Tawhid wa-l-Jihad*: 36, 38.

[2] al-Ali, Hamid. April 4, 2007. "al-Su'al: Hal man la yubayi'u (Dawlat al-'Iraq al-Islamiyya) 'usa?! Wa-hal huwa wajib al-'asr?!" *H-Alali.net*, at www.h-alali.cc/f_open.php?id=1a55240a-3422-102a-9c4c-0010dc91cf69.

[3] "Hasad al-sinin bi-Dawlat al-Muwahhidin." April 17, 2007. al-Majmu' li-qadat Dawlat al-'Iraq al-Islamiyya.

[4] Hasad al-sinin

[5] McCants, William. August 13, 2008. "Spinning the Failure of the Islamic State of Iraq." *Jihadica*, at www.jihadica.com/spinning-the-failure-of-the-islamic-state-of-iraq/.

"In the last six months, ISIL propaganda has focused increasingly on the competent, prosperous, professional Muslims living in the West—and has in all cases urged their immediate immigration and never proposed that they stage attacks in the United States or Europe."

—GRAEME WOOD

Attacks on Western Targets
What to Expect

Graeme Wood
Contributing Editor, *The Atlantic*
Lecturer in Political Science, Yale University

As of this writing, supporters of the Islamic State in Iraq and the Levant (ISIL) have conducted only a handful of attacks on Western soil. By all accounts, though, the group's foreign fighters are legion—thousands of Western men and women of fighting age have already joined ISIL, and we must assume there are thousands of other ISIL loyalists in Western countries.

Given what we know about ISIL support among foreigners, especially in Western Europe, a question proposes itself: Why have ISIL's attacks been so few and ineffective? ISIL propaganda has praised these attacks retrospectively. In a few cases, we see clear links between ISIL and the attackers themselves. These links amplify concern that attacks will become more numerous and deadly and will achieve greater damage with the blessing and material support of ISIL.

The effects of such an attack could be so severe that we have no choice but to plan for one. However, there is strong evidence to suggest that this wave of more competent attacks is not forthcoming from ISIL under current conditions, and for strategic reasons, ISIL may in fact strongly prefer continued *in*competence over competent mass attacks.

Not for the first time, our ISIL antennae require repositioning because of implicit assumptions about how the group will behave. One assumption is that the group will operate on the al-Qaeda model, under which the September 11 attacks were the ideal sort of attack. Another assumption is an effect of ISIL's graphic violence, which has persuaded many that the group is too wild and uncouth to think strategically. In fact, ISIL's ideological commitments, its public statements, and its self-interest all align, and far from requiring a spectacular attack on a Western target, they imply that ISIL might wish to avoid such an attack and instead extend its current string of blundering small ones.

Attacks Up to Now: A Review

The most sophisticated attempt to classify and enumerate ISIL attacks heretofore is by Thomas Hegghammer and Petter Nesser.[1] Hegghammer and Nesser's count shows a strong preponderance of sympathizer attacks over attacks by returned foreign fighters, and a strategy clearly focused on decentralized attacks rather than centrally planned ones. The authors note that the relatively small number of ISIL videos directly menacing Western targets tended to come just after the commencement of Western bombing and attacks against ISIL targets. They may have been, in other words, direct reactions to Western military action.

Only a small fraction of ISIL propaganda focuses on overseas operations or foreign audiences. The English-language magazine *Dabiq* is a well-known exception. The encyclicals from ISIL's spokesman, Abu Muhammad al-Adnani, also sometimes address remarks to Muslims in Western countries. The propaganda has explicitly avowed, post facto, several attacks:

> There will be others who follow the examples set by Man Haron Monis and Numan Haider in Australia, Martin Couture-Rouleau and Michael Zehaf-Bibeau in Canada, Zale Thompson in America, and Bertrand Nzohabonayo in France, and all that the West will be able to do is to anxiously await the next round of slaughter and then issue the same tired, cliché statements in condemnation of it when it occurs. The Muslims will continue to defy the kafir [infidel] war machine, flanking the crusaders on their own streets and bringing the war back to their own soil.[2]

Dabiq later mentioned Omar El Hussein, the perpetrator of the cafe and synagogue shootings in Copenhagen.[3] Notable in this list of atrocities is the limited body count: the seven attackers all died and killed six while wounding 20. If we include subsequent ISIL-linked attacks, such as Garland and Lyon, the results are even less favorable to ISIL. Garland, the attack with the most evidence of planning (including the purchase of automatic weapons and body armor), killed only the attackers themselves. Hegghammer and Nesser find that ISIL plots have killed on average 1.4 victims each.

To what do we owe this incompetence? Some of the attackers have simply been low-functioning individuals incapable of coherent planning. Others (the Chattanooga shooter might turn out to fit in this category), appeared to prefer their own martyrdom to effective mass killing on the scale of Sandy Hook or Virginia Tech, for which they had easily repeatable models and ready access to similar arms. In almost every case, the attackers had only modest means of support. None received detectable material aid from ISIL.

This parade of blundering, mentally ill, quasi-homeless losers could nonetheless be dangerous in certain circumstances. There are numerous examples—think of the shoe-bomber, Richard Reid—of simpletons who have nearly or successfully caused immense damage after being outfitted or armed by higher-functioning conspirators. And the Breivik massacre in Utøya, Norway, shows that jobless loners can kill vast numbers of people without support, if they have time and patience.

ISIL and its supporters would consider a September 11-level attack desirable in a number of ways. Their propaganda fantasizes about one, showing (for example) the White House in flames or European landmarks prominently displayed as targets. What's more, we know that new classes of commando squads are being trained to inflict precisely the kind of damage that lone wolves have thus far failed to achieve. We should ask: Why have all the ISIL-linked attacks on Western targets so far failed to kill even a tenth as many people as were slain by a single jobless Norwegian video-game addict?

A Self-Limiting Autonomous Attack

ISIL's own statements and documents prove helpful here. ISIL prefers near-enemy attacks and is principally concerned with expansion and maintenance of core territory; in this way it differs from al-Qaeda and is a much greater danger to Middle East and North Africa targets than Western ones.

The most quoted statement enjoining attacks on the West is the message titled "Indeed Your Lord Is Ever Watchful," by ISIL spokesman Adnani. Its instructions are lurid, but decidedly small-scale:

> If you are not able to find an IED or a bullet, then single out the disbelieving American, Frenchman, or any of their allies. Smash his head with a rock, or slaughter him with a knife, or run him over with your car, or throw him down from a high place, or choke him, or poison him. If you are unable to do so, then burn his home, car, or business. Or destroy his crops. If you are unable to do so, then spit in his face.[4]

But this line is anomalous in Western-directed ISIL propaganda. Much more common is the reminder of the obligation of hijrah, or immigration to ISIL territory. These messages leave little doubt that hijrah supersedes attacks *in situ* in the hierarchy of obligation. To take a representative article from the most recent *Dabiq*:

And here I call on you to make hijrah to us here in the lands of the blessed Islamic State! Do you not love Allah and His Messenger? Do you not desire to live in a land over which no rule is established other than the rule of Allah? Then come, make your way to *dārul-islām* [the abode of Islam]. And I remind you of the individual obligation on every Muslim and Muslimah to make hijrah from *dārul-kufr* [the abode of disbelief] to *dārul-islām*.

Allah says, *Indeed, those whom the angels take [in death] while wronging themselves–[the angels] will say, "In what [condition] were you?" They will say, "We were oppressed in the land." The angels will say, "Was not the earth of Allah spacious [enough] for you to emigrate therein?" For those, their refuge is Hell—and evil it is as a destination* [An-Nisā': 97]. Imām Ibn Kathīr says, "The noble *āyah* [verse] is general and refers to every person who resides amongst the *mushrikīn* [polytheists] while he is able to make hijrah and is not able to establish the religion."[5]

For every command to attack, there are literally dozens of messages like this, explaining in painstaking detail the consequences in the hereafter for failing to immigrate if possible. This trope of hijrah is relentless in the propaganda, and every supporter I have met has agreed that immigration has priority. In issue 9 of *Dabiq*, Adnani himself commanded followers: "Either one performs hijrah to the *wilāyāt* of the *Khilāfah* or if he is unable to do so, he must attack the crusaders."[6]

Supporters are aware that not all are able to immigrate, and (as with the *Hājj*) some are excused. Among these, ISIL supporters have told me, are those who truly lack the resources to fulfill the obligation. Others are ISIL supporters who are so well-known to authorities that they would be thwarted or arrested if they attempted hijrah. (The notorious UK national Anjem Choudary, who has encouraged many to immigrate, offers interdiction as the convenient but plausible excuse for his own failure to do so.)

The stress on the obligation of hijrah effectively eliminates from the ISIL overseas army anyone except for the unconvinced, the poor, the well-known, and people so isolated or incompetent that they cannot make reliable contact with the thousands of ISIL accounts out there capable of referring them to an ISIL travel-booker. Adnani's emphasis on spitting at infidels and small-scale acts of vehicular homicide is intentional as well as practical, because this is the level of play of which the remaining ISIL overseas bench is capable. In the last six months, ISIL propaganda has focused increasingly on the competent, prosperous, professional Muslims living in the West—

and has in all cases urged their immediate immigration and never proposed that they stage attacks in the United States or Europe. Losers should attack; everyone else should immigrate.

Given that ISIL's overseas agents (especially the smart ones) are among its most dangerous weapons against the West, it may appear that hijrah by non-losers, followed by burning of Western passports, is a form of unilateral disarmament— and perhaps one that should even be encouraged among those who cannot be identified and stopped. Whether the negative consequences of such a policy for ISIL's nearer-enemies would outweigh the benefits to the West is beyond the scope of this discussion. But about ISIL's own calculation there is little doubt: they believe that immigration, professionalization, and deepening the technical capacities of ISIL in its core territory is a winning, and divinely ordained, strategy.

Strategic Reasons for Self-Limiting Attacks

One of ISIL's most impressive characteristics is its ability to learn from its predecessors, most notably al-Qaeda. Its tactics in expanding through Anbar in the last year reflect the beating that ISIL's predecessors took at the hands of tribes during the Sunni Awakening. Its wariness in accepting pledges of allegiance from wannabe ISIL affiliates reflects the memory of its own misbehavior after al-Qaeda Central publicly accepted, and later regretted accepting, allegiance from Abu Musab al-Zarqawi.

No less important a lesson learned is the fallout from September 11th, and the possibility that the United States might respond with an occupying force after a similar attack. Al-Qaeda's ideologues, including Bin Laden himself, have gloated about the ease with which the September 11th attack provoked a costly U.S. overreaction. But al-Qaeda's lack of near-term state ambitions separates it from ISIL in this regard: there is little doubt that if the U.S. were to invade and occupy ISIL's main population centers, many of ISIL's supporters would regret the territorial loss and consider forfeited the caliphate's central promise of an "expanding and enduring" Islamic state. The bitterness would not be mitigated if ISIL survived as an insurgency (even if it made its conquerors live to regret their conquest).

ISIL's main interest, therefore, is a strategy that promotes its status as the most prominent and feared jihadist group, without stretching its neck out far enough to provoke a response that would exploit its key vulnerability, namely its need to control territory.

For obvious reasons, the ongoing slew of incompetent attacks fits this need perfectly. The hysterical fear of Western publics remains stoked, and the size of the public-relations bonanza that ISIL can purchase with each attack appears quite inelastic with respect to the size of the attack. The attacks remain mostly unattributable because they are autonomously conducted, and limited in size because anyone capable of larger ones should be planning to immigrate.

Conclusion

ISIL's goal is to remain in place and root itself so firmly that an invasion would be even more impractical or unwise than it currently is.

This plan may change, and it would be folly to assume it will not. However, in the interim, we should expect more of the same: persistent small-grade attacks with small numbers of fatalities. Al-Qaeda may, of course, continue to attempt spectacular attacks, although by all indications, as an organization of global reach, it is spent. For ISIL, such attacks carry great risk, and it continues to meet its main goals through the modest attacks already carried out in its name.

The consequences of failing to anticipate a competent terrorist attack would be significant, and it is unthinkable to recommend reduced vigilance in the face of a determined enemy with ISIL's capabilities. Under this frame of analysis, ISIL might just shift its efforts to targets that it bets will not provoke a response—perhaps against NATO countries less likely to mobilize against ISIL territory than the U.S.

An important corollary to this analysis is that we should expect a complex interaction between military attempts to counter ISIL and ISIL's attacks on Western targets. In the short term, attacks on ISIL are likely to increase attacks on Western targets. In the face of setbacks in its core territory, ISIL could decide to recalculate its strategy and allocate its assets to cause far greater damage than it has heretofore. I would expect ISIL to do exactly this. As the counter-ISIL efforts proceed, one might look for signs of that inflection point, for an indication of ISIL's own assessment of its fortunes and whether it continues to conceive of itself as a territory-based caliphate or whether it has given up that ambition and is preparing to enter an al-Qaeda-like phase.

Over the longer term, however, ISIL remains committed to attacking Western targets. There can be little doubt that it remains doctrinally committed to these attacks. But it will wait, if it is permitted, until a time it is strong enough to withstand the inevitable backlash.

Graeme Wood is the Edward R. Murrow Fellow at the Council on Foreign Relations. He is a contributing editor to *The Atlantic* and books editor of *Pacific Standard*, and has written for many others. He is a graduate of Harvard and The American University in Cairo and is a lecturer in political science at Yale University.

[1] Hegghammer, Thomas, and Petter Nesser. 2015. "Assessing the Islamic State's Commitment to Attacking the West." *Perspectives on Terrorism* 9 (4).

[2] "Forward." December 2014. *Dabiq*: 4.

[3] "Forward." March 2015. *Dabiq*: 5.

[4] al-Adnānī al-Shāmī, Abu Muhammad. September 21, 2014. "Indeed Your Lord Is Ever Watchful."

[5] Al-Muhājirah, Umm Sumayyah. July 1, 2015. "They Are Not Lawful Spouses for One Another." *Dabiq*: 47-48.

[6] "And Allah is the Best of Plotters." May 2015. *Dabiq*: 53.

Part 3

"There should be no assumption that the military defeat of ISIS will lead to regional stability."

—JAMES E. CARTWRIGHT

Alternative Military Strategy Options to Combat ISIS

James E. Cartwright
Harold Brown Chair
Center for Strategic and International Studies

The president has reaffirmed his strategy to degrade and ultimately destroy ISIS.[1] To degrade ISIS implies defeat is not currently an option and ultimately implies that the military intervention will conduct a holding action until the capabilities needed for defeat are available. In military parlance, this signifies a temporal mismatch between ends and means.

This chapter will look at the current strategy and two additional military strategies to bound the potential challenges of alternative ends and means associated with a military intervention into the current ISIS areas of hostility: Iraq, Syria, and Yemen. In the assessment, I narrowed the key attributes of each military intervention strategy to:

1. Forces required

2. Duration to attain the stated ends

3. Likely implications on regional stability

4. Resource implications

The analysis draws on previous gaming, modeling, and historic analogy. We sought to draw a consensus insight across the four measures for each of the chosen military strategies. Each of the strategies has different ends and means. Each of the strategies has strengths and weaknesses.

We assume the ISIS ideology has strong sectarian roots and that ISIS has capitalized on the Sunni-led uprising against Bashar al-Assad and the Sunni areas of Iraq that were neglected by Prime Minister Nouri al-Maliki.[2] We also assume that ISIS is an organization of like-minded individuals, responding to a set of underlying causal factors in Iraq and the Levant, and eliminating ISIS does not eliminate the root causes that engendered support for the movement. Removing the top leaders in ISIS does nothing to address the pull the organization has with poor, underrepresented

Sunnis in Iraq, Yemen, and Syria, or the draw it has for Muslims seeking to support a movement they believe to be for the greater good of Islam, and the world.

We assume ISIS is in the third stage of maturation of a rebel movement. The first stage is characterized by an iconic leader that is central to the continued progression of the organization without which the organization falls apart. This is not the case for ISIS. While Abu Bakr al-Baghdadi is the figurehead, Audrey Cronin in *Foreign Affairs* writes that "the group's fighters and leaders are well integrated into civilian populations," and eliminating leaders would not destroy the organization.[3] The second stage of a rebel movement is characterized by key functional and organizational players that can be replaced if lost. This is true for ISIS, which has developed a pseudo-state and governmental processes, including a leadership council and a cabinet with departments such as finance, media, and recruitment.[4] In its current state, losing top leaders in the organization may present a temporary challenge but does not create a complete vacuum of power. We assess ISIS has attained the third stage of development: the movement has central direction and decentralized execution. This organizational construct is highly adaptable and resilient and can agilely gain and sustain offensive military advantage.

We assessed three different military strategies. The first strategy is the current degrade and ultimately defeat, which addresses the military objective and seems to assume some role post conflict yet to be defined. We added an alternative military strategy to contain the conflict within existing national borders, and we dubbed this the containment strategy. In this strategy, the combatants are allowed to conclude the rebellion without an external intervention. Finally, we felt that it was reasonable to assume military defeat of ISIS envisioned in the first two strategies may be insufficient to address underlying causal factors and regional stability challenges. To address this expansion, we assumed a significant military intervention. This intervention would be designed to attain a military defeat, the removal of current governance structures, a follow-on occupation under a provisional government, and an eventual transition to self-governance, e.g., World War II. This strategy we label the defeat, occupy, and establish a provisional government.

I. Degrade and Ultimately Defeat ISIS

This is a military holding strategy. It seeks to buy time by degrading ISIS in order to generate the organic military force to destroy ISIS. In our recent endeavors to train Iraqi and Afghan forces, we trained a significant number of individuals over a period of years. However, developing the esprit and leadership across a large military force takes a significantly longer time. It should also be assumed that over the same period, ISIS forces will be growing, becoming battle hardened, and developing leaders motivated by their cause, thereby further prolonging the conflict. As a result, this will lead the coalition into an incremental employment strategy. In its worst instantiation, the coalition force will grow incrementally over time, in a reactive manner, until lack of resources and/or will lead to withdrawal. In other words, we will have prolonged the conflict and not addressed the underlying causes of the rebellion, leading to increased carnage and cost without significantly changing the end state. There should be no assumption that the military defeat of ISIS will lead to regional stability. The best result we could hope for in this strategy is for the Iraqi government to raise an effective military and police force, build an inclusive governance structure to provide a better distribution of wealth, and create a more stable governance platform under the rule of law. For Syria and Yemen, a military defeat of ISIS is not likely to change the underlying causal factors and/or end state.

II. Containment

A containment strategy, avoids direct military intervention. Instead, it seeks to stabilize the borders in the area of hostilities. Containment further seeks to deter cross-border incursions and prevent the establishment of and support for safe havens. In an ideal end state, a clear military and political winner emerges within the rebellion, with the consensus to form a governance structure that addresses the underlying causal factors, and establishes a representative and accountable governance structure in short order. In its worst outcome, a containment strategy does not get the support of regional players, generates significant humanitarian challenges, and experiences significant and prolonged challenges in transitioning from conflict to stable governance. Regional stability will be very difficult to attain if the post-war internal governance is unstable. Lack of resources along with cost, humanitarian, and duration attributes are likely to be significant barriers to a successful outcome. The reduced military coalition mission reduces resource, cost, and duration to the extent the coalition is able to not feel compelled to intervene.

III. Defeat, Occupy, and Establish a Provisional Government

A defeat, occupy, and establish a provisional government strategy seeks to mirror the strategy of WW II. This strategy imposes significant coalition force requirements both for the defeat and for a significant portion of the occupation, even if the interventions are sequenced across the three countries. In its best outcome, the military conflict leading to defeat would be swift, i.e., months. The casualties are likely to be less than the other two strategies. The costs for defeat are likely relatively low. The occupation would be prolonged. Underlying causal factors could be addressed. Regional stability could be improved. ISIS and follow-on rebellions could be defeated. Imposition of a provisional government and a transition to self-rule offer the best chance for long-term stability. On the con side of the ledger, while Iraq and Syria offer the best chances of a self-sustaining governance structure, Yemen will be harder. Regional powers may oppose an occupation force, particularly by a non-Muslim coalition, and seek to undermine the effort. The cost and resource burden may well exceed the ability and/or willingness of coalition countries.

Our assessment suggests the following:

- The current strategy of degrade and ultimately defeat has the highest probability for building a coalition. The incremental increases in mission, resource, and cost will spread the burden of support over a longer period. However, incremental intervention cedes military control of the conflict to ISIS, prolongs the conflict, and has a high probability of failing to attain the intended end state, oftentimes leading to withdrawal, without a change in the underlying causal factors.

- The containment strategy reduces coalition military and resource commitments. However, the strategy falls short in addressing humanitarian and governance concerns. It has the potential to address the underlying causal factors, but likely at high humanitarian cost. In its worst case, it implies the coalition would stand by in the face of a potential genocide.

- The defeat, occupy, establish a provisional government strategy leads to a prolonged occupation in order to address the underlying causal factors. The difficulties in this strategy are sustaining political will and the resource commitment over the life of the transition to self-governance. While the end state has the highest probability of success, the likelihood is lowest that a coalition can or would be able to enter into and sustain the prolonged resource drain.

- We believe that an integrated degrade, contain, defeat ISIS strategy has the best opportunity to match resource, political will, and capability against ISIS. Iraq has the greatest likelihood of benefiting from this approach.

We should acknowledge that Iraq will not have the esprit or leadership to conduct operations independently for many years and that incremental force application will cost more lives, dollars, and opportunity than an aggressive military intervention.

- We assess that this integrated strategy is unlikely to address the underlying causes of the conflict, or significantly reduce regional instability, and will likely prolong the rebellion. Absent a realistic defeat, occupy, establish provisional governance strategy, the integrated strategy prolongs the conflict's resolution.

- Finally, we looked at military tactics that might alter the outcome. Suffice it to say, there are no silver bullets that would somehow bring a swift end to the conflict, including abolishing the boots-on-the-ground restrictions. The force ratios necessary to conduct successful degrade, contain, defeat actions are significantly greater than what are currently envisioned by the coalition.

- Special operations forces and highly mobile forces (e.g., CAV, MEF, and armed air reconnaissance) will be most suited for the strategy. Intelligence, surveillance, and reconnaissance demand will exceed means to provide.

- Capabilities associated with the department's third offset strategy will begin to appear in this conflict and add to the capacity of the force. Full implementation of these capabilities is still years from full operational capability.

The president has reaffirmed his strategy to degrade and ultimately destroy ISIS.[5] The greatest vulnerability to the current and a broadened, integrated strategy is the time to train, equip, and develop leaders and the organizational esprit of an organic force in Iraq, Syria, and Yemen. This strategy prolongs the conflict, increasing cost, resource loss, and infrastructure destruction. While the strategy sets conditions that could permit the eventual addressal of the underlying causal factors, it creates very little leverage to compel the political outcome. The failure to aggressively address the necessary resource implications disadvantages the intervention and historically has a high probability of leading to premature withdrawal.

James E. Cartwright retired from active duty on 1 September 2011, after 40 years of service in the United States Marine Corps. General Cartwright served as Commander, U.S. Strategic Command, before being nominated and appointed as the 8th Vice Chairman of the Joint Chiefs of Staff. He became widely recognized for his technical acumen, vision of future national security concepts, and keen ability to integrate systems, organizations, and people in ways that encouraged creativity and sparked innovation in the areas of strategic deterrence, nuclear proliferation, missile defense, cyber security, and adaptive acquisition processes. General Cartwright currently serves as the inaugural holder of the Harold Brown Chair in Defense Policy Studies for the Center for Strategic & International

Studies. In addition, General Cartwright serves as a member of The Raytheon Company Board of Directors, a Harvard Belfer Center Senior Fellow, a defense consultant for ABC News, and a member of the Board of Governors for Wesley Theological Seminary. General Cartwright is also an advisor for several corporate entities involved in global management consulting; technology services and program solutions; predictive and Big Data Analytics; and advanced systems engineering, integration, and decision support services. He serves as an advisor to the Boards of Directors for Accenture Federal Services, Enlightenment Capital, IxReveal, HSH Analytics, Opera Solutions, and the Truman National Security Project. General Cartwright is also affiliated with a number of professional organizations including The Atlantic Council, Council on Foreign Relations, Global Zero, and the Nuclear Threat Initiative. He is a member of the Aspen Strategy Group.

[1] Obama, Barack. July 6, 2015. "The President Provides an Update on Our Campaign to Degrade and Destroy ISIL," at www.youtube.com/watch?v=YkJs3XU0rr4.

[2] Hubbard, Ben. November 5, 2014. "ISIS Wave of Might Is Turning into a Ripple." *The New York Times*, at www.nytimes.com/2014/11/06/world/middleeast/isis-wave-of-might-is-turning-into-ripple.html?_r=0.

[3] Cronin, Audrey. March/April 2015. "ISIS Is Not a Terrorist Group: Why Counterterrorism Won't Stop the Latest Jihad Threat." *Foreign Affairs*, at www.foreignaffairs.com/articles/middle-east/2015-02-16/isis-not-terrorist-group.

[4] "How ISIS Works." September 16, 2014. *The New York Times*, at www.nytimes.com/interactive/2014/09/16/world/middleeast/how-isis-works.html.

[5] Obama, Barack. July 6, 2015. "The President Provides an Update on Our Campaign to Degrade and Destroy ISIL," at www.youtube.com/watch?v=YkJs3XU0rr4.

"The battle needs to be joined physically and ideologically, but it must also include a heavy focus on overcoming the enemy's operations in what the Department of Defense calls the Fifth Domain of Warfare: the cyber domain."

—FRANCES TOWNSEND

The New Age of Terror

More than a decade after September 11, 2001, the world faces a growing, and adaptive, threat of terrorism

Frances Townsend
Executive Vice President
MacAndrews & Forbes Incorporated

After September 11, 2001, the United States and the world's democratic order faced a dangerous array of threats. An unconventional enemy had struck against the economic and political centers of the United States—a feat not achieved by America's conventional enemies since the British army burned down the White House in the War of 1812.

In the wake of September 11, much information came to light about the enemy and its purposes. Soon the jihadist organization responsible for the attacks was identified and isolated. Intelligence about its various plots and its vulnerabilities was rapidly acquired. Before long, al-Qaeda and its network of affiliates, including rogue states that had provided resources and safe haven, were steadily degraded and driven underground.

Almost precisely 13 years later, on September 10, 2014, President Obama announced a strategy to combat the rise of the Islamic State of Iraq and Syria (ISIS). The president's plan consisted of limited bombing raids targeting the group in Iraq and Syria, augmented by the limited use of Special Forces. This was a good idea, but too limited and only a beginning. It is still not well understood, however, that in the war on terror, the military dimension is necessary but not sufficient. An effective strategy has always required an approach that uses all instruments of natural power: military, intelligence, diplomatic, financial, and law enforcement. However, our enemy has proved adaptive, and it commands resources—literally and figuratively— that no terror group has enjoyed in the past. As a result, the U.S. and its allies are fighting an even more aggressively asymmetrical conflict than its predecessors in the global jihadist movement.

Today's terrorists have learned a great deal from the failures of their predecessors and are now less dependent on state sponsorship and a hierarchical leadership structure than in the past. (Witness the profusion of "lone wolf" attacks across the West.) The enemy is nimble, forming independent transnational networks based on religious or ideological affiliation. They actively seek to recruit members animated by a sense of perceived grievance and identity crisis. They do this by cultivating charismatic recruiters and preachers and by disseminating their message to an unfathomably large audience via the Internet and social media. All of this makes the terrorist threat considerably more difficult to detect, and prevent and combat.

The governmental response to terrorism in the first decade of the 21st century helped prevent large-scale, mass-casualty attacks on "the homeland," but it did not bring an end to the threat posed by radical Islam. A new iteration of that threat has now arisen, in the Middle East and beyond, constituting a unique challenge to the military and intelligence communities—but one that cannot be defeated by governmental forces alone.

A more comprehensive strategy is needed, one that incorporates the expertise and knowledge of the private sector and civil society. The battle needs to be joined physically and ideologically, but it must also include a heavy focus on overcoming the enemy's operations in what the Department of Defense calls the Fifth Domain of Warfare: the cyber domain. We must contest the digital battlefield of the 21st century just as we have historically contested air, sea, land, and space, by devoting the necessary resources and expertise to prevail.

The Fifth Domain

The march of technology can work for and against global security. ISIS and other jihadist groups have proven adept at exploiting the Internet to spread their messages, radicalize, recruit, and incite violence worldwide. Prior to the explosion of social media, extremists had to invest much time and effort into establishing and maintaining contact with each other. This is no longer the case. Indeed, extremists no longer even have to cross national borders to receive training that prepares them to inflict severe damage on open societies.

Radical Islam may be grounded in an ideology from the 7th century, but it is entirely modern in the way it has harnessed technology and, in the case of ISIS, put it in the service of expanding its nascent state. ISIS's Internet presence is sophisticated and all too effective. Its slick online magazines, more than 100,000 social media messages a day, and Hollywood-style production of grisly execution videos are responsible for attracting more than 20,000 recruits to the jihadist army.

The effects of this social media omnipresence, while threatening, should not distract us from the more conventional tools that extremists also rely upon. The extremist chat forums and social media presence pose a danger, but as Michael Rubin points out, ISIS also employs more traditional methods of communication. "It runs radio stations in Raqqa, Syria, and Mosul, Iraq. AM and FM radio signals from Islamic State-controlled territory reach a hundred miles into Turkey, sixty miles into Iran, and fifty miles into Jordan. This is in addition to the 48 percent of Syrians and 71 percent of Iraqis living outside ISIS control. This translates into a potential audience of 42 million."

This is reason to pursue a vigorous military strategy against ISIS in its heartland, but it is not an excuse to remain aloof from the realm where private citizens can make their influence felt. The Internet has succeeded in bringing the *umma* (the community of believers) to life in a new and potent way. Those who seek instruction in the tenets of extremist faith, or in the making of bombs, can easily receive it, allowing them to organize and plot with fellow travelers around the globe. For these reasons, the violent Islamist movement considers cyberspace to be not its enemy but perhaps its greatest ally.

This will need to change, and change quickly, if the movement is to be defeated.

The Web Response

Thanks to ISIS's impressive territorial gains in Iraq and Syria, the menace of terrorism now commands worldwide attention. Unfortunately, the world's response has been characterized by complacency and neglect. The option of deploying armed force is reserved to governments. The option of disrupting the ability of extremists to communicate and recruit is not. Depriving extremist groups of certain essential tools is an option for those in the nongovernmental and civil-societal sphere, if we choose.

In the public debate over the extremists' finely honed and accelerating use of technology, there are two primary arguments advanced in opposition to contesting the extremists' online presence. The first suggests that any such endeavor is a fool's errand. The operators behind extremist websites, this argument runs, are extraordinarily resilient: as soon as websites are disabled or taken down, they bounce back without much trouble.

But as James Van de Velde has documented in "Crash Their Comms," a recent essay for *The American Interest*—probably the best to date on contesting the jihadist web presence—this isn't quite true. "In the past, when ISPs [Internet service providers] or host countries contested some websites, many never came back at all. And those that do come back often return in a diminished manner."

The task of removing extremist content is dogged and often thankless. It is commonly characterized as a "Whac-A-Mole" game prosecuted in vain. This impression is understandable but mistaken. We must accept that the enemy will adapt to our efforts to counter its influence, but we should undertake these efforts all the same to force it to do so as quickly and as frequently as possible. This necessarily obstructs the efficiency and thus the appeal of extremist movements. While it is true that a Twitter account can come back again and again, each time it comes back a little more weakened, its influence a little more diminished.

The second argument against challenging the extremists' extensive use of the Internet holds that worse than being futile, it is positively harmful. This argument posits that interdicting extremists' presence online impairs the counter-extremist efforts of intelligence and law enforcement insomuch as it removes a valuable source of enemy intelligence.

While this argument may have had validity when there were only a few extremists using the Internet, that is no longer the case. Quality intelligence about extremists' activities and strategies is very necessary, but the most urgent need is to deprive the enemy of its ability to communicate methods and materials, attract fresh fighters, and raise money. We should not underestimate ISIS's media operation. By allowing extremists to meet online and, until recently, to plot unmolested, we have handed an immense advantage to our enemies at home and thousands of miles away.

The spectacle of extremists deploying technology that has otherwise been a force for economic, political, and social good in order to subvert and destroy the achievements of our society and its institutions is appalling. Allowing them to operate online with impunity is fighting with one hand tied behind our back, for it allows those who have declared that WE are their enemies to bend the truth 100,000 times a day in order to radicalize impressionable young people struggling for a sense of identity. This volatile combination of explosive rhetoric and a willing audience is a formula for future terrorist attacks anywhere and everywhere.

There is also the civil libertarian, 1st Amendment argument that restricting access to the cyber domain constitutes censorship, as if individuals have carte blanche to incite violence. In point of fact, there is no constitutional right to advocate and arrange support for terrorist organizations on the web. Abridging the freedom of action online does nothing to undermine Internet freedom; on the contrary, by shoring up the defenses of democracies, it strengthens it.

It is also true that the private sector possesses the majority of the infrastructure in this domain. For IT companies, then, it is not only a duty but also a right to band together in common cause to shut down these militant websites and social media accounts, just as they have done to combat child pornography, bullying, and human trafficking.

We must avail ourselves of all the means at our disposal. Adding the social tools to the military assets in our arsenal will bring us many tactical victories, but this will still not complete the phalanx of resistance to violent extremism. Any strategy that fails to take into account the driving ideology that allows extremists to recruit and motivates them to fight may be short-sighted.

Confronting the Ideology

More than a decade after September 11, 2001, the world is entering a new and possibly more dangerous phase in the war on terror. We are still confronted with a ferocious and determined foe: radical Islam, which wraps its thirst for power in the robes of religious justification. ISIS, as well as other extremist groups, actively seeks the restoration of the medieval Islamic caliphate. They demand that sharia, Islamic law, be the charter of all nations. That is old news. But with the reach of technology, the asymmetric nature of the war is magnifying, to the advantage of those who mean us harm.

The global allure of Islamist radicalism has been poorly understood in the postmodern West, not least in the political class. Ever since ISIS established its caliphate and rallied international youth to its banner, the West has struggled to come to terms with what appeal a gang of religious zealots could possibly hold for thousands of educated middle-class individuals across the world. To cite just one example, the West watches in horror the videos that capture every new ISIS atrocity. ISIS, though, makes no effort to conceal its worst deeds. To the contrary, it flaunts them worldwide in high-production quality. No act—crucifixions, beheadings, homosexuals thrown off tall buildings—is too heinous to turn off its audience, and the earned media is only a bonus.

The general response to this barbarism among the Western political class has been a form of denial. The Obama administration has been emphatic: in addition to its brutality, ISIS is guilty of false-advertising; it is not "Islamic." The extremists use this willful blindness deftly to explain that the great liberal powers traffic in bald-faced lies, and that they mean to destroy Islam.

British Prime Minister Cameron, in his recent Birmingham speech, set himself apart from this trend by grappling seriously with the threat. He recognized that Islamist terror is a potent ideology within a vast and varied religious tradition, and it purports to be a revolutionary force, propagating contempt for liberal values and offering a sense of community to all Muslims who follow the righteous path.

In point of fact, there is great danger, as well as immense opportunity, in the world of Islam. A battle for the future of the faith is taking place between reformers and reactionaries, and its outcome matters. Government has a role to play in that battle. Although Cameron put in a good word for banning violent Islamists online and in the pulpit, he did not make a vigorous case for legislation. Instead, the prime minister encouraged the private sector and universities to assume greater responsibility in countering extremist ideology in their midst. In so doing, Cameron became the first Western leader to stress that the fight against extremism must revolve around a robust partnership between government and civil society.

As the impact of ISIS grows, it is hard to imagine a good outcome to the war if we cannot bring ourselves to accept the nature of the enemy. Islamist extremism is the soil in which ISIS and its affiliates are flourishing. A strategy to counter the violent strains within Islam must acknowledge this fact. This means, for starters, countering the extremists' online presence and propaganda, as well as unleashing aggressive public diplomacy to assist liberals and reformers within Islam. Failure to do so will only put many millions—mostly Muslims—in harm's way.

Frances Fragos Townsend is an Executive VP for Worldwide Government, Legal and Business Affairs at MacAndrews and Forbes Incorporated. She works across MacAndrew's portfolio companies focusing on international, legal, compliance, and business development issues. Prior to that she was a corporate partner with the law firm of Baker Botts, LLP. From 2004 to 2008, Ms. Townsend served as Assistant to President George W. Bush for Homeland Security and Counterterrorism and chaired the Homeland Security Council. She also served as Deputy National Security Advisor for Combatting Terrorism from May 2003 to May 2004. Ms. Townsend spent 13 years at the U.S. Department of Justice under the administrations of President George H.W. Bush, President Bill Clinton, and President George W. Bush. She has received numerous awards for her public service accomplishments. Ms. Townsend is a Director on the board of three public companies (NYSE: FCX, NYSE: WU, NASDAQ: SGMS) where she serves on: compliance, compensation, and governance committees. She also serves on three private company boards where she chairs all three compensation committees and is the Chairwoman of one. Ms. Townsend serves on several government advisory and nonprofit boards. She is a trustee on the board of the New York City Police Foundation and the Intrepid Sea, Air & Space Museum. She a member of the Council on Foreign Relations and the Trilateral Commission. She is an on air Analyst for CNN and has regularly appeared on network and cable television as a foreign policy, counterterrorism, national, and homeland security expert.

"Much of the debate over how to combat the Islamic State on the ground has been binary, split between those proposing containment and those insisting on its defeat. The best strategy for fighting it online, however, is something else: marginalization."

—JARED COHEN

Digital Counterinsurgency
How to Marginalize the Islamic State Online

Jared Cohen
Founder and Director, Google Ideas
Advisor to Executive Chairman, Alphabet Inc.

Editor's Note: This is a reprint of Jared Cohen's article as it appeared in Foreign
Affairs. *The basis for this article is a paper that was originally commissioned for
the Aspen Strategy Group's 2015 Summer Workshop.*

The Islamic State, or ISIS, is the first terrorist group to hold both physical and
digital territory: in addition to the swaths of land it controls in Iraq and Syria, it
dominates pockets of the Internet with relative impunity. But it will hardly be the last.
Although there are still some fringe terrorist groups in the western Sahel or other
rural areas that do not supplement their violence digitally, it is only a matter of time
before they also go online. In fact, the next prominent terrorist organization will be
more likely to have extensive digital operations than control physical ground.

Although the military battle against the Islamic State is undeniably a top priority,
the importance of the digital front should not be underestimated. The group has
relied extensively on the Internet to market its poisonous ideology and recruit would-
be terrorists. According to the International Centre for the Study of Radicalisation
and Political Violence, the territory controlled by the Islamic State now ranks as the
place with the highest number of foreign fighters since Afghanistan in the 1980s,
with recent estimates putting the total number of foreign recruits at around 20,000,
nearly 4,000 of whom hail from Western countries. Many of these recruits made
initial contact with the Islamic State and its ideology via the Internet. Other followers,
meanwhile, are inspired by the group's online propaganda to carry out terrorist
attacks without traveling to the Middle East.

The Islamic State also relies on the digital sphere to wage psychological warfare,
which directly contributes to its physical success. For example, before the group
captured the Iraqi city of Mosul in June 2014, it rolled out an extensive online campaign
with text, images, and videos that threatened the city's residents with unparalleled

death and destruction. Such intimidation makes it easier to bring populations under the Islamic State's control and reduces the likelihood of a local revolt.

Foiling the Islamic State's efforts on the Internet will thus make the group less successful on the battlefield. To date, however, most digital efforts against the Islamic State have been too limited, focusing on specific tactics, such as creating counternarratives to extremism, in lieu of generating a comprehensive strategy. Instead of resorting to a single tool, opponents should treat this fight as they would a military confrontation: by waging a broad-scale counterinsurgency.

Know Your Enemy

The first step of this digital war is to understand the enemy. Most analyses of the Islamic State's online footprint focus on social media. In a Brookings Institution report, J. M. Berger and Jonathon Morgan estimated that in late 2014, 46,000 Twitter accounts openly supported the group. Back then, strategies for fighting the Islamic State online centered on simply removing such accounts.

Social media platforms are just the tip of the iceberg, however. The Islamic State's marketing tools run the gamut from popular public platforms to private chat rooms to encrypted messaging systems such as WhatsApp, Kik, Wickr, Zello, and Telegram. At the other end of the spectrum, digital media production houses such as the Al-Furqaan Foundation and the Al-Hayat Media Center—presumably funded by and answering to the Islamic State's central leadership—churn out professional-grade videos and advertisements.

Yet understanding the full extent of the Islamic State's marketing efforts without knowing who is behind them is not an actionable insight; it is like understanding how much land the group controls without knowing what kinds of fighters occupy it and how they hold it. An effective counterinsurgency requires comprehending the Islamic State's hierarchy. Unlike al-Qaeda, which comprises a loose cluster of isolated cells, the Islamic State resembles something akin to a corporation. On the ground in Iraq and Syria, a highly educated leadership sets its ideological agenda, a managerial layer implements this ideology, and a large rank and file contributes fighters, recruiters, videographers, jihadist wives, and people with every other necessary skill. This hierarchy is replicated online, where the Islamic State operates as a pyramid consisting of four types of digital fighters.

At the top sits the Islamic State's central command for digital operations, which gives orders and provides resources for disseminating content. Although its numbers are small, its operations are highly organized. According to Berger, for example, the origins of most of the Islamic State's marketing material on Twitter can be traced to a small set of accounts with strict privacy settings and few followers. By distributing their messages to a limited network outside the public eye, these accounts can avoid being flagged for terms-of-service violations. But the content they issue eventually trickles down to the second tier of the pyramid: the Islamic State's digital rank and file.

This type of fighter may or may not operate offline as well. He and his ilk run digital accounts that are connected to the central command and disseminate material through guerrilla-marketing tactics. In June 2014, for example, Islamic State supporters hijacked trending hashtags related to the World Cup to flood soccer fans with propaganda. Because they operate on the frontline of the digital battlefield, these fighters often find their accounts suspended for terms-of-service violations, and they may therefore keep backup accounts. And to make each new account appear more influential than it really is, they purchase fake followers from social media marketing firms; just $10 can boost one's follower count by tens of thousands.

Then there are the vast numbers of radical sympathizers across the globe, who constitute the Islamic State's third type of digital fighter. Unlike the rank and file, they do not belong to the Islamic State's official army, take direct orders from its leadership, or reside in Iraq or Syria. But once drawn into the Islamic State's echo chamber by the rank and file, they spend their time helping the group disseminate its radical message and convert people to its cause. These are often the people who identify and engage potential recruits on an individual level, developing online relationships strong enough to result in physical travel. In June, for example, *The New York Times* documented how a radical Islamist in the United Kingdom met a young woman from Washington state online and convinced her to consider heading to Syria.

Although joining the Islamic State's operations in Iraq and Syria may be illegal, spreading extremism online is not. These fighters are masters at taking advantage of their right to free speech, and their strength lies both in their numbers and in their willingness to mimic the Islamic State's official line without having to receive direct orders from its leadership.

The Islamic State's fourth type of digital fighter is nonhuman: the tens of thousands of fake accounts that automate the dissemination of its content and multiply its message. On Twitter, for example, so-called Twitter bots automatically flood the digital space with retweets of terrorist messages; countless online tutorials explain how to write these relatively simple programs. In comment sections on Facebook, YouTube, and other sites, such automated accounts can monopolize the conversation with extremist propaganda and marginalize moderate voices. This programmable army ensures that whatever content the Islamic State's digital central command issues will make its way across as many screens as possible.

Recapturing Digital Territory

Much of the debate over how to combat the Islamic State on the ground has been binary, split between those proposing containment and those insisting on its defeat. The best strategy for fighting it online, however, is something else: marginalization. The result would be something similar to what has happened to the Revolutionary Armed Forces of Colombia, or FARC, the narcoterrorist group that grabbed headlines throughout the 1990s for its high-profile kidnappings and savage guerrilla warfare. Today, the group has been neither disbanded nor entirely defeated, but its ranks have largely been driven into the jungle.

Along the same lines, the Islamic State will be neutered as a digital threat when its online presence becomes barely noticeable. The group would find it either too risky or tactically impossible to commandeer control of social media platforms and public chat rooms, and its digital content would be hard to discover. Incapable of growing its online ranks, it would see its ratio of digital fighters to human fighters fall to one to one. It would be forced to operate primarily on the so-called dark Web, the part of the Internet not indexed by mainstream search engines and accessible to only the most knowledgeable users.

Compelling terrorist organizations to operate in secret does make plots more difficult to intercept, but in the case of the Islamic State, that is a tradeoff worth making. Every day, the group's message reaches millions of people, some of whom become proponents of the Islamic State or even fighters for its cause. Preventing it from dominating digital territory would help stanch the replenishment of its physical ranks, reduce its impact on the public psyche, and destroy its most fundamental means of communication.

It will take a broad coalition to marginalize the Islamic State online: from governments and companies to nonprofits and international organizations. First, they should separate the human-run accounts on social networks from the automated ones. Next, they should zero in on the Islamic State's digital central command, identifying and suspending the specific accounts responsible for setting strategy and giving orders to the rest of its online army. When that is done, digital society at large should push the remaining rank and file into the digital equivalent of a remote cave.

The suspension of accounts needs to be targeted—more like kill-or-capture raids than strategic bombing campaigns. Blanket suspensions covering any accounts that violate terms of service could not guarantee that the leadership will be affected. In fact, as Berger and Morgan's research highlighted, the Islamic State has learned to protect its digital leadership from suspension by keeping its activities hidden behind strict privacy settings.

This is not to downplay the importance of banning users who break the rules and distribute terrorist content. Technology companies have become skilled at doing just that. In 2014, the British Counter Terrorism Internet Referral Unit, a service run by London's Metropolitan Police, worked closely with such companies as Google, Facebook, and Twitter to flag more than 46,000 pieces of violent or hateful content for removal. That same year, YouTube took down approximately 14 million videos. In April 2015, Twitter announced that it had suspended 10,000 accounts linked to the Islamic State on a single day. Such efforts are valuable in that they provide a cleaner digital environment for millions of users. But they would be doubly so if the leadership that orders terrorist content to be distributed were also eliminated.

That, in turn, will require mapping the Islamic State's network of accounts. One way law enforcement could make inroads into this digital network is by covertly infiltrating the Islamic State's real-world network. This technique has already achieved some success. In April, the FBI arrested two young women accused of plotting attacks in New York City after a two-year investigation that had relied extensively on their social media activity for evidence. Law enforcement should scale such efforts to focus on the digital domain and target the Islamic State's digital leadership, suspending the accounts of its members and arresting them in certain cases.

Once the Islamic State's online leadership has been separated from the rank and file, the rank and file will become significantly less coordinated and therefore less effective. The next step would be to reduce the group's level of online activity overall, so that it is forced into the margins of digital society. During this phase, the danger is that online, the Islamic State might splinter into less coordinated but more aggressive rogue groups. With a higher tolerance for risk, these groups might undertake "doxing" of opponents of the Islamic State, whereby the private information (such as the address and social security number) of a target is revealed, or "distributed denial-of-service attacks," which can take down an entire website.

To mitigate this threat, the digital fighters' activities need to be diverted away from extremism altogether. This is where counternarratives against violent extremism can come in. Over the last two years, several notable efforts have been launched, including video series produced by the Arab Center for Scientific Research and Humane Studies and the Institute for Strategic Dialogue. To be effective, these campaigns need to reflect the diversity of the group's ranks: professional jihadist fighters, former Iraqi soldiers, deeply religious Islamic scholars, young men in search of adventure, local residents joining out of fear or ambition. Moderate religious messages may work for the pious recruit, but not for the lonely British teenager who was promised multiple wives and a sense of belonging in Syria. He might be better served by something more similar to suicide-prevention and anti-bullying campaigns.

For maximum effect, these campaigns should be carefully targeted. An antiextremist video viewed by 50,000 of the right kinds of people will have a greater impact than one seen by 50 million random viewers. Consider *Abdullah-X*, a cartoon series marketed through a YouTube campaign funded by the European Union. Its pilot episode was promoted using targeted advertising oriented toward those interested in extremist Islam. Eighty percent of the YouTube users who watched it found it through targeted ads rather than through unrelated searches.

Given the diversity of the Islamic State's digital rank and file, however, betting on counternarratives alone would be too risky. To combat extremists who have already made up their minds, the coalition should target their willingness to operate in the open. Al Qaeda has taken pains to keep its digital operations secret and works under the cover of passwords, encryption, and rigid privacy settings. These tactics have made the group notoriously difficult to track, but they have also kept its digital footprint miniscule. Likewise, the Islamic State's rank and file should be forced to adopt similar behavior.

Achieving this will require creativity. For example, governments should consider working with the news media to aggressively publicize arrests that result from covert infiltration of the Islamic State's online network. If any new account with which a digital soldier interacts carries the risk of being that of an undercover agent, it becomes exponentially more hazardous to recruit new members. Law enforcement could also create visual presentations showing how police investigations of digital extremists' accounts can lead to arrests, thereby telling the cautionary tale that a single mistake can cause the downfall of a digital soldier and his entire social network.

Within the next few years, new high-tech tools may become available to help governments marginalize digital rank-and-file terrorists. One is machine learning. Just as online advertisers can target ads to users with a particular set of interests, law enforcement could use algorithmic analysis to identify, map, and deactivate the accounts of terrorist supporters. Assisted by machine learning, such campaigns could battle the Islamic State online with newfound precision and reach a scale that would not be possible with a manual approach.

It is worth noting that just like a physical counterinsurgency, a digital counterinsurgency is more likely to succeed when bolstered by the participation of local communities. All the online platforms the Islamic State uses have forum moderators, the equivalent of tribal leaders and sheiks. The technology companies that own these platforms have no interest in seeing their environments flooded with fake accounts and violent messages. They should therefore give these moderators the tools and training to keep their communities safe from extremist messaging. Here again, machine learning could someday help, by automatically identifying terrorist messages and either highlighting them for moderators or blocking them on their behalf.

Access Denied

At first glance, the Islamic State can look hopelessly dominant online, with its persistent army of propaganda peddlers and automated trolls. In fact, however, the group is at a distinct disadvantage when it comes to resources and numbers. The vast majority of Internet users disagree with its message, and the platforms that its fighters use belong to companies that oppose its ideology.

There is no doubt that undertaking a digital counterinsurgency campaign represents uncharted territory. But the costs of failure are low, for unlike in a real-world counterinsurgency, those who fight digitally face no risk of injury or death. That is yet another factor making the Islamic State particularly vulnerable online, since it means that the group's opponents can apply and discard new ways of fighting terrorism quickly to hone their strategy.

The benefits of digitally marginalizing the Islamic State, meanwhile, are manifold. Not only would neutering the group online improve the lives of millions of users who would no longer be as likely to encounter the group's propaganda; it would also make the group's real-world defeat more imminent. As the Islamic State's digital platforms, communication methods, and soldiers became less accessible, the group would find it harder to coordinate its physical attacks and replenish its ranks. And those fighting it online would gain valuable experience for when the time came to fight the next global terrorist group trying to win the Internet.

Jared Cohen is the founder and Director of Google Ideas and an advisor to the Executive Chairman at Alphabet Inc. He is also an Adjunct Senior Fellow at the Council on Foreign Relations and a *New York Times* bestselling author. Previously he served as a member of the Secretary of State's Policy Planning Staff and as a close advisor to both Condoleezza Rice and Hillary Clinton. Mr. Cohen is the author of four books, the most recent of which is the *New York Times* and International Bestseller (in both hardcover and paperback) *The New Digital Age: Transforming Nations, Business, and our Lives* (Knopf, 2013), which he co-authored with Google Executive Chairman Eric Schmidt. His other books include *Children of Jihad* (Gotham, 2007), *One Hundred Days of Silence: America and the Rwanda Genocide* (Rowman & Littlefield, 2006), and the forthcoming *The Accidental Presidents* (Simon & Schuster). He is also coauthor with Eric Schmidt of *The Digital Disruption: Connectivity and the Diffusion of Power*, which appeared in *Foreign Affairs* just a few months before the Arab Spring. Among his additional publications are "The Future of Internet Freedom" (*New York Times*), "The Dark Side of the Digital Revolution" (*Wall Street Journal*), "Harnessing the Power of Technology to Fight Drug Cartels in Mexico" (*Washington Post*), "Diverting the Radicalization Track" (*Policy Review*), "Iran's De Facto Opposition: Youth in Post-revolutionary Iran" (*SAIS Review*), and "Passive Revolution: Is Political Resistance Dead or Alive in Iran" (*Hoover Digest*). Mr. Cohen has conducted research in Iran, Iraq, Syria, Lebanon, Afghanistan, throughout Africa, and has traveled to 92 countries. As part of his research, he has interviewed members of Al-Qaeda, Hezbollah, the Taliban, and Somali pirates. In 2013, he was named as one of TIME's "100 most influential people." *Vanity Fair* named Mr. Cohen as a member of the "Next Establishment," *The Washington Post* and Harvard's Kennedy School of Government named him to their inaugural list of "Top American Leaders," and *Foreign Policy* listed him as one of the "Top 100 Global Thinkers." He is also one of the World Economic Forum's Young Global Leaders. He currently serves as a member of the National Counterterrorism Center's (NCTC) Director's Advisory Board. He serves on the board of advisors for several companies, including ASAPP, Rivet Ventures, SineWave, and QSI. Mr. Cohen also serves on the Board of Directors of the Tribeca Film Institute and is a member of the Berggruen Institute on Governance's 21st century Council. He received his BA from Stanford University and his M.Phil in International Relations from Oxford University, where he studied as a Rhodes Scholar. He speaks Swahili and has studied Spanish, Arabic, and Farsi.

"U.S. foreign policy has noted the correlation between good governance and stability. However, economic growth and good governance are also inextricably linked and equally necessary conditions for sustainable stability. Peace and prosperity are two sides of the same coin."

—TOM PRITZKER

A Third Pillar for the Strategy and Conduct of U.S. Foreign Policy

Tom Pritzker
Executive Chairman, Hyatt Hotels Corporation
Chairman & CEO, The Pritzker Organization LLC

If we hope to reduce the role of the military in U.S. foreign policy, we need to develop additional tools by which the president can influence outcomes in global affairs. Over the course of 2013, the Center for Strategic & International Studies (CSIS) convened a council to examine U.S. foreign policy tools through the prism of foreign assistance. These are some of our findings.

Over the past several decades, the geopolitical landscape has changed dramatically, most notably in the developing world. The level of sophistication among developing world populations and governments has undergone a paradigm shift. Knowledge and communication tools are now universally available and readily affordable. Disruptive technology is now understood to disrupt not only business models, but also Westphalian political models. Private sector trade and capital flows are now a global phenomenon and a political force. For a sense of the scale of change, in 1960, public capital accounted for seventy-one percent of financial flows in the developing world. Today, it accounts for only nine percent. Finally, developing countries are increasingly critical to global prosperity and stability. America's foreign policy tools and objectives need to adjust and respond to this new landscape.

Traditional foreign policy has relied on the two pillars of diplomacy and military power to further our national interests. Each pillar has its own methods and tactics. In the 21st century, these two pillars are necessary but not sufficient to sustain a successful foreign policy in this increasingly complex world. A third pillar of U.S. foreign policy should be a modernized approach to foreign assistance, which makes broad-based economic growth its central organizing principle.

More specifically, the CSIS council advocates a blended approach to foreign assistance that includes development, trade, and investment with three straightforward strategies:

1. Place broad-based economic growth and job creation in developing countries at the center of U.S. development and diplomatic policy.

2. Use multiple resources and incentives to strategically leverage the private sector in promoting development outcomes.

3. Facilitate wider and more effective U.S. engagement in developing countries by using trade, finance, tax policy, and other tools more cohesively.

Giving primacy to growth and job creation would have several benefits.

1. It would better align the U.S. with the core goals of many countries in the developing world. In countries of interest where respective national interests may diverge, we may find alignment around economic growth and job creation.

2. Tapping the private sector would reduce both our government's role in, and the cost of, our foreign assistance programs. This approach could relieve budget pressures while also providing our policy makers with an effective new foreign policy tool. In addition, this approach plays to America's strength. Our private sector is the global gold standard in terms of its skills, values, and know-how, which could be harnessed to drive this new concept.

3. The U.S. consumer-based economy can stimulate exports for many countries in the developing world. Our ability to channel the source country of our imports is an underutilized foreign policy tool.

4. Finally, if successful, this approach can foster both prosperity and stability within the affected countries and thereby lay the foundation for the critical building blocks of further development—including health, education, gender equality, and democracy.

This would not be the first time the U.S. has used such an approach. This concept was successfully embedded into the Iraq surge strategy of clear-hold-build. Secretary of Defense Robert Gates and General David Petraeus created a task force dedicated to commercial stabilization operations, which was integrated into both the diplomatic and military strategy. It became a key building block for the success of the surge. During the war, the task force was successful because those who owned the war effort at the time saw it as a high priority. Unfortunately, what was learned from this effort was never institutionalized within the U.S. government. That needs to be corrected. In fact, the task force was a misfit within the Department of Defense, and that impacted its sustainability after the wind down of the war. Neither the Defense Department, nor the State Department is the correct home for this effort. Each has a mission and a culture that is very different from that required to build this third pillar.

U.S. foreign policy has noted the correlation between good governance and stability. However, economic growth and good governance are also inextricably linked and equally necessary conditions for sustainable stability. Peace and prosperity are two sides of the same coin.

Some have asked if reform of governance and rule of law need to precede foreign investment efforts. Not at all. In fact, China's economic growth model, arguably the most successful of our times, saw growth and foreign investment precede rule of law and political reform. The foreign private sector traded with and invested in China in spite of its lack of rule of law as the West defines it. This was because the perceived rewards of investment in China outweighed the risks attendant to its form of governance. Furthermore, China's remarkable growth has given an ever increasing swath of its citizens an interest in the country's outcome. That, in turn, is driving the government toward rule of law. At a minimum, growth and job creation should run in the same timeframe as the development of good governance principles. We should not conceive of good governance as a precondition for the suggested approach.

President Clinton's axiom "It's the economy, stupid" is a universally applicable principle. The commercial stabilization effort during the surge in Iraq was an application of that principle. The U.S. has both the national interest and the requisite skills to support growth and job creation in developing countries. This approach can be effective at a fraction of the cost of our current foreign assistance programs.

The challenge is this: execution requires top-down leadership. Developing a third pillar for U.S. foreign policy is not a side show. In the Iraq War, we had an "owner" of the commercial effort, which secured its success. If we are to apply the lessons learned, senior leadership would need to retain the focus, influence, and drive of such a program. If done correctly, and that is no small order, this approach could open new avenues for both the conduct of America's foreign policy and the growth of its domestic economy.

Tom Pritzker was born and raised in Chicago. He holds a B.A. from Claremont Men's College, an MBA and J.D. degree from the University of Chicago. He currently resides in Chicago with his wife Margot. Mr. Pritzker is Executive Chairman of Hyatt Hotels Corporation (NYSE: H) and on the Board of Directors of Royal Caribbean Cruises LTD. (NYSE: RCL). He is also is Chairman and CEO of The Pritzker Organization, the family's historical merchant bank. In addition to the hotel business, over his career he has been involved in acquiring and building companies in a number of different industries in both the service and manufacturing sectors. He has also been a founder of significant companies in the fields of Container Leasing (Triton), biotech (Bay City Capital), and health care (Reliant Pharmaceuticals and First Health). Outside of business, Mr. Pritzker is Chairman of the Board of the Hyatt Foundation which sponsors the Pritzker Architecture Prize. He is a member of the Board of Trustees of the University of Chicago and the Center for Strategic & International Studies. He is a member of the Aspen Strategy Group. He has also organized the Pritzker Neuropsychiatric Disorders Research Consortium, which is a collaborative research effort into the genetic basis of psychiatric disorders. Mr. Pritzker is also an Honorary Professor of History at Sichuan University in China, and for the past 30 years has been leading archeological expeditions in the Western Himalayas. He has published and lectured in this field. Mr. Pritzker has also been recently elected as a Fellow of the American Academy of Arts and Sciences.

Part 4

"ISIS is not al-Qaeda. The group once led by Osama bin Laden has never sought to conquer territory or to govern, except perhaps once all its enemies within and outside the Arab world have fallen."

—DOV ZAKHEIM

ISIS Will Not Be Defeated; It Can Only Be Contained

Dov Zakheim
Senior Fellow, CNA Corp.
Senior Advisor, Center for Strategic and International Studies

Speaking to the press after the September 2014 NATO summit in Newport, Wales, President Barack Obama asserted that the United States would "degrade and ultimately defeat ISIL the same way we have gone after al-Qaeda." A year later, ISIL—or as it is more commonly known outside the U.S. government, the Islamic State, the Islamic State of Iraq and al Shams (ISIS), or Daesh (the Arabic acronym for ISIS)—has lost hundreds of square miles of territory and thousands of fighters. Yet, it is far from defeated, or even severely degraded. Indeed, al-Qaeda itself continues to operate, whether in Syria, Libya, or elsewhere, primarily through groups that have aligned themselves to its cause. And just as air attacks, drone strikes, and special forces operations have failed to quash al-Qaeda, so too is it highly doubtful that reliance on air strikes, and an even more limited use of special forces, will "degrade and ultimately defeat ISIS." The only way to defeat ISIS is to deploy hundreds of thousands of troops against it, but the American public is in no mood to support another major war in the Middle East, nor are there resources available to underwrite such a war. America and its allies would be far wiser to ratchet back their unrealistic goals and pursue a more realistic strategy of containing ISIS until it is brought down by its own flawed internal dynamic.

ISIS is not al-Qaeda. The group once led by Osama bin Laden has never sought to conquer territory or to govern, except perhaps once all its enemies within and outside the Arab world have fallen. ISIS views itself as a caliphate, one that seeks continuous expansion until, at a minimum, it governs all the lands once held by Muslims and, maximally, the entire world. It is a throwback to other extremist movements that have erupted in the Muslim world over the centuries—they conquered territory and then held it, sometimes for many decades before they were defeated. And just as al-Qaeda differs from ISIS in its very essence, so, too, the fight against ISIS must be conducted in a far different manner from that which has been undertaken against al-Qaeda.

Air strikes, the staple of the war against al-Qaeda, have little chance of affecting the fortunes of ISIS. In fact, air strikes have a long history of offering more promise than they can deliver. In 1952, hoping to force an end to the stalemated Korean War, Harry Truman authorized saturation bombing that destroyed numerous North Korean cities and towns. Air Force planners believed the attacks would prove decisive. They were wrong; the North Koreans and their Chinese allies promptly rebuilt roads, bridges, and rail lines, and the war dragged on another year.

Air power fared no better during the Vietnam War. Between March 1965 and November 1968, the United States Air Force, Navy, and Marine Corps conducted over 300,000 attack and bombing sorties in what was known as Operation Rolling Thunder. Over 900,000 tons of bombs were dropped on North Vietnamese targets, about fifty percent more than during the Korean War. Nevertheless, while the North Vietnamese sustained huge materiel and personnel losses, the attacks did not diminish their will to fight or force them to the negotiating table. In the end, the North won that war.

Four decades later, the powerful Israeli Air Force (IAF) was unable to bring Hezbollah to its knees during the 2006 Lebanon War. The IAF flew nearly 12,000 combat missions and dropped 23 tons of bombs on Hezbollah's command bunker alone. Yet, despite Israel's claim to have knocked out all of Hezbollah's medium- and long-range missile launchers, the IAF was only able to destroy some 100 of Hezbollah's 12,000 launchers for short-range Katyusha rockets. Moreover, Hezbollah later claimed to have moved most of the medium and long missiles prior to the attack and was able to increase its missile inventory subsequent to the war.

Similarly, despite the massive attacks on Hezbollah's command bunker, none of its top leadership was destroyed. Hezbollah dispersed its command and control centers, hid many of its launchers in civilian homes, and despite taking heavy losses, never gave up its will to fight. It continues to pose a serious threat to Israel's northern cities and towns.

Since the dropping of the atomic bombs on Hiroshima and Nagasaki, air power has never been the decisive factor in securing a victorious outcome on the battlefield. Indeed, in each of the three cases noted above, air power was unable to guarantee victory for the land forces with which it was operating. The current operation against ISIS, which relies primarily on air power, hardly promises to be any more successful than Korea, Vietnam, or the 2006 war. In fact, the prospects for defeating ISIS are far more grim.

To begin with, American air strikes against ISIS are nowhere near as intense as those of its previous wars. Coalition forces in Operation Desert Storm (1991) carried out over 100,000 sorties; even NATO's 2011 air war against Muammar Gaddafi totaled 26,500 sorties during a seven-month campaign. In contrast, during the twelve months beginning August 2014, U.S. and allied forces conducted only 6,200 air strikes against ISIS, an average of just 17 sorties a day. Put another way, the daily number of sorties against ISIS is one-seventh that of the Libyan campaign.

In the meantime, despite its loss of approximately one-third of the territory that it conquered in 2014, ISIS still controls and governs about one-third of all Syrian territory and much of western Iraq. It continues to find new recruits to replace the tens of thousands it has lost in air strikes and in battles with Kurdish militias in Syria and Shiite militias and government forces in Iraq. It controls nearly all of Syria's gas and oil fields, including Deir ez-Zour, one of the country's largest fields. It holds Mosul, Iraq's second largest city, and has captured Ramadi, a key city in western Iraq. It is able to fund its operations through black market oil sales, extortionist taxes imposed upon those it rules, and the ongoing flow of donations from sympathizers throughout the Sunni world, including those in Europe. Indeed, it has been argued that as many as fifty percent of all Saudis sympathize with, or actively support, ISIS. Even if that percentage is considerably smaller, it signifies a tremendous amount of ongoing support for the terrorist group and probably reflects similar degrees of financial and moral support elsewhere in the Arabian Gulf.

For its part, the Obama administration continues to refuse to send troops to fight alongside government forces in Iraq or friendly rebel forces in Syria. It will not even send spotters for its combat aircraft, rendering it even more difficult for air strikes to be effective. Though there are scattered reports that Special Forces are indeed operating on the ground in Syria, they are too few to have a decisive impact on either battlefield.

Moreover, even if the United States were to commit several thousand troops to fight ISIS, it is unlikely that the few brigades would quickly turn the tide of battle. Combatting ISIS would require troop levels comparable to those that ultimately were deployed to Iraq. Army Chief of Staff Eric Shinseki was prescient when he testified just prior to the 2003 attack on Iraq that several hundred thousand troops would be required to pacify the country. At the time he was ridiculed for his remarks, but it was only when the United States implemented its surge, which brought the total of American troops to over 166,000, in addition to approximately 50,000 coalition forces, that the Iraq insurgency was rolled back and the country enjoyed a modicum of stability.

Nothing less than a full-scale invasion is likely to bring down ISIS in the near term. Such has been the history of the rise and fall of other radical Islamist regimes that have sporadically emerged in Muslim history. For example, it took the combined forces of Christian France, Spain, and Portugal, together with an uprising by the Moroccan Almohads, to bring down the radical Berber Almoravid state in the twelfth century. Similarly, Ottoman Turkey had to launch a major invasion of the Arabian Peninsula to crush the nascent Saudi/Wahhabi state in the early nineteenth century. And the British were unable to defeat the forces of the Mahdi in Sudan until it launched a massive operation with its own and Egyptian units; then, in 1898, following the victory in the Battle of Omdurman, they were able to reconquer Sudan.

Unfortunately, it is not merely the president who is reluctant to commit large land force formations, or even smaller units, to fight ISIS. There can be little doubt that the American public is war weary, and especially tired of Middle East imbroglios. Americans are unlikely to rally behind a plan to deploy tens of thousands of troops to the region anytime soon.

Fiscal realities also constrain any possible massive redeployment of American troops to the Middle East. The Budget Control Act of 2011, which severely limits the expansion of the U.S. defense budget, remains in force. Increases beyond the budget caps outlined in the Act would result in "the sequester," which would call for cuts in virtually every defense account. Given the inability of Congress to find a permanent way out from under the shadow of the sequester, and the American public's reluctance to support a major land force commitment to the Middle East, the prospect of such a commitment is virtually nil.

The administration's policies and the attitude of the American public also render it highly unlikely that other nations will commit their own ground troops to fight ISIS. America's closest NATO partner in the Middle East, the UK, is in the midst of cutting its own land forces by twenty percent. Other European allies have also ratcheted back their defense spending.

America can expect little more from her regional allies. The Gulf states are preoccupied with the ongoing conflict in Yemen. If Saudi Arabia and her Gulf Cooperation Council (GCC) allies are likely to commit ground forces to fight outside their national boundaries, they will first dispatch them to Yemen. Jordan, which has watched developments in neighboring Syria with apprehension, likewise will not attempt to intervene in Syria with land forces of its own. Amman has to cope with hundreds of thousands of refugees, some of whom it suspects to be ISIS agents.

Moreover, King Abdullah always has to worry about his own restive population, particularly its Palestinian component. A Jordanian incursion into Syria is out of the question, even if America were to intervene with land forces, which it won't.

Syria's other neighbor, Turkey, the strongest Middle Eastern power, is more deeply concerned with the successes of the PYD (Kurdish Democratic Union) party and its YPG militias (Popular Protection Units) in their battles with ISIS than with the terrorist organization itself. The PYD and YPG are closely linked to the PKK (Kurdistan Workers' Party), with whom Turkish president Recip Tayyip Erdogan has once again gone to war in the run-up to parliamentary elections scheduled for November 2015. If Turkey were to send its troops into Syria at all, as it has frequently done in northern Iraq, it would be to fight the PKK, not ISIS. Indeed, although Turkey has finally opened its airbase at Incirlik for air operations against ISIS, and then only after numerous entreaties from Washington, its own air strikes primarily target the PKK rather than ISIS—though it has at last begun to attack ISIS as well.

Moreover, Turkey views the Assad regime, not ISIS, as its other major enemy in Syria, despite the fact that ISIS operatives planted a bomb in the Turkish (and heavily Kurdish) city of Suruc. Ankara's position stands very much in contrast with that of Washington. The United States still hesitates to attack Assad's forces directly, no doubt to not undermine its growing rapprochement with Iran, which serves as Assad's major sponsor and arms supplier, and whose ally, Hezbollah, has provided Assad with many of his toughest fighters.

Finally, America's reputation in the region as an unreliable ally further undermines its ability to marshal the forces of other Arab states—or, for that matter, potential Sunni allies in Iraq and Syria—to defeat ISIS in both countries. The Arab world has not forgotten how America abandoned the Shah in 1979, or how it turned away from Hosni Mubarak three decades later, or how it led the fight to depose Libya's Muammar Gaddafi only a few years after he agreed to terminate his program to develop a weapon of mass destruction and to halt his support for terrorism against the West. Nor have other Arab states, or the Sunni Arab "street," overlooked the fact that after prompting the Sunni Awakening by the so-called "Sons of Iraq" while surging its own forces in 2007-2008, it shortly thereafter removed all its forces from Iraq, enabling the Sh'ia Prime Minister Nouri al-Maliki to persecute Iraq's Sunni minority. Finally, Syrian Sunnis have not forgotten Washington's empty threats to remove President Assad, an Alawite, and to take military action if he employed chemical weapons. It should therefore come as no surprise that the call from Washington to help fight ISIS has met with a lukewarm response from its Middle Eastern allies or from Iraqi and Syrian Sunnis.

In light of all of the foregoing, containment is the only viable option open to Washington, other than withdrawing entirely and enabling ISIS to metastasize. Containment does not mean merely continuing to do what is already being done. From all indications, reliance on the government Army and Shi'a militias in Iraq, and on a combination of YPG militias, the al-Nusra extremists (themselves an offshoot of al-Qaeda), and the ragtag units of so-called moderates would be insufficient to contain ISIS over the long term, much less defeat it. Administration reports of progress against the extremist group are proving to be far more optimistic than the situation on the ground would warrant. Instead, containing ISIS requires a stepped-up military effort that goes significantly beyond that which is currently being undertaken.

To begin with, the air war against ISIS must be pursued with far greater intensity. The number of daily sorties should match that of the 2011 Libyan Operation. The current level of air strikes is too haphazard to inflict serious damage on a determined foe that, like the targets of other air operations, is learning to disperse its forces and to rapidly repair damage to its infrastructure. In addition, Washington should deploy spotters on the ground, who likewise would enhance the potency of air attacks on ISIS units.

Even intense and improved targeting for bombing will not contain ISIS, however. Containment can only be accomplished with reinforced, better armed land forces. Washington must commit some additional troops, including trainers, to the battlefield in both Syria and Iraq. The presence of American troops alongside them in battle can only improve the effectiveness of anti-ISIS forces.

Despite his promise to withdraw all forces from Iraq, President Obama has dispatched 3,500 troops to train the Iraqi Army. Clearly, that effort continues to fall short of expectations; the Iraqi government continues to rely far too heavily on Sh'ia militias, who have a record of pillaging the towns and villages they have nominally "liberated." Their behavior has resulted in winning more sympathy and recruits for ISIS in the Iraqi Sunni heartland.

Washington must significantly increase the number and quality of trainers it sends to Iraq, and, for that matter, to Syria. Despite years of training, the Iraqi Army has failed to dislodge ISIS from any significant portion of its territory, unless it has also had the support of Sh'ia militias and guidance from Iran's Revolutionary Guard leadership. Indeed, a good proportion of ISIS's armament consists of American equipment captured from the Iraqi Army. It is as if Washington were arming ISIS.

The program to train Syrian rebels has been so pathetic that it even pales in comparison with the Iraqi program. The $500 million effort to train the Syrian opposition to ISIS has yielded only sixty graduates, many of whom were captured by al-Nusra fighters shortly after they crossed into Syria. Moreover, both trainees and those already in the field are far less inclined to fight ISIS than to take on Assad and his Hezbollah allies.

Clearly, the training programs in both Iraq and Syria need serious review and overhaul. Too much training has been outsourced to contractors, whose commercial interests may not convey the right inspiration to those they train. Moreover, trainers rotate too quickly, thereby preventing ongoing interactions built on trust that are crucial to successful relationships in the Middle East. Finally, as noted, some number must accompany the anti-ISIS forces into battle. By doing so, they can help ensure that those forces do not break and run when confronting ISIS, as the Iraqi Army did when ISIS first appeared on the scene. The days are long gone when Western officers can command indigenous forces, as was the case, for example, at the height of Britain's raj. Therefore, the best way to ensure the cohesion and effectiveness of those forces is to have some number of active military American and coalition trainers accompany them into battle.

Although the American public clearly will not tolerate another long-term war involving forces of 100,000 or more, there is likely to be far less opposition to the deployment of several additional battalions, perhaps totaling some 5,000 troops, to support and accompany anti-ISIS forces beyond the 3,500 already deployed for that mission. These troops, primarily trainers, should be volunteers for longer-term commitments. They would, of course, be granted appropriate home leave, but they would then return to the units they have worked with. They would develop trusting relationships that could then carry into the field, where their presence would buttress the effectiveness of their indigenous counterparts.

Training anti-ISIS forces, and accompanying them on the battlefield, is not enough, however. Even with a greater American military presence on the ground in Syria and Iraq, it is unlikely that other Arab states will join the battle with ISIS. The Kurds, both in Iraq and in Syria, will remain the most capable force to confront ISIS. Unfortunately, and despite its protestations to the contrary, Washington continues to drag its feet in supplying the forces of the Kurdish Regional Government (KRG), known as the peshmerga, with modern 21st-century weaponry.

The peshmerga have played an important role in the war against ISIS not only by preventing it from seizing KRG territory, but also by fighting in support of YPG forces in Syria. The joint peshmerga-YPG units have been the only ones to roll ISIS back in Syria. Washington, in particular, could meet all their military requirements. It should do so without hesitation.

Increasing the number of trainers, accompanying anti-ISIS troops in battle, and arming the Kurds more effectively and with greater dispatch will not result in the defeat of ISIS. For ISIS to be defeated in the near term, the United States would have to commit well over 100,000 troops to the battlefield. America has neither the strategy, the will, nor the readily available resources to make such a commitment.

ISIS represents more than a rogue state. It embodies an ideology that is as intolerant as it is medieval. ISIS will only fall when it implodes due to internal fissures and it suffers an uprising by the people whose territory it has occupied, when they can no longer tolerate ISIS's radical, ideological rule. While these developments could come rapidly, it is far more likely that they will take decades. Indeed, outgoing Army Chief of Staff General Ray Odierno has predicted that the war against ISIS could last as long as twenty years, while Admiral Sandy Winnefeld, the outgoing vice chairman of the Joint Chiefs of Staff, has called it a "generational struggle."

In the interim, the United States should pursue a consistent, coherent long-term strategy that recognizes that the war against ISIS will not end anytime soon. The strategy should seek to contain ISIS, maintaining constant and unremitting pressure until this extremist force peters out of its own accord or is violently overthrown by those it seeks to rule.

Dov S. Zakheim is Senior Fellow at CNA Corp., a federally funded think tank, and Senior Advisor at the Center for Strategic and International Studies. Previously he was Senior Vice President of Booz Allen Hamilton, where he led support of US Combatant Commanders. From 2001 to 2004, Dr. Zakheim served as the Under Secretary of Defense (Comptroller) and Chief Financial Officer for the Department of Defense from 2001 to 2004. From 2002 to 2004, he also was DOD's coordinator of civilian programs in Afghanistan. During the 2000 presidential campaign, he was a senior foreign policy advisor to then-Governor Bush. From 1985 to 1987, Dr. Zakheim was Deputy Under Secretary of Defense for Planning and Resources. He is a member of the Defense Business Board, the Chief of Naval Operations Executive Panel, and the Military Compensation and Retirement Modernization Commission, and serves on several corporate boards. Previously he was a member of the Commission on Wartime Contracting in Iraq and Afghanistan, and chaired the National Intelligence Council's International Business Practices Advisory Panel. Dr. Zakheim is Vice Chairman of both the Foreign Policy Research Institute and the Center for the National Interest, and has been an Adjunct Senior Fellow at the Council on Foreign Relations and an Adjunct Professor at several universities. He earned his B.A. from Columbia College and his doctorate from the University of Oxford. He is a Fellow of the Royal Swedish Academy of Military Sciences and a Member of the Aspen Strategy Group.

"The Achilles heel of our current strategy is our reliance on local partners to do things on our behalf that run contrary to their perceived interests."

—PETER FEAVER

The Hinges of a Successful Strategy to Defeat ISIL

Peter Feaver
Professor
Duke University

What could and should the United States do with its allies to defeat the Islamic State in Iraq and the Levant (ISIL)? The choice of a successful counter-ISIL strategy swings on eight critical hinges. Some of the hinges involve bets about the nature of the threat; others involve bets about geopolitics; and still others involve implicit judgments about American priorities. Place your bets, and the resulting least-worst strategy follows fairly directly.

Defeating ISIL is putatively the goal of U.S. counter-ISIL strategy—"putatively" because the administration has also advanced as its goal to "reduce" or "degrade" or "destroy" ISIL. These terms are sometimes offered as interchangeable synonyms, but, in fact, they are different end-states that imply very different levels of effort.[1] The Army doctrinal definition of "defeat" is "A tactical mission task that occurs when an enemy force has temporarily or permanently lost the physical means or the will to fight. The defeated force's commander is unwilling or unable to pursue his adopted course of action, thereby yielding to the friendly commander's will, and can no longer interfere to a significant degree with the actions of friendly forces."[2] Defeat imposes a level of damage far greater than "reduce" (which might be thought of as the military synonym for "degrade")—any attack that destroys some ISIL positions or kills/captures ISIL fighters reduces/degrades ISIL, but to defeat ISIL requires rendering the enemy incapable/unwilling to continue fighting for a meaningful period of time. "Destroy" would greatly extend the period of incapacity. The administration bounced among various articulations of its counter-ISIL goal, and the version that has the most Google hits is the one President Obama announced in September 2014, at the start of the military campaign: "degrade and ultimately destroy." However, it appears the administration has more recently settled on "degrade and ultimately defeat" as the goal.

At the strategic level, the primary alternative goal would be to "contain" ISIL indefinitely. Containment involves preventing further significant expansions of ISIL territory and geopolitical influence, but not reversing in the short run the gains they have already made. Of course, indefinite containment could still be in the service of a desire ultimately to defeat ISIL in the distant future. That was how containment of the Soviet Union operated during the Cold War. But for the short-to-intermediate term, containment as a strategic goal is an alternative to defeat because, properly framed, containment requires a nontrivial amount of acceptance of the adversary—learning to live with the other. Depending on how limited U.S. efforts are, the administration's nominal goal to "degrade and ultimately destroy" ISIL could reduce in practice to a strategy to "contain and someday defeat" ISIL. Given ISIL's transnational and global reach, it is possible to imagine hybrid goals, such as defeating ISIL in Iraq while containing ISIL in Syria and elsewhere. How reasonable such hybrid goals are in practice depend on one's bets about the nature of the ISIL threat, discussed below.

Truly defeating ISIL would involve achieving the following objectives:[3]

1. ISIL does not and is unable to control territory.

2. ISIL does not and is unable to hold at risk the ability of lawful state leaders to govern effectively their own territory.

3. ISIL does not and is unable to recruit sufficiently to replenish its ranks.

4. ISIL is not conducting complex mass casualty attacks against the United States or its allies.

We could debate whether to add a fifth objective: ISIL does not inspire lone-wolf attacks. But I think that sets the bar too high. As awful as such attacks are, if the ISIL threat is reduced solely to that level, then we still would have secured a significant achievement for American foreign policy. Of course, the institutions of law enforcement, intelligence, and homeland security should never rest in their efforts to forestall such lone-wolf attacks, but what makes ISIL so threatening is its capacity to thwart the United States on many even more consequential levels. Indeed, as I will argue below, what helps catalyze those attacks in the first place is the perception that ISIL challenges the United States in far more fundamental ways than mere lone-wolf attacks.

The problem of defeating ISIL is far more difficult in 2015 than it might have been in 2011, when the Arab Spring upended the existing order in the region. Back in 2011, it was reasonable to believe that there was a large "moderate" faction inside Syria already mobilized, and that with deft external assistance, these moderates could hold the balance of power in Syria's civil war. The problems of creating such a counterweight seem intractable today but were far more manageable then. Moreover, in 2011, it was still possible to believe that Vice President Biden would win his wager: "I'll bet you my vice presidency Maliki will extend the SOFA in Iraq."[4] If he had done so, that would have allowed U.S. forces to remain as a hedge against Maliki's sectarian impulses, the collapse of Iraqi Security Forces (ISF), and the rise of ISIL. In 2011, it was possible to believe that the global appeal of transnational terror networks inspired by militant Islamism was waning in the wake of the double-blow—the destruction of most of the leadership of core al-Qaeda and the flowering of an alternative narrative of hope for the region in the form of the Arab Spring.

In 2015, it is not reasonable to believe any of those advantages are available, at least not in the short term. The question is, given that we are where we are, what defeat-oriented strategy will take us to a better place? The answer depends heavily on your assessment of eight hinges.

Hinge 1: How much give do we have on our other strategic goals?

The first and most important hinge is recognizing that the challenge is not defeating ISIL. The challenge is defeating ISIL while simultaneously achieving our other regional and global strategic goals: checking Iranian imperial ambitions; preventing Bashar al-Assad from winning but also not catalyzing a collapse of the Syrian political order that requires a costly occupation *à la* Iraq 2003; disposing of the lion's share of Assad's declared chemical arsenal; providing enough reassurance to Sunni partners so they will not respond to the Iran deal by demanding a similar nuclear threshold status; securing enough transactional cooperation from UN veto players without having to buy it with painful concessions on Ukraine or the South China Sea; preserving a *de facto* Middle East state structure that aligns with the *de jure* one represented in the membership of the United Nations; and so on. And the potentially insurmountable challenge is doing all of that while operating under significant self-imposed constraints that are being relaxed more slowly than the unraveling security situation may require: first, no boots on the ground in Iraq; then boots on the ground but no forward-deployed target spotters or advisors embedded in Iraqi units; then air strikes in Syria, but not against Assad; and so on.

These myriad goals are all individually reasonable, and the constraints all arise from plausible calculations, some political and others perhaps strategic, but collectively they may amount to a self-defeating effort in pursuit of an impossible dream. Our current strategy involves relying predominantly on local partners who do not share our priorities and insisting that we will only equip them with the tools they need if they fight according to our priorities. We are trying to create a capable rebel force that will fight against our enemy, not their enemy. Inside Syria, we are trying to take people who fear Assad more than ISIL and turn them into our anti-ISIL ground forces; inside Iraq, we are trying to take people who fear the sectarianism of the Iraqi government more than ISIL and turn them into our anti-ISIL ground forces. There are very capable forces that will fight exactly in the manner we want them to, but we have pledged not to use them: the U.S. military. We are backing so many horses in the Middle East—some explicitly, some implicitly—that we are almost guaranteed to find ourselves backing some losers.[5]

The problem of an inadequately resourced strategy in pursuit of conflicting goals is most vivid in the Iraq portion of the story. For understandable reasons, we are reluctant to put more American troops at risk in a ground war inside Iraq. No one wants to ask American Marines or GIs to fight to retake Fallujah yet another time. As a consequence, we rely on Iraqis to do the fighting. But the only reliable and capable Iraqi fighters are ones with a sectarian or ethnic agenda—Sunni tribes, Shia militias, and Kurdish peshmerga. The more we rely on such capable forces, the more we jeopardize our separate (and also reasonable) goal of having Iraq stay unified.

As a first-order principle, I propose the following rule: the greater the extent to which our goals push against each other, the greater the required proportion of U.S.-to-allied effort in order to achieve them. The corollary holds with equal force: the lower the available proportion of U.S.-to-allied effort, the more the United States has to sacrifice goals that are in tension with each other. To date, we as a country have not had the strategic debate about which of these conflicting goals or which of these self-imposed constraints to lift. By default, we may have settled for a strategy that is failing to deliver on any strategic goal.

Prioritizing across conflicting goals would help us answer a fundamental question begged by the quest for a counter-ISIL strategy: Is ISIL the center of gravity in this fight? That is, can we defeat ISIL without exacerbating the broader problem of radicalism in the Middle East? Or, conversely, can we confront the broader problem of radicalism in the Middle East without first defeating ISIL? To what extent is ISIL a symptom of radicalism and to what extent is it an accelerant to radicalism? Indeed, the root question may be more fundamental still: Does dealing with the problem of radicalism in the Middle East require that we reestablish the internationally recognized nation-state map, redraw that map, or reimagine a different kind of political order for the region? Can Humpty Dumpty be put back together again at an acceptable cost, or must we tolerate a generational struggle before order emerges? Can we tolerate that?

Hinge 2: How do we get our partners to do our bidding in the war?

The Achilles heel of our current strategy is our reliance on local partners to do things on our behalf that run contrary to their perceived interests. This vulnerability arises from a very understandable premise: as President Obama has put it, "ultimately it's up to the Iraqis, as a sovereign nation, to solve their problems. . . . We can't do it for them."[6] Or, as he said a year later in explaining why there has been so little progress in the fight against ISIL, "if we try to do everything ourselves all across the Middle East, all across North Africa, we'll be playing Whack[sic]-a-Mole. . . ."[7] President Obama is right, so far as he goes, but this perspective leaves unsolved the problem that has bedeviled us thus far: What if our partners are not willing to fight on the terms we want them to? How do we get others to follow an American plan?

Recent administrations have struggled with this problem and oscillated between two general approaches. One approach is premised on the claim that we get better results from others when we are leading from the front, by which I mean: (a) showing we have real skin in the game in the form of combat units or other commitments that would be sunk costs if the enterprise fails; (b) showing we will act regardless of whether they act; and (c) convincing them that we are committed to the project and will not abandon them. Another approach is premised on the claim that we get better results from others when we are leading from behind, by which I mean: (a) minimizing our skin in the game; (b) showing we will not act or will withhold acting until they do what we demand; and (c) convincing them we are committed to walking away from the project if we are unsatisfied. Advocates of the more-for-more approach argue that the second approach leads to hedging; why should our partners take risks when they have reason to believe we will abandon them? Advocates of the more-for-less approach argue that the first approach leads to free-riding; why should our partners risk anything when they have reason to believe the Americans will do the dirty work for them?

The history of U.S. relations with former Iraqi Prime Minister Nouri al-Maliki provides an interesting test of these two approaches. One can identify four distinct phases of U.S.-Maliki relations: (1) pre-surge (2006-January 2007); (2) during the Bush surge (January 2007-January 2009); (3) during the Obama surge (January 2009-December 2011); and (4) post-departure (January 2012-August 2014).[8] Each of these phases represents meaningfully different styles of American interaction with Maliki and meaningfully different estimations by Maliki as to whether he could count on the United States to "have his back."

During the first phase, mutual doubt was very high. Maliki knew that he was not America's preferred choice as prime minister, and the existing war strategy called for a rapid transition to minimal U.S. military presence. American doubts about Maliki's performance were vividly captured in a leaked White House analysis that openly asked whether Maliki's poor performance was due to weakness, ignorance (or bad advising/intelligence), or malevolence.[9]

During the second phase, U.S. leaders still harbored doubts about Maliki's competence and intentions, but President Bush had "bet on Maliki" by ordering the surge. Moreover, Bush committed to sustained and regular interactions at the leader-to-leader level—more extensive than with any other leader except Tony Blair. Maliki knew that the United States was committed to success in Iraq—America's success and his.

During the third phase, Maliki experienced a marked downgrade in relations. The Obama administration repeatedly emphasized that it thought the United States had over-invested in the Middle East, and it would rebalance America's commitments accordingly. Iraq would be exhibit A in the rebalancing. Maliki was no longer interacting regularly with the president; instead, Vice President Biden had the Iraq portfolio. While President Obama did agree to a slower withdrawal from Iraq than he promised during the campaign, the White House messaging on America's long-term commitment to the Iraq project was markedly different than it had been in the 2007-2009 period. Maliki knew that the United States was committed to ending its involvement in Iraq, period.

During the fourth phase, Maliki experienced an even sharper downgrade in relations. The stabilizing presence and influence that had come with the U.S. ground force commitment was replaced with a vacuum. The U.S. maintained rhetorical and diplomatic pressure on Maliki, but without the leverage that came with a U.S. presence.

Maliki's leadership across all four periods left much to be desired, but, to the extent to which Maliki functioned as we needed him to, it seems obvious that his performance in Phase 2 was markedly better than Phase 3, which was markedly better than Phase 4.[10] The pattern is unmistakable: the more confident he could be about American support, the better his behavior. Of course, there were other costs associated with the type of American support Maliki received during Phase 2. It could be that focusing on Maliki had the unintended consequence of boosting him at the expense of Iraqi state institutions. The optimal approach might have required supplementing the personalized support of Phase 2 with even more vigorous generalized support and engagement of the Iraqi political institutions that would be needed for an eventual post-Maliki era.

The Maliki experience may not be transferrable to every other actor on which our counter-ISIL efforts depend, but it does suggest that a strategy premised on more-for-more has a better chance of succeeding than one premised on more-for-less. Perhaps that partly helps explain why, one year into the relationship with Maliki's successor, Haider al-Abadi, we are still disappointed with the performance of the Iraqi government and obliged to rely so heavily on sub-state militias.

One practical more-for-less option is the proposal to induce better behavior from our hoped-for counter-ISIL allies by conditioning our aid on the extent to which they act as we want them to act.[11] However, this option may run afoul of the first-order principle about the relationship between U.S. effort and conflicting goals discussed above. If we were offering massive, game-changing amounts of aid, this might be a promising approach. But the more limited our offer, the less leverage we have and thus the less we can demand of the Iraqis. One reason Maliki performed better under Phase 2 than any other Phase was that what was offered to him in that period was greater than at any other period. If we need our partners to shift from courses of action they deem in their interests but we deem counterproductive, then we may need to offer much more than we have thus far.

Taking this conditional approach also requires that we tolerate setbacks that can cumulate at an alarming rate. In the first half of 2014, the Obama administration did condition its counter-ISIL aid to Iraq on political change in Iraq, and then withheld that aid even as ISIL invaded Iraq and scored impressive tactical victories. To the surprise of many, the administration even withheld the aid long enough to let ISIL seize and consolidate control over the second city of Iraq, Mosul, in June 2014. As ISIL gained territory, the Obama administration continued to condition its assistance on Prime Minister Maliki stepping down. Finally, faced with a Benghazi-like prospect of ISIL sieging Erbil in the Kurdish region (putting at risk substantial U.S. personnel who were on the ground), the administration acted *even though the condition had not been met—Maliki was still prime minister*. U.S. intervention catalyzed the political shift that the Obama administration had wanted—U.S. airstrikes began on August 8, 2015, and Maliki stepped down on August 14, 2015—but it is hard to code this as a clean success for a policy of conditionality because the United States eventually had to relax the conditionality to forestall a catastrophe.[12] Moreover, sticking with conditionality as long as we did surrendered substantial momentum to ISIL and imposed considerable setbacks to our side, showing conditionality to be an especially high-cost strategy (see related discussion later in this chapter).

Once we have determined what we will offer, we have to confront the problem of shrinkage—the term businesses give to shoplifting, employee theft, fraud, and other ways in which a business strategy is degraded by the malfeasance of others. Since our strategy depends so heavily on others, we are especially at risk of shrinkage. Indeed, one reason that the U.S. effort to build an indigenous Syrian counter-ISIL ground force has been so paltry—a force of only 60 fighters after spending $240 million (of a $500 million authorization)—has been the great lengths the administration has gone to avoid shrinkage with vigorous vetting.[13] It may be very hard to find Syrians willing to risk their lives to fight ISIL but *not* Assad—and to do that without any guarantee of protection from the United States once launched into the fight.

All shrinkage is unfortunate, but not all of it may be fatal. For instance, it is unfortunate but probably not fatal that the Tajik commander we trained went over to ISIL.[14] Shrinkage much closer to fatal is the utter collapse of the ISF and the way our material assistance to ISF inadvertently made us the arsenal of ISIL.[15] The difficult question is determining where to draw the line of acceptability between those two extreme examples.

Hinge 3: What is an acceptable-achievable outcome in Syria?

The challenges outlined in the first two hinges come to a head in Syria, where the contradictions between the myriad U.S. objectives are especially vivid. The United States wants Assad to lose power, but not in a way that would create a political vacuum that would exacerbate the civil war and necessitate a costly post-conflict occupation. The United States wants Assad to stop using chemical weapons, but not badly enough to punish him when he violates his commitments.[16] The United States wants a capable ground force to be the anvil against which our airpower could hammer ISIL, but does not want to work with any of the capable militant Islamist ground forces that are hammering ISIL. The United States does not want to stand idly by as it witnesses cultural genocide against Christians in the Middle East, but nor does it want to take sides in the religious-sectarian divisions that plague the region. And so on.

ISIL's very rise in Syria derived from the way the United States was paralyzed into inaction (or ineffective minimal action) by the contradictory goals. The administration's arms control deal with Syria defused the 2013 redline crisis, but in a way that made the United States effectively Assad's partner and regime guarantor.[17] Our inability to figure out how to create a capable indigenous moderate rebel force inside Syria without *de facto* intervening in the Syrian civil war left us hamstrung when we decided that ISIL had moved from being a junior varsity to a varsity-level threat.

Syria also tragically demonstrates that American inaction can play a role in catalyzing an ethno-sectarian civil war that results in millions of refugees and hundreds of thousands of fatalities—a butcher's bill that resembles one traditionally blamed on American action (Iraq). Indeed, in Syria, the local, regional, and international communities have already collectively paid many (though not all) of the costs usually attributed to outright external military intervention.

This price has been paid as the international community has shown the strategic patience to wait for Assad to realize that he is on the wrong side of history. This has taken much longer than most observers expected. In the process, the problem has metastasized into one that senior military officials now concede could last not years but decades.[18] This is not a wildly unreasonable estimate, but it far exceeds the politically relevant timeline that will guide U.S. strategic choices.

Iraq is not the only negative example that is instructive for the Syrian problem. Although heralded at the time as a great success, in hindsight the Libyan case reteaches the painful lesson about the consequences of failing to develop a robust Phase IV plan.[19] Whether we topple a regime by airpower or landpower, if U.S.-backed actors do not control the inevitable post-conflict contest for political power, then the chaos will favor the agenda of transnational terror networks of militant Islamists. Yemen may be even more instructive, because in explaining his approach to confronting ISIL, President Obama explicitly invoked the strategy "we have successfully pursued in Yemen."[20] To those who doubted that our approach would lead to success against ISIL, President Obama effectively said, "look at Yemen." Within months, Yemen looked neither like a success nor an attractive model—evidence more for those who doubted our counter-ISIL strategy than for those promoting it.

Finally, consider also the role of Turkey, arguably our most capable potential local partner. From the American perspective, Turkey has grossly underperformed in the fight to defeat ISIL. On the margins, Turkey has actually empowered ISIL, viewing it as a useful weapon against two higher-priority enemies, Assad and the Kurds. Turkey has also successfully turned the tool of conditionality against the United States: it has withheld the use of assets like the airbase in Incirlik in an effort to get the United States to accept Turkey's strategy of creating a safe zone protected by a no-fly zone. According to some reports, Turkey has succeeded;[21] but according to other reports, the U.S.-Turkey deal is still very much a moving target.[22] Peering through the confusion, one thing is clear: the two putative partners do not share a common vision, and each is trying to cajole the other into doing its bidding, but without committing the requisite resources to make the cajolement effective. The establishment of such a safe zone could be a promising step toward a more successful strategy to defeat ISIL, especially if it slows down Turkey's unhelpful escalation against Kurdish ground forces. On the other hand, if this is a reluctant, halting step toward committing the United States to effecting (versus merely wishing for) Assad's collapse, then it raises more questions than it answers.

One question looms above all others: Can the United States defeat ISIL in Syria without increasing U.S. involvement in Syria—and does increasing our involvement implicate us in a generational struggle for political order in that broken society?

Hinge 4: How does the Iran deal affect our counter-ISIL effort?

The Iran deal is an especially important hinge for the counter-ISIL strategy. Let's bracket off the question of whether the deal makes sense when viewed narrowly as a way to put Iran's nuclear ambitions in a box for a non-trivial amount of time. Reasonable people differ on that narrow question, but for our purposes, the more urgent question is the broader one of whether this helps or hurts a counter-ISIL strategy. The answer to the broader question does not hinge on your answer to the narrow one.

Advocates of the Iran nuclear deal make a case that it will help U.S. efforts against ISIL.[23] Iran hates ISIL and the deal makes Iran stronger; ergo, a stronger Iran will be better able to fight ISIL. Moreover, perhaps the successful negotiations will usher in an era of good feelings, which will make Iran more pliant on other issues. One of those issues has been Iran's support for Assad, in particular Assad's strategy of tacitly coordinating with ISIL to destroy all moderate opposition to his regime. Perhaps Iran will trust the United States more and be more willing to accommodate U.S. interests in Syria. Another way a more accommodating Iran could help would be to lean on the Iraqi regime to pursue a less sectarian agenda and to reach out more effectively to disaffected Sunnis. Even if one does not buy into the optimism of the deal yielding peace for our time in this fashion, we still could end up with better Iranian cooperation if, having successfully dealt with the nuclear problem, the United States would no longer need to tiptoe on these other issues. During the delicate negotiations phase, the United States had to temporarily alleviate diplomatic pressure on Iran on other concerns, but now that the deal is done, the United States can more vigorously pressure Iran on these other issues, and perhaps that will yield better results. Indeed, this last line of reasoning was frequently presented by administration sources seeking to reassure skeptics over the last several years of negotiations.

Skeptics of the Iran nuclear deal make the opposite case. The windfall of the nuclear deal will be translated into greater support for Iranian-backed terrorist and militia groups, thus exacerbating the sectarian conflict in which ISIL flourishes. The dramatic concessions the United States had to make to secure the nuclear deal will fuel concerns about America's global retreat, and those concerns will translate into the very hedging behavior by regional partners that ISIL has exploited in its rise. The most dramatic concession was U.S. acquiescence to terms that specify a date to end the embargos on conventional arms and missile sales to Iran without any corresponding concessions from Iran on the non-nuclear regional threats. This is a concession administration supporters had promised skeptics they would never make, and it raises serious questions about the viability (existence?) of a larger regional strategy to defend American interests from the Iranian challenge. Interestingly, the Assad regime apparently has voted with the skeptics rather than the advocates, arguing that the Iran deal will oblige the United States to align itself more closely with Syria.[24] Ongoing challenges implementing the deal will force the United States (at least under the current administration) to continue tiptoeing around Iranian support for extremist groups lest American hawkishness drive the Iranians to abandon the deal. The dirty secret of the Iranian deal is that the benefits to Iran are front-loaded and the much-heralded snap-back sanctions mechanisms would not be reassembled very snappily, especially if the United States could credibly be blamed for provoking a crisis.[25]

It is hard to point to any concrete example in the weeks since the deal was announced in which Iranian action has buttressed the case of the advocates. If the nuclear deal will eventually catalyze a new era of U.S.-Iranian cooperation, the best case one can make right now is that this achievement is not yet evident.

For this reason, despite the superficial similarity that advocates of the deal find so attractive, the deal with Iran is likely to have the opposite geostrategic effect that the Nixon-Kissinger rapprochement with China helped catalyze. Triangular diplomacy did juggle geopolitics in ways ultimately conducive to American interests. As Michael Green and Gabriel Scheinmann explain,[26] however, the factors that made the China gambit work are weaker or entirely absent in the Iran case. To be sure, Iran and the United States both view ISIL as an enemy, as the United States and China viewed the

Soviet Union, but the similarities mostly end there. The Iran deal may be a price worth paying to delay the Iranian nuclear program by a decade, but the price will likely be a more daunting geostrategic picture in the Middle East, not a more favorable one.

My own view is that we need to be more Churchillian and less Rooseveltian in how we leverage ISIL's enemies. When circumstances require, we can exploit co-belligerency with unreliable partners in the service of a larger strategy. But we should not confuse co-belligerency for budding partnerships. It is fine to accept tactical assistance from even unsavory co-belligerents—e.g., targeting assistance from the Taliban or timing our airstrikes to take advantage of ground-based counter-ISIL attacks from Iranian forces—but it is naive to think that this is a promising basis for a broader rapprochement with these groups. We need to make sure that our tactical coordination does not prevent us from rapidly confronting the threats posed by our erstwhile co-belligerents, even as we also deal with ISIL.

Hinge 5: How geographically limited can our strategy be?

A reasonable person might assume that the more geographically limited our strategy, the better the prospects for success. Isn't it easier to attempt less than to attempt more? The last several years, however, have suggested the opposite may be more accurate: we cannot have a successful strategy that is arbitrarily limited to a certain country.

For instance, we may not be able to defeat ISIL in Iraq while ignoring ISIL in Syria; indeed, as the last year has shown, we may not be able to defeat ISIL in Iraq with only an air campaign against ISIL in Syria, and a relatively ineffective one at that. First, strength in one country is a function of the safe-haven and support it can receive from neighboring countries; ISIL's operations in Iraq depend on the strategic resources it can mobilize from within Syria. Similarly, ISIL's success in Syria has been augmented by its ability to relieve pressure on its operations there as the counter-ISIL coalition scrambles to respond in Iraq. Second, ISIL has proven itself nimble enough to jump from host to host. There are now viable ISIL elements stretching from West Africa all the way to Afghanistan/Pakistan.

I do not know of any reason why even that span forms the limit of ISIL's global reach. Al-Qaeda showed a capacity to reach all the way to the Philippines and Indonesia, and ISIL is on track to eclipse al-Qaeda on most important metrics—why not geographic scope? Certainly strategists in Southeast Asia are concerned about our inability to check the rise of ISIL and what that means for their security interests.[27] If one adds in the foreign fighter problem, the containment problem escalates dramatically. To be sure, during the Cold War, the United States did mount a global containment strategy. But the Cold War experience rather proves the point: the United States thought about the communist threat in global terms.

The Cold War analogy suggests one further insight: while we must approach the ISIL threat regionally, if not globally, we should not make the Cold War error of ignoring local differences. ISIL offers a transnational ideological appeal with common features across the board, but each local actor reflects idiosyncratic features. The precise formula optimized for Iraq may not work in Syria, let alone in Libya or Egypt.

Hinge 6: How much does ISIL depend on momentum?

ISIL clearly benefits from momentum, where tactical success breeds further tactical success culminating in operational or even strategic success. Part of the reason would-be jihadis flock to ISIL is that ISIL appears to be on a winning streak. ISIL has stolen market share from al-Qaeda and other older terrorist groups by generating more recent battlefield successes than ISIL's rivals have achieved.

But does ISIL *depend* upon momentum? Is the only plausible way ISIL can win strategically by giving the impression that it is winning tactically, thereby swelling its ranks, paralyzing its more materially powerful foes, and convincing them to back down? In theory, there is another possibility: perhaps ISIL wins not by winning, but simply by not completely losing—by living to fight another day?

Which of these interpretations seems true depends on whether or not you believe ISIL offers an intrinsically appealing ideology that over time can win in the marketplace of ideas. If that is the case, ISIL simply needs to hang on. If, on the other hand, ISIL's ideology has limited intrinsic appeal, then it needs the force multiplier of momentum. Why, for instance, have former Baathist regime elements joined ISIL? The reason likely has less to do with the religiously grounded ideology of the self-proclaimed caliph and more to do with the pragmatic calculation that ISIL represents the strongest horse running against their several foes: the legitimate Iraqi government, the Kurds, and the United States.

Put another way: if ISIL's appeal is intrinsically limited—if local populations will quickly tire of ISIL's brand—then it depends on the multiplier effect of momentum to bring in new recruits who will help suppress local discontent. If, on the other hand, local populations are inclined to see ISIL as attractive enough to be the lesser evil (or even better than that), then merely seeking to contain ISIL and deny it new tactical successes could lock us into an enduring conflict. These time-frame judgments matter more than the popular commentary admits. Communism turned out to have the inherent flaws the early architects of containment identified, but it also turned out to have far more staying power because of its intrinsic appeal than the early containment architects realized. The ideological contest ended in a U.S. victory, as the containment policy foresaw, but at a much longer time frame and a much higher cost in U.S. blood and treasure than expected. What started out as a call for short-term patience morphed into the expectation of a multigenerational ideological struggle. Those who advocate containment today may have similarly miscalibrated expectations. And perhaps even if ISIL is credited with only an intrinsically limited appeal, it may still have longer staying power than other limited-appeal tyrannies; sitting atop oil reserves might allow them to buy a long life.

An ISIL that depends on momentum will be put on a trajectory toward defeat once it starts to suffer pronounced, sustained, and repeated tactical setbacks. Just as ISIL benefited from the falling dominoes of 2014, ISIL could be undone by being forced into serial and cumulative retreat from those same territories. An ISIL that wins by hanging on can quickly turn tactical setbacks in one geographic area into tactical gains in another.

At some point, ISIL may gain momentum simply from holding territory, i.e., demonstrating ongoing tactical success by rebuffing efforts by the United States and its partners to free territory under ISIL control. Fidel Castro gained enormous prestige simply by defying the U.S. containment strategy. Of course, ISIL is unlikely to enjoy the blandishments of a superpower patron, but it could benefit, as Castro did, from growing weariness (if not outright defections) in the containment coalition. The Cuban experience is a cautionary tale for those who believe we can diminish ISIL's appeal simply by preventing any future gains and containing ISIL within its existing territory.

Hinge 7: How reversible are our own tactical setbacks?

Regardless of the extent to which ISIL *depends* on momentum, defeating ISIL may require that the United States and its allies not suffer any further tactical setbacks of our own. Historically, the United States has shown remarkable resilience, overcoming tactical setbacks in most of the wars it eventually won. Perhaps the fight against ISIL will fit that pattern. But it is possible that our existing strategy against ISIL is much less resilient than the American historical norm. It may be that every setback makes victory much harder to achieve even when we adjust our approach because (a) our strategy is particularly dependent on getting others to fight on our behalf, and (b) we seem to have a historically unprecedented intolerance for paying the human costs of war.

Consider just one example: the United States had ample opportunity to blunt ISIL's advance before the fall of Mosul. We chose not to for understandable reasons—we were trying to incentivize the government of Prime Minister Maliki to make political concessions to the Sunnis by withholding our aid until he reformed. He did not adjust his behavior in time, Mosul fell, and some weeks later Iraqi leaders finally took the steps we insisted they take, thus triggering more robust U.S. aid. As of early fall 2015, Mosul still is in the hands of ISIL, but we have plans to help the Iraqis retake it in 2016. In previous wars, such an ebb and flow on the battlefield would not be decisive, but in our current conflict the price of delay could be more significant. Is there a world of difference between never losing Mosul and losing but then retaking it, or are they essentially equivalent?

Or consider another question: Does the 2007-2009 success of the Iraq surge demonstrate that the United States can manage the coalitional politics of gaining the cooperation of Iraqi government forces and Sunni militias? Or does our failure once we left Iraq to force Maliki to continue honoring the commitments he made during the surge's heyday mean that another surge-cum-tribal-awakening is foreclosed?

Put another way, are tactical setbacks like a broken bone, which gets stronger when it heals, or like a sprained ankle, which will stay weaker for a very long time once it has suffered the damage?

Hinge 8: Does ISIL pose a qualitatively different lone-wolf threat?

America has long had a lone-wolf terrorism problem, all the way back to Timothy McVeigh and the 1995 attack in Oklahoma City. We also know that Americans have tolerated the intolerable threat of gun violence from deranged individuals. Yet the public views the threat of those kinds of attacks when inspired by militant Islamist networks of extremists as qualitatively different from the older—dare we say, more native?—form of lone-wolf problems. Why?

Part of the reason—an unattractive part—may be xenophobia, viewing one sort of evil as domestic, a tragic legacy of our own history, and another sort of evil as alien, a tragic legacy of someone else's history. Part of the reason may be the more acceptable notion that there seem to be practical limits to the kinds of mayhem that a villain in the mold of a Charleston shooter might threaten, whereas it is hard to know the limits to the kinds of mayhem that the Chattanooga shooter represented. Even when the domestic lone wolf results in al-Qaeda-scale casualties—note that McVeigh's single attack killed several multiples more Americans than the combined post-9/11 attacks on U.S. soil by al-Qaeda and ISIL followers—Americans perceive the threat differently, presumably because McVeigh did not have an army of followers, whereas al-Qaeda and now especially ISIL does. ISIL seems poised to tap a formidable arsenal of individuals who left their home country and flocked to fight on ISIL's behalf. ISIL's ability to attract at least 25,000 foreign fighters from 100 countries has created a vast pool of potential hard-to-track future terrorists, elevating the ISIL threat into a qualitatively different category.[28]

Whatever the reason, it matters for our counter-ISIL strategy that Americans deem ISIL to be a higher-priority national security threat than other lone wolves. For ISIL has shown greater success in inspiring such lone-wolf attacks than its militant Islamist predecessors. A strategy aimed at defeating ISIL has to wrestle with how to counter this threat. And a strategy aimed only at containing ISIL is even more on the hook for a response.

I have indicated that we may only be able to reduce and not eliminate this lone-wolf threat, but what can we do to reduce it? Slowing down ISIL's momentum is the most important first step, but it is not the last. Likewise, putting ISIL on the defensive in social media, degrading its use of other Internet tools, and making more headway in the war of ideas will surely make it harder to recruit ISIL wannabees. As the last line of defense, we should bolster the FBI's ability to track social media interactions and improve the funding and training for local law enforcement to engage local communities in well-considered counter-radicalization efforts.

Conclusion

There are doubtless more hinges worth considering, but these eight go some way in distinguishing among plausible strategies. For my part, I make the following bets:

1. We do not have much give on our other strategic goals. We need to defeat ISIL *and* achieve the other goals, and we should be willing to pay the higher cost that will require.

2. We get others to do more by doing more ourselves.

3. Eventually, defeating ISIL will require defeating it inside Syria *and* facilitating the establishment of a post-Assad regime.

4. The Iran deal on balance sets back our counter-ISIL effort.

5. We can afford to sequence our efforts geographically, but we cannot truncate them geographically.

6. ISIL depends heavily on momentum and the prestige that comes from holding territory.

7. Given the serious tactical setbacks we have suffered in recent years, we cannot suffer many more without markedly undermining our prospects for victory.

8. It is appropriate to view the ISIL (and other militant Islamist) lone-wolf threats as qualitatively different from the threats posed by other domestic terrorists.

This leads to the conclusion that we cannot defeat ISIL with the strategy we currently are following in the early fall of 2015. We must do more, including committing a significant U.S. ground presence beyond what we have hitherto been willing to contemplate, or we must accept a goal short of "defeat ISIL." The strategy these bets lead to looks a great deal like the one recently outlined by Michèle Flournoy and Richard Fontaine, which suggests that it might have bipartisan appeal.[29]

Note: these bets do not necessarily lead inexorably to Operation Iraqi Freedom 2.0, but they might lead to a strategy that involves far more ground force risk than the administration has been willing to contemplate thus far. For instance, these bets might lead to a strategy that involves more operational raids within ISIL territory, more ground commitment to secure some high-profile territorial ISIL setbacks (e.g., Mosul), and more safe areas within Syria to better protect, cultivate, and eventually mobilize Syrian refugees.

A common thread stitches together the bets I would make: thinking through the problem from both our own *and* the enemy's perspective rather than from just our own. Viewed only from our own perspective, it would be highly desirable to be able to defeat ISIL without a ground commitment, to be able with a minimum of leverage to induce partners to act according to our preferences rather than their own, and to discover that we can suffer repeated setbacks without materially affecting our chances for ultimate victory. But when one looks at the problem from the perspective of ISIL—what does ISIL need to prevail against the United States?—some of those bets seem more grounded in hope than in reality. Turning my assignment on its head like this might well reveal that ISIL has the potential to achieve something it would define as victory.[30]

Once you have picked your strategy, how will you assess its effectiveness? It is easy to measure degrading: weapons caches bombed, mobile refineries taken out of commission, fighters captured/killed. But measuring progress toward defeat is harder. Viewed narrowly in terms of metrics of degrading, the U.S. effort has some things to boast about.[31] The problem is that while the administration claims ISIL's control over territory—and ability to threaten other territory—has diminished, it has not diminished proportional to the progress the administration claims on the metrics of degrading. It is possible the kinetic campaign against ISIL follows the familiar nonlinear pattern of aerial bombardment: a sustained period of minimal effect followed by rapid collapse of the enemy.[32] If so, it may be premature to conclude that ISIL is proving resilient. On the other hand, control of territory is the key metric of a strategy to ultimately defeat ISIL. Until that metric trends more favorably for the United States, it is certainly premature to claim we are winning.

This brief survey left plenty of grist for a future mill. What is the domestic and international legal basis for the various forms of counter-ISIL strategies?[33] How does Israel factor into the ISIL strategy? If you believe Sykes-Picot is fundamentally obsolete, what, besides chaos, do you see as the substitute?

And, above all, what are the costs of the various strategies? Expectations of cost may in practice be the decisive hinge. Advocates of the current strategy say doing anything more is prohibitively expensive, beyond what is politically palatable. Advocates of an even more modest containment strategy likewise cite cost as its chief selling point.[34] Polls suggest that the public could be persuaded to support a more vigorous strategy than our current one, but only if they were led by an administration fully committed to that higher-cost strategy. The public may not be war-weary, but it is certainly war-wary. Before we commit the country to a strategy to defeat ISIL, we must realistically estimate the cost and prepare to justify that to the American people. And if we commit the country to a less ambitious strategy, we should be similarly rigorous and clear-eyed in communicating the costs of that course of action, namely the sacrifice of goals.

In closing, we should remember that a successful strategy avoids two pitfalls of our own making. The first pitfall is having a strategy that is only backward looking—one so focused on the mistakes of the past that it misses the opportunities of the future. In a sense, we are in the predicament we are in today because we gave into this temptation in recent years. America's Middle East strategy has been overly focused on "avoiding another Iraq," meaning avoiding another major U.S. ground commitment to a shooting conflict.[35] We managed to avoid that but in the process did not pay adequate attention to all the unintended costs of such a strategy.

Today it is quite clear that the effort to "avoid another Iraq" directly contributed to the problems we face, including the rise of ISIL. Outgoing Army Chief of Staff Ray Odierno is only the most recent respected voice to acknowledge the obvious: that had the United States not withdrawn entirely from Iraq in 2011, we would have been in a much better position to prevent the subsequent rise of ISIL.[36] Likewise, it is evident that factors that were deemed showstoppers in those earlier years—such as the desire to have immunity protections enshrined in law by the Iraqi parliament rather than merely guaranteed by executive authority—somehow became finessable once the need to return to Iraq was apparent to all.[37]

A backwards-looking focus would indeed reveal a laundry list of missed opportunities and unfortunate decisions in recent years, but the urgent challenge is salvaging a viable way forward today. In the middle years of the Iraq war, it was customary for critics of the Bush administration to respond to requests for advice on alternative strategies with some variant of the old joke about the Vermonter giving the hapless out-of-towner driving directions: "How to get there? Well, I wouldn't start from here." Answering a question about how to win in Iraq in 2005 or 2006 with "don't invade Iraq in 2003" was of limited utility, however sincerely it may have been felt. Similarly, pointing out all the ways in which our recent decisions have been flawed is at best only a modest start to figuring out what to do now.

The second pitfall is one of despair. As daunting as the challenges are, the United States does have cause to be reasonably optimistic about the medium and long term. Ironically, the most frustrating aspect of the setbacks the United States has suffered geopolitically is how few of them were truly beyond our ability to influence or forestall. We have suffered defeats of choice, not of necessity. We have suffered setbacks not because of inherent material weakness of the United States or material strength of our adversaries, but because of deliberate bets we have made. At the geostrategic level, looking to the long term, America has the stronger hand. I would be surprised if any member of the Aspen Strategy Group would rather play another actor's hand, even in the counter-ISIL game where we have struggled so painfully in recent years. Partisans on both sides may find short-term advantage in describing the world in turmoil in vivid terms, but the situation today is still less daunting than the one confronting American strategists in the 1970s when the seeds of the Aspen Strategy Group were planted. America struggled with those challenges, but with wise political leadership dealt with them far more successfully than many expected. I do not see why wise political leadership could not do the same again today.

Peter D. Feaver is a Professor of Political Science and Public Policy at Duke. He is Director of the Triangle Institute for Security Studies and of the Duke Program in American Grand Strategy. His principal area of research is the politics of American foreign policy, particularly civil-military relations, public opinion and war, grand strategy, and nuclear proliferation. Dr. Feaver is an author: *Armed Servants* (Harvard, 2003) and *Guarding the Guardians* (Cornell, 1992). He is a co-author: with Christopher Gelpi and Jason Reifler, *Paying the Human Costs of War* (Princeton, 2009); with Susan Wasiolek and Anne Crossman, *Getting the Best Out of College* (Ten Speed Press, 2008, 2nd edition 2012); and with Gelpi, *Choosing Your Battles* (Princeton, 2004). He has also published on other topics: strategic planning, cybersecurity, IR theory, and the gap between academics and policymakers. From June 2005 to July 2007, Dr. Feaver served as Special Advisor for Strategic Planning and Institutional Reform on the National Security Council Staff at the White House, where his responsibilities included the national security strategy, regional strategy reviews, and other political-military issues. In 1993-94, Dr. Feaver served as Director for Defense Policy and Arms Control on the National Security Council at the White House, where his responsibilities included the national security strategy review, counterproliferation policy, regional nuclear arms control, and other defense policy issues. He is a member of the Aspen Strategy Group, blogs at shadow.foreignpolicy.com, and is a Contributing Editor to *Foreign Policy* magazine. He received a Ph.D. from Harvard in 1990.

I thank Emma Campbell-Mohn and Luke Maier for research assistance on this project.

[1] Feaver, Peter. September 10, 2014. "A Simple Goal for the President's Speech: Clarity on the Objective." Shadow Government at ForeignPolicy.com, at foreignpolicy.com/2014/09/10/a-simple-goal-for-the-presidents-speech-clarity-on-the-objective/.

[2] ADRP 1-02. February 2015. *Terms and Military Symbols*, at armypubs.army.mil/doctrine/DR_pubs/dr_a/pdf/adrp1_02.pdf.

[3] The precise wording of the objectives is intentional. We could consider ISIL defeated if it is no longer in the business of conducting complex mass casualty attacks even if, in some hypothetical sense, it still has some residual capacity to do so. At some point, the line between "complex mass casualty" attacks and "lone wolf" attacks blurs into obscurity. For instance, one plausible way that ISIL could launch a complex mass casualty attack on U.S. soil would be through geographically dispersed simultaneous lone-wolf attacks, such as several coincident shootings at large public gatherings throughout the United States. Since I do not think it is possible to eliminate entirely truly lone-wolf attacks, as I explain later in the text, some residual threat of the former may also be irreducible.

[4] Quoted in Gordon, Michael R. September 22, 2012. "In U.S. Exit from Iraq, Failed Efforts and Challenges." *New York Times.*

[5] The list of explicit partners is daunting enough: Sunni allies (those in the Gulf States who are not supporting ISIL), Kurdish forces, Turkey, Jordan, Israel, the Shia-dominated Iraqi government, Iraqi Sunni tribes, and secular rebels in Syria. However, by virtue of our arms control agreements, we are also implicitly partnered with the Assad regime in Syria and also now with the Iranian regime; both have also been implicit partners in counter-ISIL efforts. There are real tradeoffs, where aid to one of these partners reduces the relative gains of aid to other partners; for instance, aid to Turkey reduces the impact of aid to Kurdish forces and vice versa.

[6] Obama, Barack. June 13, 2014. "Statement by the President on Iraq, Delivered on the South Lawn of the White House," at www.whitehouse.gov/the-press-office/2014/06/13/statement-president-iraq.

[7] Obama, Barack. July 6, 2015. "Remarks by the President on Progress in the Fight Against ISIL, Delivered at the Pentagon," at www.whitehouse.gov/the-press-office/2015/07/06/remarks-president-progress-fight-against-isil.

[8] Additional phases might be Maliki before and after the 2010 Iraqi parliamentary elections, but I stick with the demarcations based on changes in U.S. strategy, given the focus of this chapter.

[9] Gordon, Michael R. November 29, 2006. "Bush Aide's Memo Doubts Iraqi Leader." *New York Times.*

[10] Reasonable people can differ as to where to put Phase 1 in the rankings. It doesn't matter for my argument.

[11] Chollet, Derek, and Robert Ford. July 26, 2015. "Call to Action: The Iraq Strategy America Really Needs." *National Interest,* at nationalinterest.org/feature/call-action-the-iraq-strategy-america-really-needs-13421.

[12] See Feaver, Peter. August 15, 2014. "Obama's Concession on Iraq Might Be a Turning Point for His Foreign Policy." Shadow Government on ForeignPolicy.com, at foreignpolicy.com/2014/08/15/obamas-concession-on-iraq-might-be-a-turning-point-for-his-foreign-policy/. In some of the popular commentary, the timeline gets confused and the sequencing reversed. See Ignatius, David. August 21, 2014. "The New Battle Against Evil." *Washington Post,* at www.washingtonpost.com/opinions/david-ignatius-obamas-correct-approach-to-battling-the-evil-islamic-state/2014/08/21/4fdef9ea-296a-11e4-958c-268a320a60ce_story.html?hpid=z3. And Krauthammer, Charles. August 21, 2014. "Stopping the Worst People on Earth." *Washington Post,* at www.washingtonpost.com/opinions/charles-krauthammer-goal-of-us-airstrikes-is-stopping-the-worst-people-on-earth/2014/08/21/2417619a-2964-11e4-958c-268a320a60ce_story.html.

[13] Wright, Austin. July 8, 2015. "Price Tag for Syrian Rebels: $4 Million Each." *Politico,* at www.politico.com/story/2015/07/price-for-syrian-rebels-4-million-each-119858.html.

[14] Solovyov, Dmitry. May 28, 2015. "Commander of Elite Tajik Police Force Defects to Islamic State." *Reuters,* at www.reuters.com/article/2015/05/28/us-mideast-crisis-tajikistan-idUSKBN0OD1AP20150528.

[15] Conflict Armament Research. September 2014. *Islamic State Weapons in Iraq and Syria.* London: Conflict Armament Research, at www.conflictarm.com/wp-content/uploads/2014/09/Dispatch_IS_Iraq_Syria_Weapons.pdf.

[16] Entous, Adam, and Naftali Bendavid. July 23, 2015. "Mission to Purge Syria of Chemical Weapons Comes up Short." *Wall St. Journal,* at www.wsj.com/articles/mission-to-purge-syria-of-chemical-weapons-comes-up-short-1437687744.

[17] Hamid, Shadi. September 14, 2013. "The U.S.-Russian Deal on Syria: A Victory for Assad." *Atlantic,* at www.theatlantic.com/international/archive/2013/09/the-us-russian-deal-on-syria-a-victory-for-assad/279680/. See also, Doran, Michael. February 2, 2015. "Obama's Secret Iran Strategy." *Mosaic Magazine,* at www.hudson.org/research/10989-obama-s-secret-iran-strategy.

[18] Mehta, Aaron. July 17, 2015. "Odierno: ISIS Fight Will Last '10 to 20 Years.'" DefenseNews.com, at www.defensenews.com/story/defense/2015/07/17/odierno-isis-fight-last-10-20-years/30295949/.

[19] Contrast the following two pieces, which mark the evolution of administration thinking on Libya. Daalder, Ivo H., and James G. Stavridis. October 30, 2011. "NATO's Success in Libya." *New York Times;* Ernst, Jonathan. April 17, 2015. "Obama Urges Gulf Nations to Help with Chaos in Libya." *Reuters,* at www.reuters.com/article/2015/04/17/us-libya-security-italy-usa-idUSKBN0N820D20150417.

[20] Obama, Barack. September 10, 2014. "Statement by the President on the State Floor," at www.whitehouse.gov/the-press-office/2014/09/10/statement-president-isil-1.

[21] Barnard, Anne, Michael R. Gordon, and Eric Schmitt. July 27, 2015. "Turkey and U.S. Plan to Create Syria 'Safe Zone' Free of ISIS." *New York Times.*

[22] Rogin, Josh. July 28, 2015. "U.S. Shoots Down Idea of Syria Safe Zone." *Bloomberg View*, at www. bloombergview.com/articles/2015-07-28/u-s-shoots-down-idea-of-syria-safe-zone.

[23] Parsi, Trita. June 30, 2015. "Iran's Nuclear Talks: Five Reasons a Deal Would Be Good for the U.S." CNN. com, at www.cnn.com/2015/06/30/opinions/iran-nuclear-talks-parsi/.

[24] Al-Khalidi, Suleiman. July 23, 2015. "Syria Sees West Easing Tough Stance After Iran Deal: Assad Aide." *Reuters*, at news.yahoo.com/syria-sees-west-easing-tough-stance-iran-deal-171643092.html.

[25] Feaver, Peter D., and Eric Lorber. July 21, 2015. "Do the Iran Deal's 'Snap-back' Sanctions Have Teeth?" Shadow Government on ForeignPolicy.com, at foreignpolicy.com/2015/07/21/do-the-iran-deals-snapback-sanctions-have-teeth/.

[26] Green, Michael, and Gabriel Scheinmann. July 27, 2015. "The Iran Deal Isn't Anything Like Nixon Going to China." *Foreign Policy*, at foreignpolicy.com/2015/07/27/the-iran-deal-isnt-anything-like-nixon-going-to-china/

[27] Paddock, Richard, and I-Made Sentana. July 17, 2015. "Fears Grow Over Islamic State's Influence in Southeast Asia." *Wall St. Journal*, at www.wsj.com/articles/fears-grow-over-Islamic-states-influence-in-southeast-asia-1437106924.

[28] Lederer, Edith M. April 1, 2015. "UN Report: More than 25,000 Foreigners Fight With Terrorists." *AP*, at bigstory.ap.org/article/cec52a0dbfab4c00b89bc543badf6c20/un-report-more-25000-foreigners-fight-terrorists.

[29] Flournoy, Michele, and Richard Fontaine. June 24, 2015. "To Defeat the Islamic State, the U.S. Will Have To Go Big." *Washington Post*, at www.washingtonpost.com/opinions/to-defeat-the-Islamic-state-the-us-will-have-to-go-big/2015/06/24/fccb9f46-19e2-11e5-ab92-c75ae6ab94b5_story.html.

[30] Arango, Tim. July 21, 2015. "ISIS Transforming Into Functioning State That Uses Terror as a Tool." *New York Times*.

[31] These are helpfully tabulated on Operation Inherent Resolve's webpage: www.defense.gov/home/features/2014/0814_iraq/. See also, Hesterman, John. June 5, 2015. "Department of Defense Press Briefing by Lt. Gen. Hesterman Via Telephone from the Combined Air and Space Operations Center, Southwest Asia." Broadcast from the Pentagon Press Briefing Room, at www.defense.gov/Transcripts/Transcript.aspx?TranscriptID=5637.

[32] See, for instance, Cohen, Eliot A. 1993. *Gulf War Air Power Survey*. Washington, DC: U.S. Government Printing Office.

[33] A containment strategy that does nothing more than wait for ISIL to collapse probably has the easiest legal bar to clear, but anything more vigorous raises serious legal questions, especially since President Obama predicated his strategy on a request for a new AUMF—a request Congress has yet to honor.

[34] Cronin, Audrey Kurth. March/April 2015. "ISIS is Not a Terrorist Group." *Foreign Affairs*, at www. foreignaffairs.com/articles/middle-east/2015-02-16/isis-not-terrorist-group.

[35] Feaver, Peter. 2013. "Has the Obama Response to the Arab Revolutions Been Effective? Yes, Not Really, and Probably Too Soon to Tell." In *The Arab Revolutions and American Policy*, edited by Nicholas Burns and Jonathon Price, 49-70. Washington, DC: Aspen Strategy Group.

[36] Griffen, Jennifer, and Lucas Tomlinson. July 22, 2015. "Army chief Odierno, in exit interview, says US could have 'prevented' ISIS rise." FoxNews.com, at www.foxnews.com/politics/2015/07/22/exclusive-army-chief-odierno-in-exit-interview-says-us-could-have-prevented/.

[37] See Feaver, Peter, and Mitchell Reiss. November 19, 2014. "What Happened to Immunity for U.S. Troops in Iraq." Shadow Government on ForeignPolicy.com, at foreignpolicy.com/2014/11/19/what-happened-to-immunity-for-u-s-troops-in-iraq/.

"If we have learned anything since 9/11, it should be that we need to deny sanctuary to a terrorist group that wreaks unspeakable violence and brutality against all except those who share its tortured worldview."

—MICHÈLE FLOURNOY & RICHARD FONTAINE

An Intensified Approach to Combatting the Islamic State

Michèle Flournoy
Chief Executive Officer
Center for a New American Security

Richard Fontaine
President
Center for a New American Security

In the eleven months since President Obama committed the United States to "degrade and ultimately destroy" the Islamic State, the group has expanded its international reach, metastasized to form offshoots across multiple regions, and increased its perceived momentum. While U.S. government officials cite the reduction in the overall size of the group's geographical sanctuary in Iraq and Syria and the killing of thousands of ISIS fighters on the battlefield, the fall of Ramadi and much of Anbar province to the Islamic State served as a wakeup call that current efforts to counter ISIS are not adequate to the task.[1] Meanwhile, the threat that the terrorist group poses to Americans appears to be growing, as ISIS-inspired individuals conduct attacks targeting Westerners around the globe, including here in the United States.

While President Obama has articulated a fairly comprehensive strategy against ISIS, the United States and the 60-nation coalition it has formed to fight ISIS have not translated the President's words into an effective campaign on the ground. The military dimensions of the strategy have been under-resourced. And many of the nonmilitary lines of operation remain underdeveloped.

This paper explores the threat posed by ISIS, assesses the administration's efforts to date, and recommends what the United States and its partners can do to make our efforts to counter and ultimately destroy ISIS more effective.

The ISIS Threat

The Islamic State is at once a terrorist organization, a proto-state, and an ideological movement. In its effort to establish a caliphate and inspire Muslims around the world to join its cause, the group combines extreme violence, savvy use of social media, a jihadist narrative, an ability to seize and hold territory, and explicit hostility to the West.[2] Unlike al-Qaeda, which maintains strict criteria and protocols for membership, asserts centralized control, and focuses on conducting carefully planned, spectacular attacks, the Islamic State has adopted a "let a thousand flowers bloom" approach that invites geographically disperse, self-proclaimed affiliates and inspires uncoordinated attacks.

Its hallmark attack outside the Middle East has thus far been of the "lone wolf" variety. The Islamic State has called on sympathizers to attack Westerners and their property wherever they can be found. Of the eleven attacks that occurred in the West between May 2014 and February 2015, ten were carried out by individuals.[3] The Islamic State has carried out or inspired attacks in Tunisia, Kuwait, Egypt, Saudi Arabia, Canada, Australia, France, Denmark, and other countries, including the United States.[4] The threat to the homeland appears to be growing: after an Islamic State-inspired attack in Texas in May, the FBI reported foiling several July 4th-related plots in what its director described as "crowd sourcing terrorism."[5] Future attacks may not be limited to lone-wolf efforts; according to one counterterrorism analyst we interviewed, "ISIS is just one Mohammed Atta away from a 9/11-type attack in the United States."

In Syria and Iraq, some 22,000 foreign fighters have joined the Islamic State from 100 different countries,[6] and thousands of these people have Western passports that enable them to travel freely within and between Europe and the United States. And ISIS's threat to Iraq's stability is clear. In addition to seizing Mosul and Anbar, the group poses a grave threat to other parts of the country; currently, for instance, more than 40 percent of Iraqi security forces are assigned to the Baghdad operations command, an indication of the government's fear for its capital.[7]

While ISIS has suffered recent setbacks in both Iraq and Syria, its presence elsewhere is growing. The group has established a haven in Libya and the Sinai Peninsula and is attempting to establish footholds throughout the Middle East and in the Caucasus, Southeast Asia, Afghanistan, Nigeria, and elsewhere. Its ambitions—and the scope of its threat—appear to grow along with its capacity and reach. Driven in part by a sense of competition with al-Qaeda, the threat posed by the Islamic State to the United States may grow over time as it becomes more entrenched in more places and as it attracts and trains more sophisticated fighters.

U.S. Strategy to Counter ISIS: Strong in Theory, Inadequate in Practice

Despite repeated charges that his administration lacks a strategy, President Obama has on several occasions articulated U.S. efforts to combat the Islamic State. Over the past year, the administration has assembled a 60-nation coalition to conduct a long-term, multidimensional campaign to defeat ISIS. The key elements of this campaign include:

- The deployment of U.S. and coalition military teams to train and equip local forces in Iraq and from Syria, and the provision of air support to help the Iraqi Security Forces and Peshmerga push ISIS out of key terrain it has occupied in Iraq.

- Air strikes in both Iraq and Syria against ISIS senior leaders, infrastructure, fighting positions, convoys, equipment, and oil and gas facilities that provide the group with a source of revenue.

- Information sharing with partners to help them strengthen border security to stem the flow of foreign fighters into Syria and Iraq, and then back to their home countries.

- Multilateral cooperation to track and disrupt illicit financing of ISIS.

- Diplomatic efforts to press Iraqi Prime Minister Abadi to build a more inclusive central government that represents and serves all Iraqis—Shia, Sunni, and Kurd—and devolves more authority and resources to the provinces.

- Discussions with partners regarding a negotiated transition to a post-Assad government in Syria.

- Efforts to discredit ISIS's narrative and counter its propaganda online.

- Measures to strengthen U.S. homeland security to prevent ISIS attacks.

In principle, all of these elements must be part of an effective American strategy to combat ISIS, but in practice, the whole has been less than the sum of the parts. Many of these efforts remain more aspirational than real. In some cases, they have been woefully under-resourced; in other cases, the president's rhetoric has not been translated into effective programs and actions.

In practice, American efforts to combat the Islamic State thus far convey a sense of creeping incrementalism. For example, in recent weeks, the administration has announced the dispatch of 450 additional troops to Iraq—only 50 of which are trainers, with the remainder as support—to train Iraqi troops, bringing the total U.S.

commitment to 3,550.[8] Meanwhile, a year-old DoD training effort has yielded just 60 anti-Islamic State fighters currently in training for deployment in Syria.

These and other moves simply will not turn the tide given ISIS's spread and momentum. For the president to realize his ambition of ultimately destroying the Islamic State—or even of containing ISIS gains or rolling them back—a broader and more intensive effort is needed.

Toward a More Robust and Effective Effort

A more robust campaign to counter ISIS should start with intensifying and fully resourcing our efforts in Iraq. To date, the counter-Islamic State strategy in Iraq has lacked the urgency and resources necessary for success. A re-energized and more forward-leaning approach should combine the following elements:

- **Intensify U.S. diplomacy in support of an integrated political-military plan for Iraq.** Iraq is the locus of the current U.S. military effort against the Islamic State, and the administration's strategy of working with and through Iraqi forces is the right one to achieve gains that are sustainable over the long term. But these efforts require better coordination between the military and diplomatic lines of effort. An integrated political-military plan should include stepped-up diplomacy with Baghdad to push for greater Sunni inclusion, devolution of authority and resources to provinces such as Anbar, and the establishment of a national guard as a vehicle for Sunni tribal militias to become part of the Iraqi security forces.

  Shia party leaders in Baghdad must be made to understand two fundamental facts: failure to adopt more inclusive policies with regard to the Sunni population risks the dissolution of Iraq as a unitary state, and relying predominantly on Iranian-backed Shia militias to clear ISIS out of Sunni areas will only further alienate the Sunni population and create fertile soil for ISIS's return. Given Iran's military operations and outsized influence in Iraqi politics, Tehran will be a major factor in the sustainability of a multi-sectarian Iraq. The United States should urge Iraqi leaders to make clear to Tehran that a zero-sum approach to sectarian conflict in Iraq risks the country's further fragmentation, increased ISIS influence, and deeper tension with the United States.

- **Intensify U.S. and coalition outreach to and support for the Sunni tribes.** While Shia-dominated Iraqi Army units may not have the "will to fight" to regain Sunni areas from ISIS, Sunni militia would be willing to take up arms against ISIS provided two key conditions are met: first, they must be convinced that Baghdad will provide them with more autonomy and resources to govern themselves at the provincial level, and second, they must believe that the U.S.-led coalition will provide them with the military and financial support necessary to enable their success against ISIS. Both conditions will be difficult to attain given the previous Sunni tribal alliance with the United States during the Anbar Awakening and the failure to translate those gains into greater Sunni political representation in a federalized Iraq.

Washington should clarify its willingness to provide operational support to Sunni tribal fighters and redouble its efforts to get Arab partners, who have largely sat on the sidelines and watched Iran fill the vacuum in Iraq, to provide Iraq financial support that is conditioned on greater inclusion of the Sunni population there.

- **Provide arms directly to Sunni tribes and the Kurdish Peshmerga.** The pipeline of weapons through Baghdad to those Sunnis and Kurds willing to take on the Islamic State has often been slow and inadequate, undermining the effectiveness of both training and operations against ISIS. The United States should speed the supply of arms and equipment directly to local tribal militia and Peshmerga units, while holding out the prospect that arms will flow through Baghdad if and when the central government establishes a reliable process for their transfer and passes legislation to include these fighters in the Iraqi security forces. Providing this assistance directly could also incentivize Shia politicians in Baghdad, who have thus far been reluctant to pass legislation establishing an Iraqi National Guard, to support the new law to ensure these local forces ultimately fall under the control of the Iraqi Security Forces.

- **Embed Special Operations forces at the battalion level and allow them to advise Iraqi commanders during operations.** The Iraqi Security Forces' will to fight has faltered repeatedly in the face of Islamic State advances, and yet it is difficult to bolster morale, stiffen backbones, or adjust a battle plan from a training base. When Iraqi units are trained, equipped, and ready for combat, U.S. military advisers should be allowed to embed with Iraqi battalions and advise Iraqi commanders during operations from "the last point of concealment"—i.e., a protected position closest to the fighting.

While this would increase the risk to some U.S. personnel, it would likely have a marked impact on the combat-effectiveness of Iraqi forces battling ISIS.

- **Intensify the coalition air campaign and deploy forward air controllers to call in close air support during combat missions.** The air campaign against the Islamic State has thus far been the centerpiece of U.S. strategy, yet as currently structured, it is unlikely to turn the tide. Since August 2014, the U.S.-led coalition has conducted over 2,600 air strikes against ISIS targets in Iraq and over 1,600 in Syria. But the intensity of the air campaign has been far less than in previous air campaigns and has been somewhat hampered by both a lack of intelligence on ISIS targets and lack of nearby basing to allow more responsive strikes on emergent or fleeting targets. Employing more U.S. air assets based in Iraq or neighboring partner countries, rather than on distant aircraft carriers, would enable far more strikes per day in both Iraq and Syria. Turkey's recent decision to open Incirlik Air Base for U.S. aircraft conducting operations against ISIS could be an important step in this regard. Authorizing U.S. forward air controllers to accompany Iraqi forces into the fight to identify targets and call in close air support for Iraqi units under fire would also make those forces far more effective.

At the same time, the United States should also intensify its efforts to counter ISIS in Syria. Specifically, the U.S. should:

- **Redouble efforts to aid the Syrian opposition.** The Islamic State will pose an enduring threat to Iraq and other countries as long as it enjoys a safe haven and base of operations in Syria. The continued leadership of Bashar al-Assad remains the fuel that fires the sense of Sunni disaffection in Syria and pulls that population toward its purported Islamic State protectors. Current U.S. policy requires oppositionists seeking training to target only the Islamic State and not the Assad regime. It is small wonder that just 60 potential fighters are currently undergoing training in the DoD-led program.

The DoD training mission should cease its insistence on the Islamic State as the sole target and begin training and equipping moderate opposition fighters who wish to take on the Assad regime as well. It should also begin providing anti-aircraft artillery to the moderate opposition to counter the regime's continued use of barrel bombs against the civilian population. As part of this effort, the United States should leverage its increased commitment to persuade Gulf States and Turkey to back the American effort rather than those of Jaish al-Fatah and other extremist groups in Syria.

The United States should aim for a resolution in which Assad is no longer in power but the Syria state retains the basic structures of government and avoids disintegration. This is a difficult and risky objective, but the alternatives promise endless bloodshed and fuel for ISIS's continued growth. Moving U.S. policy in this direction would allow Washington to better coordinate with regional states that wish to more vigorously oppose Assad, including Jordan, Saudi Arabia, and Qatar. It may also induce Turkey to enhance its border controls to better prevent the flow of foreign fighters into Syria. Indeed, the recently reported (and then officially denied) U.S.-Turkish buffer zone on the Syrian-Turkish border could be an element in such an approach. Specifically, the U.S. should:

- **Set the conditions before attempting a settlement in Syria.** A flurry of rumors suggests that, following the agreement on Iran's nuclear program, the administration may attempt a multilateral peace negotiation aimed at ending the Syrian civil war. Yet no political solution will be possible so long as the key parties—including Assad, the Islamic State, and other jihadist groups—believe they can win. The lack of serious U.S. engagement to date means that we would have little leverage in such a negotiation if it began tomorrow, and the parties we wish to see prevail—moderate rebels—are in fact the weakest on the field.

  Setting the table would first and foremost mean strengthening the elements in Syria who are best placed to govern a post-Assad Syria, and building support among the Gulf partners and Turkey for such a force. It would also include raising the costs for Iran both in Syria and across the region by more aggressively using military and intelligence tools to counter Iran's surrogates and proxies, jointly with Arab partner militaries. And it would mean engaging in a dialogue with Iranian officials to detect any changes in their calculus with respect to Assad and his regime's future.

- **Employ a "tourniquet strategy" around Syria.** While the United States takes more affirmative steps to achieve an acceptable endgame in Syria, it should also lead the coalition in a collective effort to keep the civil war from destabilizing countries on its borders, especially Turkey, Jordan, and Lebanon. Each of these countries is being overwhelmed by the largest refugee crisis since World War II: more than 4 million refugees have left Syria, with 1.8 million going to Turkey, nearly 1.2 million in Lebanon, and some 630,000 in Jordan. These states need more assistance from the international community to deal with this humanitarian crisis and counter ISIS efforts to launch attacks and gain a foothold on their territory. The U.S.-led effort should bolster the resilience of these border states in the face of unprecedented pressure. The reported plans to establish a "safe zone" in Syria along the Turkish border could be a step in the right direction, though militarily difficult to achieve and defend.

Neither the United States nor the international community can afford to focus only on countering ISIS where it is strongest—in Syria and Iraq. As the group seeks to establish affiliates in places as far flung as Afghanistan, Libya, Nigeria, and Yemen, the United States should seek to prevent it from creating additional safe havens from which it can conduct attacks. The United States and its partners should:

- **Intensify the global campaign against the Islamic State.** An enhanced strategy that combines military, intelligence, diplomatic, and economic efforts will be necessary to prevent ISIS from becoming the new al-Qaeda—a terrorist organization with global reach and ambitions to attack Americans at home and abroad. Many tools will be familiar from that fight, including counter-threat financing, building partnership capacity, intelligence sharing, and targeted counterterrorism operations. The United States should leverage the tools it has honed and the lessons it has learned to keep ISIS from establishing itself as a viable terrorist organization in countries beyond Syria and Iraq.

  In Afghanistan, the rise of the Islamic State's efforts to recruit disaffected Taliban and create a rival organization also offers one more reason to abandon the calendar-based withdrawal of U.S. forces from that country by the end of 2016. Instead, the United States should adopt a more forward-looking approach that would keep a modest force in place to advise and assist the Afghan National Security Forces and conduct joint counterterrorism operations to safeguard both countries.

- **Counter ISIS's narrative on social media.** ISIS reportedly puts out nearly 90,000 messages a day on social media outlets ranging from Facebook to Twitter to YouTube to WhatsApp.[9] The group is highly effective in using the Internet and social media to disseminate propaganda, radicalize and recruit followers, provide operational support to foreign fighters, and inspire "lone wolves" to conduct jihad. To date, U.S. and coalition efforts to counter ISIS messaging have been inadequate and ineffective.

A more coordinated digital effort is needed, one that includes not only other countries but also key partners in the private sector and NGO community. This counter-messaging campaign should include efforts to amplify more moderate voices within Islam who discredit ISIS's extremist views and calls to violence. It should also disseminate tales of disaffected former Islamic State fighters to better reveal the reality of ISIS and dissuade others from joining. While the efforts of partner governments like the UAE and Tunisia will be particularly important, it is imperative that the U.S. also engage key private sector and NGO partners to bolster their efforts. To cite one example, Google regularly reviews videos posted on YouTube and removes those that show or aim to incite violence. In addition, the company has recently connected YouTube stars skilled in reaching younger audiences with NGOs working to counter ISIS narratives. These and other creative approaches should be encouraged and supported.

Beyond these near-term steps to intensify the campaign against ISIS, the United States needs to revisit and revitalize efforts that aim to address the conditions that create fertile soil in which violent Islamic extremism can take root and grow. Such efforts are sometimes referred to as "draining the swamp." On the face of it, steps such as empowering more moderate voices within Islam and building the resilience of communities at risk of radicalization seem like no-brainers and entirely noncontroversial. But translating those generalities into specific policies can quickly become quite controversial. For example, should the United States press Saudi Arabia to stop its export of Wahhabism across the Islamic world? Should U.S. leaders openly call for the separation of the state and religion in the Muslim world? Should we give greater priority to addressing the failure of states across the Arab world to meet the basic needs and address the grievances of substantial segments of their populations? Should the U.S. renew its push for democratic reform in the Arab world, even among friendly autocracies, or count on them to impose stability through repression? Should we press European allies who have failed to integrate Muslim immigrant populations into their societies to take a different approach? And are we willing to scrutinize our own treatment of U.S. Muslim communities and change course where heavy-handed surveillance has trumped community engagement and alienated the very communities we are seeking to make resilient to radicalization? There are few easy answers to these questions, but they are central to the long-term effort to combat the Islamic State—and the successors and offshoots of it that will emerge as long as violent extremism remains an attractive ideology to motivated individuals.

Together, these steps would mark a significant intensification in the campaign against the Islamic State in Iraq and Syria and globally. They would involve putting a small number of U.S. "boots on the ground" and would expose American troops to greater risk. Yet the risks of inaction are greater still. If we have learned anything since 9/11, it should be that we need to deny sanctuary to a terrorist group that wreaks unspeakable violence and brutality against all except those who share its tortured worldview.

Most Americans regret having permitted al-Qaeda to establish a sanctuary in Afghanistan in the 1990s. Years from now, we do not want to look back with regret at this period of time when the Islamic State is creating its own havens. In the Middle East and elsewhere, we have imperfect and disorganized partners, but they are partners nonetheless. Now is the time to intensify our efforts to help lead them in a common campaign to defeat the Islamic State.

Michèle Flournoy is Co-Founder and CEO of the Center for a New American Security (CNAS). She served as the Under Secretary of Defense for Policy from 2009 to 2012. She was the principal adviser to the Secretary of Defense in the formulation of national security and defense policy, oversight of military plans and operations, and in National Security Council deliberations. She led the development of DoD's 2012 Strategic Guidance and represented the Department in dozens of foreign engagements, in the media, and before Congress. In January 2007, Ms. Flournoy co-founded CNAS, a non-partisan think tank dedicated to developing strong, pragmatic and principled national security policies. She served as CNAS' President until 2009. Previously, she was senior adviser at CSIS for several years and, prior to that, a distinguished research professor at the National Defense University. In the mid-1990s, she served as Principal Deputy Assistant Secretary of Defense for Strategy and Threat Reduction and Deputy Assistant Secretary of Defense for Strategy. She has received several awards from the Secretary of Defense and the Chairman of the Joint Chiefs of Staff. Ms. Flournoy is a member of the President's Intelligence Advisory Board, the Defense Policy Board, the DCIA's External Advisory Board, and is a Senior Fellow at Harvard's Belfer Center. She serves on the boards of The Mitre Corporation, Amida Technology Solutions, The Mission Continues, and 12 CARE, and is a Senior Advisor at the Boston Consulting Group. Ms. Flournoy earned a bachelor's degree from Harvard University and a master's degree from Balliol College, Oxford University. She is a member of the Aspen Strategy Group.

Richard Fontaine is the President of the Center for a New American Security (CNAS). He served as a Senior Advisor and Senior Fellow at CNAS from 2009-2012 and previously as foreign policy advisor to Senator John McCain. He has also worked at the State Department, the National Security Council (NSC), and on the staff of the Senate Foreign Relations Committee. Mr. Fontaine served as foreign policy advisor to the McCain 2008 presidential campaign and, following the election, as the minority deputy staff director on the Senate Armed Services Committee. Prior to this, he served as associate director for Near Eastern affairs at the NSC from 2003-04. He also worked in the NSC's Asian

Affairs directorate. During his time at the State Department, Mr. Fontaine worked in the office of former Deputy Secretary of State Richard Armitage and in the department's South Asia bureau, working on issues related to India, Nepal, and Sri Lanka. Mr. Fontaine began his foreign policy career as a staff member of the Senate Foreign Relations Committee, focusing on the Middle East and South Asia. Mr. Fontaine graduated summa cum laude with a B.A. in International Relations from Tulane University. He also holds a M.A. in International Affairs from the Johns Hopkins School of Advanced International Studies. He is a member of the Council on Foreign Relations and has been an adjunct professor at Georgetown University. He also served as the chairman of the World Economic Forum's Global Agenda Council on the United States.

[1] Administration officials report the loss of more than a quarter of the populated areas the Islamic State seized in Iraq. See Obama, Barack. July 6, 2015. "Remarks by the President on Progress in the Fight Against ISIL," at www.whitehouse.gov/the-press-office/2015/07/06/remarks-president-progress-fight-against-isil.

[2] For useful descriptions of the Islamic State, see, *inter alia*, Rasmussen, Nicholas J. February 12, 2015. "Current Terrorist Threat to the United States," hearing before the Senate Select Committee on Intelligence; Wood, Graeme. March 2015. "What ISIS Really Wants." *The Atlantic*; Cronin, Audrey Kurth. March/April 2015. "ISIS Is Not a Terrorist Group." *Foreign Affairs*; Fishman, Brian. June 24, 2015. "The Next Decade: Aligning Strategy Against the Islamic State," hearing before the House Armed Services Committee; and Robinson, Linda. June 24, 2015. "An Assessment of the Counter-ISIL Campaign," hearing before the House Armed Services Committee.

[3] Rasmussen, 2015.

[4] Ibid.

[5] Edwards, Julia, and Mark Hosenball. July 9, 2015. "FBI says it thwarted Islamic State-inspired July 4 attacks," *Reuters*.

[6] Johnson, Jeh. May 29, 2015. "United Nations Interior Ministerial Security Council Briefing on Countering Foreign Terrorist Fighters," at www.dhs.gov/news/2015/05/29/remarks-secretary-homeland-security-jeh-charles-johnson-united-nations-interior.

[7] Robinson, 2015.

[8] Carter, Ashton. July 7, 2015. "Statement on Counter-ISIL before the Senate Armed Services Committee," at www.defense.gov/Speeches/Speech.aspx?SpeechID=1956.

[9] Schmitt, Eric. February 16, 2015. "U.S. Intensifies Effort to Blunt ISIS' Message." *New York Times*.

"At a minimum, the policies the U.S. would adopt on 'the day after' an ISIS-caused catastrophe must be readied now. Even if the all-out effort is not deployed, it would be inexcusable if plans were not ready."

—PHILIP ZELIKOW

U.S. and Coalition Strategy Against ISIS

Philip Zelikow[1]
Professor
University of Virginia

Perhaps a more effective U.S.-led strategy against ISIS is slowly taking shape. There are promising signs of ferment. This chapter suggests where that transition in strategy might lead. It calls out some of the assessments and choices that might help inform a more effective policy.

The current strategy has several "lines of action." But an effective strategy also has concrete, operational objectives. An effective strategy embodies credible theories about how these objectives will be attained in the desired timeframe with available means. An effective strategy includes designs to make good on these theories, designs to mobilize capabilities and choreograph their use.

As of September 2015, to an outsider the strategy seems like it could be boiled to: Iraq first; stay out of the Syrian civil war; little territorial rollback of ISIS; time not important; and mainly rely on airpower.

- The principal theater of U.S. combat operations in the world is in Afghanistan, directed mainly against the Taliban side in the Afghan civil war. But the more dangerous threats to the United States and the largest humanitarian crisis in the world are now both probably centered in the Levant, boiling out of the Syrian cauldron.

- In the U.S.-led fight against ISIS, the main effort seems concentrated in Iraq. But the ISIS center of gravity is in Syria.

- Within Iraq, the main effort seems concentrated in the south, in Anbar province. But even within Iraq, the area in the north, around Mosul, is much more important to ISIS.

- In the coalition fight against ISIS, the main argument seems to be about more or less U.S. military presence. But a principal obstacle to success is not military but political: the absence of a credible political strategy to rally and organize Sunni Muslim allies in Syria and in Iraq.

- In public arguments, a principal assumption is that the U.S. must choose between military escalation and better diplomacy. But in this case, a stronger military commitment is actually the enabler for stronger diplomacy, not an alternative to it. While Americans debate, Russia and Iran have redoubled their military commitment to the faltering Assad regime, reenergizing their diplomatic efforts. And, while Americans debate, the best Iraqi leader in more than ten years is struggling to enact vital political reforms. In other words, a weak military commitment hamstrings the effectiveness of American diplomacy, discourages humanitarian help, and makes peaceful solutions less likely.

Here I offer key assessments, the elements of a strategy, and suggestions about process. The strategy I propose will require a much larger political and military commitment to the effort against ISIS. But this is not a reprise of the earlier massive U.S. efforts. The effort suggested here would require a U.S. troop commitment that is a small fraction–less than ten percent–of the scale of earlier interventions in Iraq and Afghanistan.

No sensible American wants to see U.S. forces reinvade the Middle East. Yet the surest road to that dreadful outcome is if the anti-ISIS operations fail and disaster follows.

In August 2014, President Obama made the decision about combat operations against ISIS. So for a year, Americans have been killing members of ISIS where they live, killing them in the thousands.

In that year, ISIS has actually gained strength. Now the issue is not whether to reengage in combat in the Middle East but how to win. To put it even more clearly: how Americans and our allies can decisively defeat ISIS before its adherents can do to us some portion of what we are already doing to them, before the human chaos coming out of Syria and Iraq puts even more pressure on the stability of other nations. Any strategy that involves the Syrian civil war must also now reckon with Russia's decision to make a significant military commitment to defend the embattled Assad regime.

American politics have instead been embroiled in another debate, about the nuclear arms control agreement with Iran. Yet that debate is less about the technical qualities of the deal and more about whether America is halfhearted in confronting Iranian sponsorship of so much of the violence spreading across the Middle East.

That, then, is another reason why the U.S. should choose this moment to develop a maximum effort to defeat ISIS in Syria as well as Iraq. Such a strategy would confront

Iranian ambitions in both places. It would be the ideal companion to the diplomacy to curb an Iranian nuclear threat.

Key Assessments

#1: How serious a threat does ISIS pose to the United States?

The current level of U.S. effort is about what would be expected against a threat regarded as serious but not vital. The fear has mainly been about "lone offender" attacks of the kind that sadly are becoming endemic. Yet for some time now, this threat assessment has been in transition.[2]

ISIS is at war with the United States. It has a larger safe haven than al-Qaeda did before 9/11. It has more recruits—including foreign recruits—than al-Qaeda did at its peak. Still, the public assumption has been that it does not yet pose that level of threat. It is worth recalling that al-Qaeda was not described as posing a catastrophic threat either, until catastrophe struck.

Some observers have assumed that the ISIS cult of ultraviolence will doom such a crazed, Khmer Rouge-like organization. They assume that antibodies are bound to rise up and topple it. These predictions have not been borne out.[3]

In late July, the FBI director said publicly that the threat from ISIS now eclipsed that from al-Qaeda.[4] A useful thought experiment for each reader is to ask yourself: If next week ISIS carried out attacks that killed 1,000 (or even 100) Americans, what do you think the United States government would do about it?

Do you believe that the president and his advisers would then say to themselves and to the country that the status quo level of effort has been and remains satisfactory? That it is all that can be done?

I do not believe they would say that.

For more than three years, between 1998 and 9/11, the U.S. government floundered in developing options to deal with the al-Qaeda menace that could find some effective middle ground between a "Normandy invasion" and a "fly swatter." Several mid-range options were worked up in the bowels of the bureaucracy. None gained high-level attention.

The assessment is only partly about today's threat. Americans should also ask themselves what they think the threat may be like in 2016 or 2017, given current trends and with a widening refugee crisis. To put this point in historical perspective: the 9/11 hijacker-pilots left Germany for Afghanistan about two years before 9/11. Back then they thought they were volunteering to fight against Russia. Time passed; plans evolved.

The U.S. is making policies now that will take years to play out. The enemy is doing the same.

After 9/11, many people asked themselves: Could America's leaders have done more? My staffers and I heard plenty of those reflections when we interviewed those leaders in our 9/11 Commission work. And of course, the answer we frequently heard from them was: yes, we could have done more. All sorts of options seemed obvious on the day after 9/11 that had seemed inconceivable or too risky the day before.[5]

At a minimum, the policies the U.S. would adopt on "the day after" an ISIS-caused catastrophe must be readied *now*. Even if the all-out effort is not deployed, it would be inexcusable if plans were not ready. And the process of readying such plans will clarify today's choices.

#2: Are present trends tolerable? In other words, is the threat likely to ease in an acceptable timeframe without much more U.S. effort?

A somewhat comforting assessment might be that ISIS is effectively contained. This view could hold that U.S. airpower and the many local fights are sufficiently degrading the organization's capabilities and distracting its attention so that it cannot metastasize. The situation does not look so sanguine to me.

But there are dangers beyond that of an attack on Americans or the erosion of global values from the unchecked reign of such a barbarian regime. Consider the broader trends developing now in one of the world's great conflicts: the struggle for the future of the Muslim world.

As others have pointed out, this struggle is reminiscent of the agonizing wars of religion that ranged across Western Europe for nearly 150 years.[6] The now-bucolic fields of rural Holland were once the landscapes of living nightmares, the monsters in the art of Hieronymus Bosch.

The Muslim world, especially the Arab Muslim world, is engulfed in an awful era of strife about community identity and the character of authority. Millions of Muslims live in communities that for years, in some cases more than a decade, have been scoured by death squads, torture houses, and innumerable forms of privation, abuse, and sudden death.

In the wars within Islam, ISIS has a basic strategy that goes back to when Abu Musab al-Zarqawi was leading its precursor organization. The strategy above all is one of division and polarization. This is what Arabs mean when they use the derisive description of these groups as *takfiri*. ISIS wants to drive the Muslim world into a zero-sum war of Sunni versus Shia and Islam versus America. In that war, ISIS hopes to be seen as the purest and most terrifying sword of the prophet.

For ISIS, a trend line toward the triumph of sectarian extremism validates this basic narrative. So if Shia extremists attack them and pillage cities like Fallujah and Ramadi, this short-term setback for ISIS could be a net advance for its cause. ISIS is already gaining a worrisome level of popular support among the population of Saudi Arabia.

This polarization is occurring among both Sunnis and Shia. It is advancing fast. After ISIS conquered Mosul in 2014, Iraq's Grand Ayatollah Ali al-Sistani called for jihad. Shiite preachers in Najaf put on military fatigues and called on worshippers to fight for Iran's supreme leader, Ayatollah Ali Khamenei, against these satanic Sunnis.

A top commander of the Badr Organization marveled that no one, not even Iran's Ayatollah Ruhollah Khomeini, had ever before dared to declare an open-ended jihad against a Sunni enemy. In the recruiting centers, walls are covered with portraits of Iran's Ayatollah Khamenei and Iraq's Ayatollah al-Sistani. To the Badr leader, Khamenei is now "the *wali amr al-muslimeen*, the legal ruler of all the Muslim lands." On billboards in Baghdad, portraits of the late Ayatollah Khomeini with a map of Iraq in his hands are now openly displayed. Iran's Islamic Revolutionary Guard Corps (IRGC) commander Qassem Suleimani openly tours the frontlines where IRGC troops fight alongside the "Popular Mobilization Forces."[7]

Notice too how the ISIS attack on Suruc in Turkey has so roiled Turkish domestic politics (with some help from Turkish President Recep Tayyip Erdogan). Notice how the ISIS attack on Tunisian beachgoers strategically targeted the vital tourist industry of that promising country (while also being the worst terrorist attack against British citizens in ten years). Notice how an ISIS attack in Kuwait, hitting a Shia mosque, struck at the core of that country's delicate domestic balance. And these are just early skirmishes.

Some Americans may find this trend to be sad but tolerable. After bitter experience, many Americans have internalized a great humility about their country's capacity to make things better in these faraway places of which they know so little. Which then leads to the third key assessment . . .

#3: Must—can—the U.S. play favorites among so many "bad guys"?

One reason Americans are so reluctant to get more deeply involved in fighting ISIS and leading a coalition to resolve the Syrian civil war is because they perceive—with cause—that all the groups are tarnished. Some may wish, above all, just to stay out of such a mess.

For generations, a classic dilemma of U.S. foreign policy has arisen from America's eternal quest for the good moderates, the "third force" between tyrants and zealots. The U.S. seems to always find itself bolstering flawed leaders, compromised factions, and faltering regimes. But if the leaders weren't flawed, the factions compromised, and the regimes faltering, the place probably wouldn't be imploding. There wouldn't be a crisis to draw America's attention.

So the usual, tortured choice is either to bolster flawed friends or abandon them. Both alternatives are usually problematical: hence the dilemma.

America's potential allies in the struggle against ISIS are all deeply flawed. So taking their side requires an assessment that ISIS is worse—distinguishably worse.

Just because ISIS is much worse does not mean that the other players are "moderates." After years in the crucible, there are few moderates still fighting in Syria or Iraq (or Libya, etc.).

None of the factions has a system for administering justice that adheres to nominal world standards for human rights. Truly disordered communities never do. When formal justice systems prove dysfunctional or irrelevant in handling threats to the community, informal—sometimes tribal—systems of justice take their place.

That still does not mean that all the groups are equally bad. But it does mean that principled outsiders, trying to help, shoulder a stressful burden of murky, relative moral judgments.

Yet most local inhabitants, and outsiders tuned to them, can tell which groups respect the norms of their community. For example, in Sunni-majority Iraqi communities in provinces like Anbar and Diyala, Americans eventually realized that there was a difference between insurgent groups like the 1920 Revolution Brigades and an organization like Al-Qaeda in Iraq (AQI). The 1920 Brigades usually had tribal roots and were opposed to outside control in all forms—Americans or AQI.

To some Americans, all the insurgents seemed to be the same. They were not. In 2006 and 2007, Americans—and Iraqis—finally learned how to make necessary differentiations and forge political understandings even in places that had been among the most dangerous in Iraq, like Ramadi (in Anbar) or Baqubah (in Diyala). If local people could recover control of their own communities, accepting reasonable limits on their authority, a basis could be found for common action against a common enemy.

My premise is that ISIS is indeed special. It has fed off and occasionally allied itself with homegrown insurgencies, but it is really more akin to a force of foreign raiders and plunderers, with a strong sense of common identity. This identity is founded on an exclusive sense of divine mission and a devotion to the logic and imagery of empowering savagery. Enslaving captives, including young girls, is only part of that attraction.

The movement's top leaders are creatures formed out of the region's decades of brutality. At the very top of ISIS, they are alumni of AQI and Saddam Hussein's gestapo. Tens of thousands of foreign recruits, attracted from around the world, provide the shock troops of the movement.

The attractions of ISIS are difficult to understand for people whose values and notions of rationality are infused by contemporary liberal civilization. But the surge in foreign fighters (there were hardly any in 2012) did not happen because the ideology changed or because the movement began using social media. As an anonymous writer in a *New York Review of Books* article put it, "The only change is that there was suddenly a territory available to attract and house them. If the movement had not seized Raqqa and Mosul, many of these men might well have simply continued to live out their lives with varying degrees of strain—as Normandy dairy farmers or council employees in Cardiff."[8]

It is not enough for the U.S. and its friends to be able to distinguish among Sunni Muslim factions and single out ISIS and its affiliates. The coalition also has to be able to distinguish among the enemies of the Sunni Muslims.

For Sunni Muslims who might be willing to sacrifice their lives to defeat ISIS, their gallery of monsters is clear. For them, Bashar al-Assad's regime in Syria and the Shiite extremists in Iraq are at least as bad.

And these Sunni Muslim concerns are credible. There is no need to recount the record of the Assad regime, whose horrors have been discussed in mass media for the last four years. Yet, Sunni Muslim concerns about Shia terrorists are not so well understood.

To take one notable example: in 2005 and 2006, Shia death squads in Iraq, some of them organized with help from forces in the Iraqi government's Interior and Health ministries, were regularly kidnapping, torturing, and murdering Sunni Arabs. One especially notorious torturer and killer was Mahdi al-Gharawi, who in 2006 was a senior commander in the Iraqi National Police.

Finally, aided by U.S. pressure, the Iraqi government arrested Gharawi and charged him with torture and murder. Gharawi went free, however, since Iraqi Prime Minister Nouri al-Maliki would not allow him to be prosecuted. In 2012, Prime Minister Maliki appointed Gharawi as the principal security commander for Mosul, with the rank of lieutenant general.[9]

Stories like this are why the inhabitants of Mosul are afraid not just of ISIS terror. They are perhaps even more afraid of what will happen to them if the Baghdad forces come back.

Elements of the Strategy

#1: Political objectives that attract those who will do most of the fighting.

Whatever the U.S. can do with its airpower, forces will still have to go in on the ground. The U.S. preference will be that local fighters do that work.

Most of the Kurds have little appetite to give their lives to reconquer the Sunni portion of Mosul and beyond. Many Shia see little point in fighting on Sunni lands. They don't want to lay down their lives in order to sort out which Sunni Arab will rule Ramadi or Haditha.

True, there are Shia and Kurdish extremists who want to conquer some Sunni lands and towns. Where they have been successful, they do their own ethnic cleansing. That is not the victory the U.S. seeks.

Therefore, to head off the dreaded scenario of very heavy U.S. ground force involvement, an effective anti-ISIS coalition probably should rely, above all, on Turkey and Sunni Muslim allies in Syria and Iraq. Some of these allies are Islamist. Some, like the YPG Kurds (Kurdish People's Protection Units), are secularist.

For almost all these potential partners, the defeat of ISIS must be associated with the defeat of the Assad regime.[10] If one is achieved without the other, the outcome will not have the balance that Sunni Muslims need to make the fighting worthwhile. In that case, the U.S. will have difficulty finding adequate ground partners to do most of the fighting.

All the allies should be able to agree that, as a companion to the disintegration of ISIS, they will also oppose Syrian government forces under the authority of Assad. The liberation of Aleppo would be a key step.

In Iraq, Sunni Muslims will not fight to subordinate themselves to a Baghdad regime they understandably distrust. That distrust has not been ameliorated by the U.S.-forced replacement of Maliki with that good and well-meaning man, Haider al-Abadi.

Within Iraq, Sunni Muslims might be persuaded to fight for the autonomy of local leaders they respect in provincial Ninewa and Anbar governorates dominated by other Sunnis. Kurds would have to tolerate an autonomous, largely Sunni-governed, Ninewa.

Baghdad may not want a truly autonomous Anbar province, and the Kurds of Erbil do not currently want a Sunni-governed Ninewa province. But allowing such autonomy may be the only way to preserve even the semblance of a unified Iraq. The likely alternatives are either partition or a Shia absolutism at gunpoint in ruined cities.

#2: Operational objectives to guide coalition action.

The July 2015 agreement with the Turks to clear ISIS from border areas in northern Syria, protected by U.S., Turkish, and perhaps other allied airpower, may be a landmark. But the allies have not even agreed on a safe zone. And if they did, that would still only be a staging area, a place to gather refugees, from which to contemplate the moves to come.[11]

The summer of 2015 is becoming a moment in which the key players should make up their mind about what they really want to do. The U.S. government has seemed uncertain.

But the Turkish government is at least as confused. It seeks Assad's ouster; strikes at its PKK (Kurdistan Workers' Party) enemies (who are also fighting ISIS with U.S. support); and half-heartedly attacks ISIS too. The Erdogan government is beset domestically. Yet, there is broad public support in Turkey for steps that will contain or end the Syrian civil war. Nor is ISIS popular among most Turks.

To mount an effective military coalition against ISIS, the U.S. should prioritize the reduction of ISIS control in its core sanctuary and foreign fighter conduit in Syria, then Iraq. This can be expressed as *an operational objective that by the end of 2017, if not sooner, the coalition should at least end ISIS control of the cities and road network on the axis of Aleppo–Raqqah–Deir es-Zour–Mosul.*

A second operational objective should be that by the end of 2017, if not sooner, the coalition should seek to end the current phase of the Syrian civil war, opening up a fresh chance for broad negotiations about a political transition in Syria. A new diplomatic process got underway in October 2015, in Vienna, that can provide a forum for this work. The U.S. does not need to have a strong view of its own about whether or how the Syrian state should be reconstituted.

#3: Commit enough Americans, on the ground, to ensure military success and gain needed political insight and influence.

In its Syrian and Iraqi core areas, ISIS is not at all like al-Qaeda was in Afghanistan or Pakistan. As Audrey Kurth Cronin wrote in a *Foreign Affairs* article, "Terrorist networks, such as al Qaeda, generally have only dozens or hundreds of members, attack civilians, do not hold territory, and cannot directly confront military forces. ISIS, on the other hand, boasts some 30,000 fighters, holds territory in both Iraq and Syria, maintains extensive military capabilities, controls lines of communication, commands infrastructure, funds itself, and engages in sophisticated military operations."[12]

At least in the current stage, the war against ISIS and the war against Assad are conventional military operations, clearing fielded military forces—often foreign forces—out of the towns and road networks they are trying to hold.[13] Some of the defenders are fanatical, dug in with extensive use of mines and IEDs, and well-armed. Dislodging them will be difficult.

The attacker can just try to obliterate everything and everyone in its way, as the Assad regime has attempted to do in some of its offensive operations. The alternative is tough urban fighting.

This kind of U.S. support can work. Local forces can fight and defeat ISIS and the Assad regime's forces. Recent experience supporting the YPG Kurds in northern Syria has proven it.

That kind of military task requires and rewards:

- combat aggressiveness;
- high-quality capabilities, such as armored vehicles, jammers, overhead surveillance, precisely targeted munitions, sniper overwatch, communications among the components, quick-reaction forces, and medevac capabilities;
- field training; and
- skillful, conscientious leadership at the small-unit level (brigade-level and below).

As mentioned earlier, the main fighting must be undertaken—if it will happen at all—by local forces, visibly made up mostly of Sunni Muslims. There are not yet ground forces that are ready for this task.

The United States and other coalition partners can provide the needed support. The question is whether the U.S. can provide adequate support if it relies mainly on airpower and does not have significant forces that are deployed on and near the battlefield.[14]

The United States has been at war against violent Islamist extremists in many settings since 1998, continuously so since 2001. Over this time, many lessons have been painfully learned. One of them driven home again and again, in military operations and in policing, is that school training—whether Americans training foreigners or Americans training Americans—is no better than a baseline. The critical training is in the field, where what was learned in the school is customized or junked.

To avoid U.S. forces doing all the work, the U.S. has learned to leverage combat, police, and intelligence advisers operating in the field. After one very successful advisory team—about 10 soldiers advising an Iraqi battalion of about 500 in Anbar province—completed its work in 2006, its team leader carefully noted what he had learned for the record. "[U.S.] soldiers are trained according to a plan dictated by higher, yet 85 percent of it was not needed. . . . Advisors must live and work with their Iraqi counterparts. Training them to perform missions but refusing to join them on those missions is counterproductive."[15] His words have been echoed by many others; his lessons have been learned over and over and over again.

The argument starts in military and intelligence gains. But it cycles very quickly into political outcomes. Direct U.S. military partnerships can improve results on the ground because the learning process can run both ways.

The local partner gauges the American commitment; the Americans learn vastly more about what is really going on. If they do their job, the Americans are also there as civilians. They gain insights that instantly carry over into their political effort, identifying viable sources of local authority and engaging with the credibility that comes with granular local knowledge.

There are already Americans on the ground near northern Syria and in Iraq. Putting aside the current operations in Anbar, probably the Americans who are now closest to serving in field advisory roles are working secretly. Outsiders cannot evaluate the scope or quality of their work. They should not feel bad about that. Most of the insiders can't evaluate it either.

But my assumption is that these secret advisory efforts are not nearly sufficient to achieve the operational objectives suggested here. Nor do they seem likely to be sufficient to provide the local insight and political leadership needed to cement a workable and effective coalition.

To achieve the operational objectives suggested here, substantial local ground combat forces, numbering at least in the tens of thousands, will be needed in northern Syria and in northern Iraq beyond the "green line" that separates Iraqi Kurdistan from the rest of Iraq.

In addition, the U.S. may need to prepare an effort on the scale of that now deployed in Afghanistan. This could entail the deployment of at least 10,000 soldiers, airmen, and Marines with three brigade combat-team equivalents based in Turkey, the Syrian safe zone, Iraq (in Iraqi Kurdistan, the current al-Taqaddum Air Base, and perhaps at the old Tal Afar and al-Asad bases), and possibly Jordan, as well as in the existing bases in the Gulf states.[16]

This would be a major U.S. commitment. Certainly Americans will be killed and injured. The U.S. will be accused of entering another Middle Eastern quagmire. So it's best to address the "quagmire" argument head-on.

The Quagmire of the Status Quo

For a lesson on how the U.S. can wage war inconclusively, dealing out death and destruction month after month while the war goes downhill, consider the past year of U.S. combat operations in Iraq and Syria. The U.S.-Turkish wish to clear Syrian border areas and the intensified Turkish role in attacking both Syrian Kurds and ISIS have now raised the stakes. The political contest for who will rule in the cleared zones will escalate. The Turkish government may be tempted to intervene in ways that could make ISIS even stronger.

Airpower can be more effective than current efforts if U.S. aircraft fly missions out of Turkish bases and get more timely and accurate intelligence to guide their missions. These efforts may also do more to disrupt the flow of foreign recruits to ISIS. That is on the plus side.

But these intensified efforts are not likely to provide local ground forces with the capabilities they will need to dislodge ISIS from its strongholds. It may not be enough to dislodge the Assad regime.

So there is a danger that the U.S. finds itself still more embroiled in another kind of quagmire, much more draining and dangerous than the ongoing "fly swatter," twilight wars the U.S. is waging in Somalia and Yemen. Time is not making these problems easier to solve. The humanitarian disaster in Syria has already spread to Europe. An emboldened Russian government is conducting air strikes in Syria and pouring more military supplies to the Assad regime and its Iranian allies. Political stability in neighboring countries is buckling.

Perhaps the next prediction of ISIS collapse will come true. But it seems at least equally likely that the U.S. would get more responsibility without more influence. Washington could become even more of a hostage to fortune.

Fundamentally, I am arguing for accepting a higher level of U.S. engagement and short-term risk in order to reduce the long-term risks. One of the long-term risks is that the U.S. will be pulled into a full-scale invasion, with even heavier responsibilities, in the aftermath of some catastrophe. This was the pre-9/11 dilemma. Can the U.S. securely judge that this danger is less serious than that one was?

Confronting Iran . . . and Enabling Diplomacy

Iran is already playing a large role in military campaigns in Syria with its Hezbollah expeditionary forces and direct IRGC advisors. In Iraq, the IRGC and Hezbollah advisors are also deployed in support of Shiite supporters. The strategy suggested here necessarily confronts Iran's interventions in both countries and more generally in the region. Iran's activism may escalate in 2016 if it gains access to its currently blocked billions.

Neither of the objectives proposed here would eliminate Iranian influence in Syria and Iraq. The U.S. and its allies would instead be trying to check Iranian ambitions in both countries and persuade Iran to be more discriminate in its support.

The U.S. had similar objectives in Iraq in 2007 and 2008. Having organized a diplomatic opening to Iraq in the newly created P5 + 1 process during 2006, the U.S. and its allies were able to win passage of the landmark UN Security Council (UNSC) resolution to curb Iranian nuclear ambitions (UNSC Res. 1696, July 2006) and also developed an ingenious and powerful financial sanctions strategy underpinned by this resolution.

In Iraq, the U.S. used its greater influence to contain (not erase) Iranian influence in the Iraqi government. The U.S. had to fight Iran's proxies in the country, which led to the heaviest fighting during the surge. Eventually, the Iraqi government became emboldened enough during 2008 to clean out the worst of the Iranian-supported militias that had dominated Basra and much of southern Iraq.

Iran remained very influential in Iraq. But at least this reset mitigated some of the worst sectarian violence and gave a stabilized Iraq a chance to get back on its feet.

A much more powerful U.S.-led coalition effort now in Syria and Iraq can actually enable diplomacy. Iran, and the IRGC, respect strength on the ground. If the U.S. and its allies can create a credible counterweight, and also take on some enemies that the Iranians also despise, Iranian officials could be open to discussions about how each side can reasonably protect its legitimate interests in the region.

Managing a Transformed Strategy

In preparing for an effort on the scale envisioned here, the U.S. will need a stronger and more integrated political-military effort. The most recent successful model was the joint campaign plan developed and implemented by Ryan Crocker and David Petraeus/Ray Odierno in 2007 and 2008.

Today, the U.S. government has a State Department special envoy for the anti-ISIS coalition: retired General John Allen. He is based in Washington. The U.S. has another special envoy for Syria and an ambassador in Iraq. The military has a newly appointed commander for the anti-ISIS effort, Lieutenant General Sean MacFarland, who will reportedly be based in Kuwait under CENTCOM.

The political-military leadership for the anti-ISIS coalition and campaign, whether that is Allen and MacFarland or someone else the president may select, should be based together. Their joint headquarters should be in the region, probably in Turkey or in Iraqi Kurdistan. The center of the U.S. military effort should probably be relocated accordingly.

The Crocker-Petraeus team created a joint campaign plan that was developed by a very strong Joint Strategic Assessment Team (JSAT) that did its work during the spring of 2007. The team of about twenty experts was co-led by an Arabic-speaking foreign service officer (currently ambassador to Greece), David Pearce, and by then-Colonel (now Lieutenant General) H.R. McMaster.

Political experts on the team included Robert Ford and Toby Dodge. The team led with a political framework for the campaign. Having led or helped lead prior reviews of Iraq strategy, I believe this JSAT model was a good way to do this work—in the field and with the right people involved.

Meanwhile, Washington also reorganized its management of the effort. In the spring of 2007, then-Lieutenant General Douglas Lute was detailed to the White House from the Joint Staff, where he had been serving as the J-3. Lute became a deputy national security advisor responsible for oversight of the wars in both Iraq and Afghanistan, a job he retained into the Obama administration.

Bob Gates offers a good description of why Lute's job was created:

> In my job interview, I had raised with the president the need for stronger coordination of the civilian and military efforts in the war, and for the empowerment of someone in Washington to identify bureaucratic obstacles to those efforts and force action. I saw this person as an overall coordinator on war-related issues, someone who could call a cabinet secretary in the name of the president if his or her department was not delivering what had been promised. I told the press on April 11 [2007], "This czar term is, I think, kind of silly. The person is better described as a coordinator and a facilitator . . . what Steve Hadley would do if Steve Hadley had the time—but he doesn't have the time to do it full-time.[17]

The "Lute position" was effectively abolished at the White House when Lute left at the end of President Obama's first term. It may have been abolished in the expectation that the war in Iraq was over and the war in Afghanistan was winding down. Times have changed. The process needs to adapt along with the strategy.

Philip Zelikow is the White Burkett Miller Professor of History at the University of Virginia. He has also served as the dean of the Graduate School at Virginia. Having begun his career as a trial and appellate lawyer in Texas, and after a stint teaching for the Navy, Dr. Zelikow became a career foreign service officer. He served overseas and on the NSC staff in the White House of President George H.W. Bush. He then became a professor, at Harvard and then at Virginia. His books include *Germany Unified and Europe Transformed* (Harvard UP, with Condi Rice), *The Kennedy Tapes* (Harvard UP and Norton, with Ernest May), and *Essence of Decision* (Longman, with Graham Allison). While at Virginia, he directed the 2001 Carter-Ford commission on national election reform, which led directly to the landmark Help America Vote Act of 2002. More recently, he helped lead a bipartisan group setting an agenda for America's economic future amid the digital revolution, Rework America, organized by the Markle Foundation. He drafted the group's new book, *America's Moment: Creating Opportunity in the Connected Age* (Norton). Dr. Zelikow returned to full-time government service in 2003-2004 to direct the 9/11 Commission. In 2005-2007 he returned to State as Counselor of the Department, a deputy to Secretary Rice. He has also served on the President's Intelligence Advisory Board for President George W. Bush (2001-2003) and for President Barack Obama (2011-2013). He currently serves on the Defense Policy Board that advises Secretary of Defense Ashton Carter. He is a member of the Aspen Strategy Group.

1 No classified information was used or reviewed in the preparation of this paper. I'm grateful for suggestions I received from James Jeffrey and a few other knowledgeable people.

2 "We remain mindful of the possibility than an ISIL-sympathizer could conduct a limited, self-directed attack here at home with no warning," the National Counterterrorism Center director announced six months ago. Back then he added: "We also remain concerned that ISIL may place a greater priority on more organized attacks on the West, as opposed to propaganda-driven, lone-offender attacks. The group's ambitions have grown in parallel with its capabilities; it sees itself in competition with core al-Qaeda and could develop its own anti-Western plotting capability and draw from some of the thousands of foreign fighters in theater." Rasmussen, Nicholas. February 12, 2015. "Current Terrorist Threat to the United States." Statement for the Senate Select Committee on Intelligence, at www.nctc.gov.

3 This is the thesis in: Anonymous. August 13, 2015. "The Mystery of ISIS." *New York Review of Books*, p. 27. The editors describe Anonymous as someone with "wide experience in the Middle East and was formerly an official of a NATO country." The Khmer Rouge regime was eventually toppled only by a Vietnamese invasion of Cambodia.

4 Paletta, Damian. July 26, 2015. "U.S. Security Conference Reveals Islamic State as Confounding Foe." *Wall Street Journal*; Dilanian, Ken. July 22, 2015. "FBI chief: Islamic State group bigger threat than al-Qaida." *Associated Press*, at bigstory.ap.org/article/5f7dcc94a52442d3aa93ff01bf24cdf6/fbi-chief-islamic-state-group-bigger-threat-al-qaida.

5 The anti-al-Qaeda defense plans, with their blustery codename "Infinite Resolve," did not even deserve to be called "plans," the then-commander of CENTCOM, Tommy Franks, later told me. A number of ideas had been tossed around by officials in the Office of the Secretary of Defense, the Joint Staff, and Special Operations Command. None received serious high-level consideration. "At no point before 9/11 was the Department of Defense fully engaged in the mission of countering al-Qaeda, though this was perhaps the most dangerous foreign enemy then threatening the United States. The Clinton administration effectively relied on the CIA to take the lead in preparing long-term offensive plans against an enemy sanctuary. The Bush administration adopted this approach, although its emerging new strategy envisioned some yet undefined further role for the military in addressing this problem. Within Defense, both Secretary [William] Cohen and Secretary Donald Rumsfeld gave their principal attention to other challenges." 9/11 Commission. 2004. *9/11 Commission Report*. New York, NY: Norton, pp. 351-52.

6 See Owen IV, John M. 2015. *Confronting Political Islam: Six Lessons from the West's Past*. Princeton, NJ: Princeton University Press. An essay that excerpts the book: Owen IV, John M. May/June 2015. "From Calvin to the Caliphate: What Europe's Wars of Religion Tell Us About the Modern Middle East." *Foreign Affairs*, p. 77.

The Thirty Years' War, centered in Bohemia and German lands between 1618 and 1648, was only the final conflagration in a series of wars of religion that began in the 1540s. During the 1500s, the two great cockpits of fighting were the Netherlands and France. Those internal wars lasted from the 1560s to the 1590s, with frequent interventions by outsiders. The religious issues also were the great backdrop of the contest between Spain and England, including the attempted Spanish invasion of England in 1588, battles in the Western Hemisphere, and various fights in central Europe, in places like Hungary.

For those who follow contemporary Iraqi politics, the French wars of religion may have particular resonance. In France during the 1580s, there were really *three* parties to that struggle, not two. There were the Catholic extremists—the Catholic League, backed by Spain and the pope. There were the Protestant Huguenots—usually backed by the Dutch, English, and their hired German and Swiss mercenaries. And in the middle there were the royalist moderates (usually Catholic) who were anxious above all to recover the central kingly power and rebuild a coherent French state—a kingly power that both of the extreme factions wanted to hamstring or destroy. Sound familiar?

In France it was this third faction that finally prevailed. And hence the tremendous, even obsessive, French concern throughout the following 17th century with building up absolutist royal power in France.

[7] Pelham, Nicolas. June 4, 2015. "ISIS & the Shia Revival in Iraq." *New York Review of Books*, p. 30. Pelham's observations were in April-May 2015.

[8] Anonymous, 2015, p. 29. There is no obvious correlation between home country policies and ISIS recruitment. The most successful political transition in the Arab Spring has been in Tunisia. Tunisians are, nevertheless, among the most numerous recruits in the ISIS ranks.

[9] Slater, Andrew. June 19, 2014. "The Monster of Mosul: How a Sadistic General Helped ISIS Win." *The Daily Beast*. Slater had worked on the Gharawi case while serving in Baghdad. For more background, see also, Gordon, Michael, and Bernard Trainor. 2012. *The Endgame*. New York, NY: Pantheon, pp. 361-62, 509.

[10] See, for example, the May 13 statement of a broad group of Syrian factions: Lund, Aron. May 15, 2015. "'Syrians have overthrown Staffan de Mistura:' An Interview with Subhi al-Refai." Carnegie Endowment for International Peace, at carnegieendowment.org/syriaincrisis/?fa=60103; and the evolution of de Mistura's position: Siegel, Jacob. June 3, 2015. "U.N. Envoy to Syria: Assad Must Go." *The Daily Beast*.

[11] For some ideas elaborating on the need for humanitarian relief of the Syrian refugee crisis and on the need for renewed effort to "stabilize a shattered Syria" with a "major shift in the level and nature of international engagement," see Burns, Nicholas, and David Milliband. July 9, 2015. "Syria's Worsening Refugee Crisis Demands Action from the West." *Washington Post*.

[12] Cronin, Audrey Kurth. March/April 2015. "ISIS Is Not a Terrorist Group: Why Counterterrorism [on the model of AfPak or Somalia] Won't Stop the Latest Jihadist Threat." *Foreign Affairs*, p. 88.

[13] This paper therefore does not need to litigate the argument about whether the U.S. can or should master "counterinsurgency." There were a set of strategies needed in Iraq to pacify several different local wars that blended anti-American insurgency and civil wars among a variety of combatants in various regions. The Afghanistan-Pakistan war was a very different kind of struggle, and in my view, the strategies sometimes employed with success in Iraq were usually not well suited to it.

The war against ISIS that the U.S. began waging in 2014 is different yet again. Although, as I stress, there are some broad lessons of great value to take away about the nature of effective advising and the sources of political influence, the ISIS war requires its own campaign plan.

[14] I therefore agree with arguments that local Muslim forces must be seen to be bearing the main burden of the fight against ISIS. See, for example, Clark, Howard Gambrill. July/August 2015. "Go Local." *The American Interest*, p. 25. However, I disagree with Clark's assumption that adequate U.S. support can be provided "silently and invisibly" (p. 30) by CIA operatives and U.S. Special Forces. If only.

I am also sympathetic to analyses that take into account the requirements for urban warfare and the shortcomings of the current Iraqi Security Forces. See, for example, Johnson, David E. Spring 2015. "Fighting the 'Islamic State': The Case for US Ground Forces." *Parameters*, p. 7. I am not yet convinced, however, that the "advisor option" is not feasible, especially if—as in Afghanistan today—the local forces are backed by a small but capable core of U.S. combat units, both ground and aviation.

[15] Lieutenant Colonel Michael Troster's July 2006 after-action report, quoted in: West, Owen. 2012. *The Snake Eaters: Counterinsurgency Advisors in Combat.* New York, NY: Simon & Schuster, pp. 220-21. This excellent book is partly a memoir; West was one of Troster's successors in leading an advisory team for this particular Iraqi battalion, which was stationed in the Habbaniyah area of Anbar in 2005-2007.

[16] For a brief summary of an analogous set of proposals, which would likely entail a comparable scale of effort, see Flournoy, Michele, and Richard Fontaine. June 24, 2015. "To defeat the Islamic State, the U.S. Will Have to Go Big." *Washington Post.*

[17] Gates, Robert. 2014. *Duty: Memoirs of a Secretary at War.* New York, NY: Knopf, pp. 66-67. General Petraeus immediately encountered friction with CENTCOM leader Admiral William "Fox" Fallon. By his account, Gates took steps to shelter that general's autonomy within his area of responsibility.

"Time is another challenge for CVE, because addressing the underlying drivers of violent extremism is a generational effort. Trust between historically marginalized communities and security forces takes years to build; habits of public corruption do not easily disappear; and credible local voices need time to find the courage and message to confront violent extremist propaganda head-on."

—SARAH SEWALL

The Challenge of Violent Extremism

Sarah Sewall
Under Secretary of State for Civilian Security, Democracy, and Human Rights
U.S. Department of State

Stemming the rise of violent extremism is among the most urgent and complex challenges of our time. From neo-Nazi actors in the United States and Europe to radical Islamic movements in the greater Middle East to extremist Buddhist networks operating in parts of Southeast Asia, no region, country, or community is immune to this threat. While violent extremism is not new, over the last decade it has become a global cancer with no simple diagnosis or cure.

Once violent extremism has infected a region or community, it becomes extremely difficult to root out. This hard reality has pushed the United States and the international community to seek ways to not only *respond* to violent extremist acts but also do more to *prevent* the spread of violent extremist influence, actors, and networks.

The U.S. government recognizes that while our military, intelligence, and law enforcement tools are vital to reducing the immediate threat posed by current violent extremist groups, we need a broader set of tools and actors to address the underlying dynamics that help create and sustain these groups. We call this broader effort Countering Violent Extremism (CVE). CVE's emphasis on prevention is ambitious and challenging, but also potentially more effective at securing Americans at home and promoting stability abroad by getting ahead of the next generation of threat.

There are many factors that can aid the spread of violent extremism at the individual, local, national, or regional levels. Therefore, we must develop tailored approaches that draw on the full range of governmental and nongovernmental tools. For that reason, our approach to CVE in our foreign policy has several distinct elements.

A primary element of CVE is countering the lies and propaganda violent extremists use to recruit vulnerable individuals and align with aggrieved communities. For example, violent extremists "pull" individuals toward their views by appealing to personal desires for spiritual guidance and purpose, adventure, friendship, or ideology.

Addressing this "pull" dynamic means empowering credible voices to counter violent extremist communication, monitor web traffic, and engage proactively on social media. Defectors from violent extremist groups are especially effective at this work, so rehabilitating and reintegrating those who no longer pose a threat to society is critical to CVE. Mainstream religious and local leaders who educate vulnerable youth about tenets of faith or help them find meaningful roles in their communities can also reduce the pull of violent extremism.

At the same time, CVE requires addressing underlying "push" factors—the gaps in human needs and lack of respect for human rights that violent extremists exploit. Some of these deficits are harder to identify than others, making it difficult to predict who will become radicalized to violence and why. The absence of security, equality, justice, or other "goods" is common where citizens are marginalized, repressed, or lack essential services and economic opportunity. The rise of al-Shabaab or the rapid expansion of ISIL in Iraq and Syria illustrate how these deficits—whether real or perceived, and whether experienced directly or witnessed from afar—can make individuals or entire communities vulnerable to adopting violent extremist ideology or aligning with violent extremist groups.

It is impossible, of course, to eliminate all gaps in human needs and ensure complete respect for human rights. Moreover, no single push factor explains violent extremism. Many terrorist recruits come from relatively free, affluent, and well-governed societies. Corruption, poverty, or marginalization may make individuals more susceptible to violent extremist ideology. Yet each case of personal or community radicalization is the result of context-specific interaction between "push" and "pull" factors.

With that said, neither concrete grievances nor ideology can ever justify violent extremism. And when extremists use or threaten violence, a military or law enforcement response is essential. We nonetheless have learned that governments may inadvertently feed violent extremist narratives and increase their security vulnerabilities by tolerating or perpetrating bigotry, marginalizing segments of society, or by failing to ensure that security and police forces respect the rights of citizens.

The U.S. seeks to better understand the complex and context-specific interplay of factors that make people vulnerable to radicalization to violence and then help local communities, international development organizations, the private sector, nongovernmental organizations, and other actors better prevent and counter violent extremism.

This recent but critical phase in our evolving CVE effort emphasizes building resilience within individuals and communities against radicalization, recruitment, and mobilization to violence. That means not only exposing the dead end of violent extremism, filling specific gaps in human needs, and addressing the lack of respect for human rights, but also building credible and positive alternatives for the populations extremists target—from expanding political and economic opportunities to improving governance and the rule of law to promoting voices of peace and tolerance. This adaptive approach to CVE both advances global security and reinforces core international norms and law.

An Evolving Threat and Response

The Obama administration's counterterrorism policy initially focused on dismantling al-Qaeda and its affiliates. This approach included a significant focus on strengthening the capacity of our international partners to address terrorist threats within their borders. At the time, the U.S. government recognized the need to complement "hard security" actions drawing on military, intelligence, and law enforcement tools with a broader approach that emphasized diplomacy, development, human rights, good governance, the rule of law, and universal values. It would take time, however, before we began concerted efforts to integrate this broader approach at scale.

As the U.S. targeted al-Qaeda, the organization decentralized and dispersed, adopting new strategies to reconstitute its recruits, resources, and safe havens. Al-Qaeda remnants began portraying themselves to communities as protectors from ethnic, sectarian, or tribal opponents as saviors from an abusive or corrupt government, or as providers of basic services and employment. At times, al-Qaeda ideologues and operatives joined with indigenous militants to form affiliates, creating networks that could exploit local grievances about insecurity, unemployment, sectarianism, or marginalization while maintaining connection to centralized know-how, guidance, and financing. Wielding flexible appeals, these actors found especially fertile soil in the Arabian Peninsula, Horn of Africa, Maghreb, Sahel, and the Lake Chad Basin Region and merged with local militias, criminal networks, and insurgencies in these areas. For example, al-Qaeda in the Islamic Maghreb (AQIM) affiliated with marginalized Tuaregs to establish new bases of operation. Later, Ansar al-Sharia exploited post-Gaddafi power struggles to ensconce itself in Libya. More recently, ISIL capitalized on Sunni political disenfranchisement to expand its base of operations in Iraq. These violent extremists have further destabilized many of the world's most weakly governed, conflict-ridden, and poverty-stricken regions. ISIL, Boko Haram, and other groups use brutality, slavery, and sexual violence against women to terrorize foes and recruit fighters.

Though many of these groups, including ISIL, also threaten direct attacks on the U.S. homeland, they now appear focused on destroying local states and controlling territory. Groups like ISIL, al-Shabaab, and Boko Haram have embedded themselves in local insurgent and criminal networks, threatening global security as they continue to propagate extremist narratives, sow regional instability, and perpetrate egregious violations of international law.

To address these threats, the U.S. and its global partners have dramatically increased dedicated military and intelligence capabilities since 9/11. The Department of Defense (Defense) embarked on major capacity-building efforts with international partners, while the Department of State (State) and other agencies strengthened foreign law enforcement and justice capacities and improved information exchanges. But as violent extremism became a more geographically dispersed, organizationally flexible, and locally rooted threat, the U.S. mobilized new tools and actors, improved interagency coordination, and catalyzed similar approaches by foreign governments and multilateral bodies.

For example, the Trans-Sahara Counterterrorism Partnership was launched in 2005, and the Partnership for East Africa Counterterrorism in 2009. These U.S. initiatives brought Defense, State, and the U.S. Agency for International Development (USAID) together to support at-risk regions. USAID undertook what might now be called CVE efforts, working with communities vulnerable to violent extremism to develop new programs tailored to address "push" factors like socioeconomic inequality, corruption, conflict, repression, and poor governance. In 2010, the Center for Strategic Counterterrorism Communications (CSCC) was created to contest extremist propaganda and misinformation in Arabic, Urdu, Punjabi, and Somali across a range of digital environments.

State leveraged relationships with foreign governments to create multilateral approaches to CVE. The Global Counterterrorism Forum (GCTF), launched in 2011, emerged as a multilateral platform for civilian-led approaches to counter terrorism, such as strengthening rule of law-based criminal justice systems, improving border security, and enhancing community-oriented policing. The GCTF in turn helped inspire the creation of three institutions: *Hedayah*, the first international CVE training and research center; the Global Community Engagement and Resilience Fund, the first public-private fund that will provide local NGOs with small grants for community-based CVE projects; and the Malta-based International Institute for Justice and the Rule of Law to train criminal justice and law enforcement practitioners, especially in countries in transition, on the importance of respecting human rights in their work. In 2011, USAID issued a guide clarifying how development assistance should be tailored to address violent extremism. USAID also launched a range of CVE initiatives, from reintegrating marginalized communities in northern Mali targeted for recruitment by AQIM to countering radicalization among Somali youth by providing them with outlets to peacefully express grievances and learn marketable new skills for employment. In 2011, State's Bureau of Counterterrorism (CT), which had previously focused on information exchange and capacity building with foreign law enforcement, also began pilot programs supporting community-based CVE initiatives.

The Bureau of International Narcotics and Law Enforcement (INL) began using programs to improve prison management to help prevent radicalization among inmates in at-risk countries. The Bureau for Education and Cultural Affairs began bringing together women, youth, and religious leaders to learn from one another's experiences in building community resilience to violent extremism. The Bureau of Democracy, Human Rights, and Labor (DRL) harnessed support for civil society and marginalized communities to further CVE goals.

CVE nonetheless remained a niche activity dwarfed by more traditional counterterrorism activities and capacity building of foreign state partners. Moreover, large segments of the international community—particularly those reluctant to engage in hard security activities—had not become engaged in preventive CVE efforts. Major development and investment resources from states, international institutions, and the private sector, along with many local and international civil society organizations who could be partners in prevention, remained on the sidelines of the struggle to contain and reverse the spread of violent extremism. The continued expansion and shocking brutality of groups like ISIL and Boko Haram, however, revealed violent extremism as a global threat that required a broader and more proactive approach.

To that end, the president convened the White House Summit on Countering Violent Extremism in February 2015, in which over 60 countries, 12 multilateral bodies, and representatives from civil society, business, and the faith community launched a global "whole-of-society" effort to tackle a broader range of "push" and "pull" factors fueling violent extremism.

The summit shifted the global conversation about violent extremism in three important ways. First, it expanded *how* we address violent extremism, by more explicitly targeting the underlying drivers that feed it. Second, the summit expanded *who* must lead this effort, by emphasizing the critical roles of local and nongovernmental actors. Third, it expanded *where* CVE efforts should be prioritized, highlighting communities on the periphery of active conflict that are aggressively targeted by violent extremists for recruitment and expansion. This comprehensive approach seeks to both limit the growth of current extremist groups and prevent new ones from emerging.

Summit participants outlined a concrete action agenda with nine pillars related to preventing and countering violent extremism: (1) promote local research and information-sharing on the drivers of violent extremism; (2) empower civil society; (3) strengthen relations between at-risk communities and security and police forces; (4) promote counter-narratives and weaken the legitimacy of violent extremist messaging; (5) promote educational approaches to build resilience to violent extremism; (6) enhance access to mainstream religious knowledge; (7) prevent radicalization in prisons and rehabilitate and reintegrate violent extremists; (8) identify political and economic opportunities for at-risk communities; and (9) strengthen development assistance and stabilization efforts.

President Obama challenged summit participants to meet again at the United Nations General Assembly (UNGA) in six months to chart their progress in advancing this agenda. State established a CVE Coordination Cell, directed by Eric Rosand, chief architect of the GCTF, to help states draft national CVE action plans and organize regional CVE summits, direct resources to civil society leaders to engage in CVE Summit activities, and foster global discussion on a range of CVE topics, such as the economic drivers of violent extremism and the role of international financial institutions in CVE.

When participants gathered again in September, the global CVE movement had grown to 100 countries, 20 multilateral bodies, and over 120 civil society groups with much to report. Governments in Albania, Algeria, Australia, Kazakhstan, Kenya, Mauritania, and Norway had hosted regional CVE summits to engage additional states, municipal governments, and civil society and private sector participants in preventive approaches to violent extremism. A number of countries had developed National CVE Action Plans charting their way forward. On the margins of UNGA, mayors from around the world launched a new Strong Cities Network to identify and share community-level best practices for building social cohesion and resilience against violent extremism. Young people gathered at the first-ever Global Youth CVE

Summit to showcase innovative tools for countering the appeal of violent extremism among their peers. Local researchers launched the RESOLVE Network (Researching Solutions to Violent Extremism) to connect with policy institutes and methodologists around the world to better understand the community-level factors fueling violent extremism and the best evidence-based approaches to address them. Civil society organizations have joined in all of these events and initiatives, further amplifying the chorus of voices to counter violent ideologies on the ground. The Intergovernmental Authority on Development sponsored a new CVE Center for Excellence and Counter Messaging for the East Africa region. The Government of Albania is spearheading an initiative to build regional capacity and cooperation around CVE, for example by supporting CVE-related research and counter-messaging. These new networks and platforms will be vital to sustaining the global momentum for CVE in the years ahead.

For its part, the U.S. has taken several concrete steps to broaden its own CVE approach over the last year. The CSCC is now doing more to empower nongovernmental voices to push back against violent extremists online, recognizing that they have greater credibility to influence at-risk individuals. This year, the U.S. also partnered with the United Arab Emirates to launch the Sawab Center—the first multinational online messaging and engagement hub to challenge extremist propaganda and narratives.

Also in 2015, the Bureau of Conflict and Stability Operations (CSO) built a new unit to analyze the underlying drivers of violent extremism in different global contexts. This CSO analysis feeds into a new State initiative to design and implement CVE programming through an integrated and holistic process. State is launching CVE pilot programs focused on the most at-risk communities and key drivers of radicalization with carefully tailored, evidence-based approaches. In recent months, State has also helped to develop a working definition for CVE ("undermining the attraction of and recruitment by violent extremist movements and ideologies that seek to promote violence against the United States and its interests") to help guide the efforts of U.S. agencies at home and abroad. State has engaged new governments, multilateral bodies, and nonprofit organizations about the critical role of development in this work. The most recent Quadrennial Diplomacy and Development Review designated CVE, and especially its emphasis on prevention, as one of State and USAID's top global policy priorities.

While this multifaceted activity is positive and hopeful, we remain sober about the challenges ahead. The multiple and often opaque factors that can enable radicalization to violence make it considerably harder—though not impossible—to measure the impact of CVE efforts. As our many recent CVE efforts grow, we will continue

216 Blind Spot: America's Response to Radicalism in the Middle East

to use concrete metrics and coordinate within government to minimize redundancy and maximize results. In addition, we will continue to provide support to other governments—for example, by assisting them in developing and implementing their national CVE action plans.

Time is another challenge for CVE, because addressing the underlying drivers of violent extremism is a generational effort. Trust between historically marginalized communities and security forces takes years to build; habits of public corruption do not easily disappear; and credible local voices need time to find the courage and message to confront violent extremist propaganda head-on. This long-term campaign will require sustained political support and leadership.

The United Nations (U.N.), which has long emphasized the importance of preventing rather than responding to conflict, will help sustain global momentum for CVE because it is uniquely positioned to convene a broad range of stakeholders, codify CVE approaches through international norms and law, coordinate related efforts, and undertake projects to enhance the capacities of member states. Building on the General Assembly's 2006 U.N. Global Counter-Terrorism Strategy, the U.N. Security Council adopted Resolution 2178 in September 2014 to increase international focus on countering foreign terrorist fighters. The Human Rights Council passed Resolution 30 in October 2015 to codify the importance of a holistic, human rights-based approach to preventing and countering violent extremism. In the coming months, Secretary-General Ban Ki-moon is expected to present his plan of action, building on the White House Summit process, to outline the U.N.'s role in preventing and countering violent extremism, along with recommendations for member states to support this effort.

Conclusion

As violent extremism evolves into a broader and more complex threat, the global community must continue developing strategies and tools to both defeat its current forms and prevent its future expansion. Though the U.S. has long appreciated the limits of force in defeating violent extremism, today we are much closer to a holistic, preventive approach and have begun scaling the diplomatic and development coordination required.

Through the summit process, American leadership has helped spark conversations around the world, from Algeria to Australia, and Kazakhstan to Kenya, about the need to mobilize new tools and actors to undermine violent extremist narratives and address factors that can fuel the spread of violent extremist ideology. These efforts have facilitated dialogue between historically marginalized communities and their governments, new national strategies that emphasize both civilian and military approaches to violent extremism, and new platforms for researchers, cities, and youth to collaborate on CVE efforts.

Events over the past decade show that we must embrace a long-term and holistic approach that empowers new states and actors, emphasizes preventive action, and champions our universal values of human rights and the rule of law. In pushing for this broader approach, the Obama administration has successfully reimagined the fight against violent extremism to advance both our security and our values, while ensuring that we will have global partners in this generational struggle.

Sarah Sewall is Under Secretary of State for Civilian Security, Democracy, and Human Rights. Dr. Sewall spent the previous decade on the faculty of the Harvard Kennedy School of Government, where she was Senior Lecturer and Director of the Carr Center for Human Rights Policy. She also served on the Defense Policy Board and spent a year as Minerva Chair at the U.S. Naval War College. She served as the Pentagon's inaugural Deputy Assistant Secretary for Peacekeeping and spent six years as Senior Foreign Policy Advisor to U.S. Senate Majority Leader George Mitchell. Dr. Sewall has served on corporate and non-profit Boards ranging from the Center for Naval Analyses to Oxfam. She is a graduate of Harvard College and Oxford University.

Blind Spot: America's Response to Radicalism in the Middle East

FOREWORD BY JOSEPH NYE AND BRENT SCOWCROFT

Blind Spot:
America's Response
to Radicalism in the
Middle East

EDITED BY NICHOLAS BURNS AND JONATHON PRICE

For More Information, Please Visit:
http://blindspot.aspeninstitute.org/

Also Available on Amazon.com:
http://amzn.com/089843629X

Or visit JSTOR in the coming weeks

For Bulk Orders, Please Contact:
Jonathon Price
Phone: 202-736-5808
E-mail: jonathon.price@aspeninst.org
 @AspenStrategy

aspen strategy group